Alphaвet city SIX

culture тheory politics

D0841770

OPEN CITY

Issue Editor
John Knechtel

Editorial Board
Ian Balfour
Rebecca Comay
Deborah Esch
John Knechtel
Detlef Mertins

Editor
John Knechtel

Managing Editor
Zoë Newman

Design Concept and Direction
Lewis Nicholson

Design
Lewis Nicholson *with* Gilbert Li

Production
Gilbert Li

Cover Design & Wordmark
Gilbert Li, Gottschalk+Ash
International

Typesetting
Richard Hunt

Associate Editors
Michael Bresalier
Heather Cameron
Len Guenther
Cornelius Heesters
Rafaël Newman
Kelly O'Brien
Tim Owen
Elias Polizoes
Micheil Russell
Ann Shin
Julija Sukys
Deborah Viets
Kyla Wazana

Contributing Editors
Sharon Brooks
Diana Fitzgerald Bryden
Susan Ehrlich
John Graham
Rachel Gray
Alison Hahn
Dianna Ilk
Tom Keenan
Rita Leistner
Sean Meagher
Andrew Ross
Jim Shedden
Nigel Smith
Karen Valihora
Caroline Wiedmer

Editorial Advisory Board
Svetlana Boym
Natalie Zemon Davis
Atom Egoyan
Gayatri Chakravosty Spivak
Samuel Weber

Alphabet City thanks the following
institutions and individuals:
The Graham Foundation of Chicago;
The Ontario Arts Council; The Social
Sciences and Humanities Research
Council of Canada; Gottschalk+Ash
International (Stuart Ash, Principal);
Moveable Type, University of Toronto
School of Architecture and Landscape
Architecture (Larry Richards, Dean);
York University Department of English
(Maurice Elliott, Chair); University
of Toronto Office of the President
(Robert Pritchard, President).

Marilyn Booth, Eugenia Canas,
Tessy Chakkalakal, Michael Davis,
Tom Lackey, Michael Lenaghan,
Michael McMahon, Martha Sharpe,
Melony Ward, Justin Young.

House of Anansi Press acknowledges
the Canada Council for the Arts and
the Ontario Arts Council for their
support of our publishing program.

Content created by Alphabet City Magazine of Toronto, Inc., a not-for-profit
organization built with volunteer labour.

Alphabet City
Box 387 Station P
Toronto, ON, Canada M5S 2S9

This issue is published in 1998 by
House of Anansi Press Limited
1800 Steeles Avenue West
Concord, ON, Canada L4K 2P3

Distributed in Canada by General
Distribution Services Inc.
30 Lesmill Road
Toronto, ON, Canada M3B 2T6
Tel. (416) 445-3333, Fax (416) 445-5967

Printed and bound in Canada

**Canadian Cataloguing in Publication
Data**

Alphabet city

Annual, 1991–
No. 1 (summer 1991)
Each issue also has distinct title.
ISSN: 1183–8086
ISBN: 0–88784–621–1 (1998 issue)

P87.A56   051   C94–300833–6

Permissions & Credits
Cover photograph: by Rita Leistner.
Taken in Toronto, 4 a.m., May 26, 1996,
westbound on Dundas, just past Shaw.

Inside Covers photograph: by Hugo
Glendinning.

p. 10: Coxwell Sanitary Trunk Sewer,
1960. Photograph courtesy of the City
of Toronto Archives.

pp. 12–27: *Générations d'une ville*, by
Jacques Derrida, was originally
published in *Lettre Internationale* 33,
summer 1992, 23–27.

pp. 104–113: Excerpt from
No Lease on Life © 1997 by
Lynne Tillman, published by
Harcourt Brace.

pp. 134–147: Images courtesy of the
Artist and Galerie Lelong, New York.

p. 148: Image by Mike Hoolboom.

pp. 152–157: Photographs by
Renate Berg.

p. 159: Photographs by
Adrian Blackwell.

pp. 160–171: All photographs by
Hugo Glendinning.

p. 177: Photograph by Phil Jackson.

pp. 188–191: Images courtesy of the
Artist.

pp. 216–217: MVRDV: Winy Maas,
Jacob van Rijs, and Nathalie de Vries
with Tom Mossel. Based on a study
by Indesen-group 1995 at Technical
University, Delft, tutored by Jean
Attali, Winy Maas, and Jacob van Rijs.
Photograph is by Vendex driehoek
© Dijkstra.

pp. 218–232: Photographs are of
Toronto's Nordheimer Ravine and the
Castle Frank Brook. The numbered
sign boards within these photographs
indicate they are from a series of some
thirty images which were taken in the
mid 1950s as part of the reconnaissance
that occurred in advance of the proposed Spadina Expressway. Due to citizen protests the expressway was never
built south of Eglinton Avenue, but the
brook was concealed in a storm sewer
in preparation for construction. Images
courtesy of the City of Toronto Archives.

pp. 302–315: Panorama of the Pariser
Platz, Berlin, January 1996, by Heather
Cameron. Text by permission of Johns
Hopkins University Press.

pp. 316 & 319: Photograph by Richard
Barnes.

OPEN CITY

Contents

Contributors

Stan Allen is an architect based in New York and teaching at Columbia University. He recently edited *Sites & Stations: Provisional Utopias*. Two books of works and writings are forthcoming, *Practice* and *Points and Lines*.

Renate Berg studied architecture at the University of Kassel in Germany. She works as an architect in Berlin and is active in urban development and contemporary social movements.

Maurice Blanchot is a philosopher and writer, many of whose texts have been translated into English, including *The Madness of the Day*, *The Writing of the Disaster*, and *The Unavowable Community*.

Roland Brener studied at St. Martin's School of Art in London, England. Currently living in Victoria, British Columbia, Brener represented Canada in the Venice Biennale in 1988 and the Sao Paolo Biennale in 1987.

Catherine Bush is the author of the novel *Minus Time*, which is currently being adapted for film. Her nonfiction has been published in the *New York Times Book Review*, *The Globe and Mail*, and other venues. She is working on a second novel, *The Rules of Engagement*, and teaches creative writing at Concordia University in Montréal.

Heather Cameron is a photographer and doctoral candidate in Social and Political Thought at York University, Toronto. She currently lives in Berlin.

Constantine P. Cavafy was born in Alexandria, Egypt in 1863. He never published a volume of poems and, aside from occasional contributions to periodicals, he preferred to circulate broadsheets or privately printed pamphlets of select poems among friends and relatives. His 154 "collected poems" were published posthumously in 1935. "Waiting for the Barbarians" was written in 1898 and circulated in pamphlet form, possibly in 1904.

Rebecca Comay teaches philosophy and literary studies at the University of Toronto and writes on contemporary philosophy and critical theory.

Lynn Crosbie is a writer and critic who has published several collections of poetry and a novel, *Paul's Case*. She has edited several anthologies: *The Girl Wants To*, also *Plush*, and *Click*, and is working on a novel called *Dorothy L'Amour*.

Jacques Derrida teaches at the École des Hautes Études en Sciences Sociales and at the University of California, Irvine. His recent books include *The Politics of Friendship*, *Le monolinguisme de l'autre* and *Adieu: à Emmanuel Levinas*.

Rodolphe el-Khoury teaches in the Graduate School of Design at Harvard University. His latest books include a translation and critical edition of Jean Francois de Bastides: *The Little House: An Architectural Seduction*, *Architecture: In Fashion*, and *Monolithic Architecture*.

Aris Fioretos has published several books of fiction and scholarship in his native Sweden — most recently *En bok om fantomer* ("A Book about Phantoms"). Forthcoming in English translation is his book-length literary essay, *The Gray Book*, the second installment in a "gray trio."

Vivian Flynn studied at the California Institute of Arts, The Rhode Island School of Design, and the Otis Art Institute. Flynn was the recipient of a National Endowment for the Arts Grant through the Foundation for Art Resources in 1979. She now lives in Los Angeles.

Forced Entertainment, a performance group based in Sheffield, U.K., mixes high and low tech, bitterness and poetry, and is increasingly involved with cross-disciplinary art practice; moving from theatre towards installation and works for broadcast. **Hugo Glendinning** is an arts and editorial photographer who has worked closely with the company since 1986.

Foreign Office Architects, located in London, won the competition to design Japan's Yokahama International Port Terminal and is competing for the redevelopment of Link Quay waterfront area of Santa Cruz de Tenerife, Canary Islands.

Mike Hoolboom has made forty experimental films since 1980, which have appeared in over two hundred festivals. He is the author of *Inside the Pleasure Dome: Fringe Film in Canada* (1997).

Paulo Lemos Horta is a doctoral candidate in English at the University of Toronto, where he works on Salman Rushdie. He has translated *The Conquest of the Marvellous*, forthcoming from the University of California Press.

Dianna Ilk is an artist living in New York City. She teaches at Rutgers and works as a film and video editor. Her current project will be screening in NYC in the Spring of 1998.

Phil Jackson is a sometime photographer born in Manchester U.K. and resident in Toronto. His most recent exhibition at the Garnet Press Gallery in Toronto was entitled "Would You Turn Back."

Guntar Kravis is a photographer whose range of work includes images for books, advertising and new media, as well as stills for the Canadian Film Centre and various Toronto theatres. He has exhibited in solo and group shows in Toronto.

Denis Lago is founder of Public Thing International, a Toronto group focused on the art and design of public space which is currently developing a proposal for a sound garden in memory of Japanese composer Toru Takemitsu.

Rita Leistner is a photographer and writer based in Toronto. Her current projects take her to Cambodia, France, and Britain.

MVRDV is a Rotterdam architectural firm founded in 1992 by Winy Maas, Jacob van Rijs, and Nathalie de Vries. Besides designing buildings, MVRDV is involved in the development of master plans, interior design, and furniture design.

Eric Miller teaches at St. Thomas University. His work has appeared in numerous periodicals, including *Descant*, *The Malahat Review*, and *Brick*.

Edward Mitchell is an architect based in New Haven and teaching at the Pratt Institute in New York. His recent projects include the Cedar Hill Neighborhood Planning Study in New Haven with Architecture Theatre pro.ME.THE.US, Public Space in the New American City for the Atlanta Olympic Games, and Top Dog State Park.

Yelda Nasifoglu was born in Istanbul and lives both there and in NYC. She received her bachelors degree in architecture from the Pratt Institute in 1997.

Philippe Petit holds a PhD in philosophy and is a journalist at "Idées" and at "L'Événement du Jeudi."

Pina Petricone is an intern architect teaching at the University of Toronto School of Architecture and Landscape Architecture. Her STUDIO *P2* designs furniture and buildings as well as writing critical texts.

Luca Pocci is a doctoral candidate in comparative literature at the University of Toronto and is writing a dissertation on Italo Calvino and John Barth.

Elias Polizoes is a doctoral candidate in comparative literature at the University of Toronto. His dissertation, "Beautiful Enigma," is a study of Cavafy, Seferis, T.S. Eliot, and Montale.

Bruce Robbins teaches English and comparative literature at Rutgers University, and is a coeditor of the journal *Social Text*, coeditor of the forthcoming *Cosmopolitics*, and author of the forthcoming *Internationalism in Distress*.

Andrew Ross teaches American studies at New York University. His books include *The Chicago Gangster Theory of Life* and the forthcoming *Real Love: In Pursuit of Cultural Justice*.

Richard Sanger is the author of *Shadow Cabinet* (Véhicule, 1996), a book of poems; he is currently working on a new play entitled *Two Words for Snow*. His poems and reviews have appeared in many publications, including *The Globe and Mail* and *The Times Literary Supplement*. He lives in Toronto with his wife and son.

Saskia Sassen teaches in the Department of urban planning at the School of International and Public Affairs at Columbia University. Her most recent book is *Globalization and Its Discontents* (New York: New Press, 1998).

Julija Sukys is a doctoral candidate in comparative literature at the University of Toronto. She writes on nationalism and literature.

Lynne Tillman's books include the novels *Motion Sickness* and *Cast in Doubt* and an essay collection, *The Broad Picture*. Her new novel, *No Lease on Life*, from which her piece in *Alphabet City* was excerpted, appeared from Harcourt Brace in January.

Paul Virilio, before being appointed director of l'École spéciale d'architecture in Paris, studied war architecture. His publications include: *Vitesse et politique*; *L'Espàce critique*; *La vitesse de la libération*.

Krzysztof Wodiczko won widespread acclaim for his "public projections," political images projected onto monumental buildings. He is now Director of the Center of Advanced Visual Studies at Massachusetts Institute of Technology.

Introduction

In the summer of 1925, Walter Benjamin and Asja Lacis travelled to Naples and wrote about the city for the *Frankfurter Zeitung*. The area's light, Vesuvian rock inspired their central figure: porosity. "As porous as this stone is the architecture," they discovered, and extended the image to Neapolitan commerce, gestures, ideas. Interruption, mobility, improvisation — these attitudes were to be found everywhere in the streets of Naples. The city's porosity spoke to a dense, interpenetrating open — an open that was not abstract but one, rather, that could be read in the minutiae of everyday life.

In this Naples, the open was immediate and sensuous. "So everything is joyful and mobile. Music, toys, ice cream circulate through the streets." If the open opens itself through the pleasures of sensory surprise, then the tongue, too, is challenged to taste this fluidity: "Day and night the pavilions glow with the pale, aromatic juices that teach even the tongue what porosity can be."

While the tongue, it is hinted, may possibly have a future, its access to the porous is subject to one restriction: "The stamp of the definitive is avoided. No situation appears intended forever, no figure asserts its 'thus and not otherwise.'" The porous tongue "demands that space and opportunity be at any price preserved."

An ideal instrument for building the open city might then be said to be a tongue both impoverished and porous, a tongue with a "passion for improvisation," labouring to construct a "theatre of new, unforeseen constellations." This is the double condition of our ethical relation to the city: to take responsibility for building while protecting the always unknown, to resist mastery in the present in favour of the freedom of a future we ourselves may never inhabit or recognize.

—J. K.

Générations d'une ville : mémoire, prophétie, responsabilités

Jacques Derrida

Generations of a City: memory, prophecy, responsibilities

Jacques Derrida

Translated by Rebecca Comay

Liminaire

Qu'est-ce qu'un *seuil*, pour une ville ? Une porte, des murailles, une frontière administrative, une enceinte naturelle, les limites d'un poste douanier ? Suffit-il de dire le seuil pour dire l'identité d'une ville ? Et comment transposer cette figure du seuil de l'espace à l'histoire ? Parfois une ville se trouve aussi *au seuil*, non seulement dans la figure du seuil mais au seuil d'une figure nouvelle, d'une configuration encore invisible qu'elle doit *se donner* elle-même, c'est-à-dire ne pas se laisser imposer par la loi d'un autre. Qu'est-ce que la loi d'un autre ? La loi d'un autre peut être ici la loi de l'étranger, d'un nouveau maître politique, mais cela peut être aussi la loi d'une autre logique que celle de la ville elle-même, si elle en a une et qui lui soit propre, une autre logique politique, militaire, policière, économique, touristique, qui viendrait rompre l'idéal *autonomique* de la ville pour en défigurer le plan propre.

En exergue de ces quelques réflexions innocentes — et par là j'entends d'abord *incompétentes* —, incompétentes et préliminaires, au seuil de ce seuil, au seuil de cette marche liminaire qu'est Prague et que veut dire le nom de *Praha* je rappellerai quelques lignes d'un écrivain qui, pour avoir été un éminent Pragois,

Liminal

What is a *threshold*, for a city? A gate, walls, an administrative border, a natural enclosure, the limits of a customs post? Is it enough to speak of the threshold to speak of the identity of a city? And how are we to transpose this figure of a spatial threshold to history? Sometimes a city is also to be found *at the threshold* — not simply inscribed within the figure of the threshold but at the very threshold of a new figure, of a still invisible configuration which it must provide for itself, and this precisely that it not be subject to the law of another. What is the law of another? The law of another can here be the law of a stranger, of a new political master, but it can also be the law of a logic other than that of the city itself, if it indeed has one, and which would be proper to it, another logic — at once political, military, police, economic, touristic — which would come to rupture the autonomous ideal of the city in such a way as to disfigure its own plan.

As a prelude to these few innocent reflections — by which I mean, in the first place, *incomplete* — incomplete and preliminary, at the very threshold of this threshold, at the threshold of this liminal border region which is Prague and which the name of *Praha* means, I will recall several lines of a writer who, for all

n'écrivit ni dans votre langue, ni dans la mienne — ce qui pose un premier problème, le problème *babelien* qui lie la structure de cette ville-ci à l'histoire, voire parfois à la concurrence hyperbolique de plusieurs langues... Et même de plusieurs langues dont toutes ne sont pas européennes: qui oserait affirmer que la responsabilité, les tâches et les actes de mémoire que nous assigne une ville s'inscrivent, au présent, au futur ou au passé, dans des pierres muettes plutôt que dans la rumeur des idiomes qui la hantent ?

Dans ses *Cahiers divers et feuilles volantes*, sans doute en 1922, donc peu de temps après la guerre, à la naissance toute récente et fragile de la Tchéco-Slovaquie — nous y sommes encore, nous y voici revenus et la re-naissance est tout aussi fragile —, Kafka écrit ceci, peut-être en relation avec le texte extraordinaire intitulé *Recherches d'un chien* :

> Dans notre ville, on bâtit continuellement. Pas pour l'agrandir, elle suffit à nos besoins, il y a longtemps que ses limites n'ont pas changé, il semblerait même qu'on éprouve une certaine appréhension à l'agrandir, on préfère se restreindre, on bouche les places et les jardins avec des édifices, on pose de nouveaux étages sur de vieilles maisons, mais en fait ce ne sont pas du tout ces constructions nouvelles qui forment la part principale de la perpétuelle activité du bâtiment. Celle-ci se propose plutôt, si on peut provisoirement s'exprimer ainsi, de consolider ce qui existe déjà. Non qu'on eût construit moins solidement autrefois qu'aujourd'hui et qu'on se trouve ainsi sans cesse amené à corriger d'anciennes erreurs. Sans doute, il règne toujours chez nous une certaine negligence — difficile de discerner ce qui est là légèreté d'esprit et ce qui tient à l'inquiétude d'un caractère trop grave —, mais c'est justement dans le bâtiment qu'elle a le moins l'occasion de se faire sentir. Nous vivons en effet dans le pays des carrières, nous bâtissons presque uniquement en pierre, même le marbre est à notre disposition, et ce que les hommes peuvent laisser échapper en construisant,

that he was an eminent Praguian, wrote neither in your language nor in my own — which poses an initial problem, the Babelian problematic that binds the structure of this city to history, indeed at times to the hyperbolic simultaneity or concurrence of several languages.... And even of several languages not all of which are European: who would dare claim that the responsibility, the tasks and the acts of memory that a city assigns to us are inscribed, in the present, in the future, or in the past, in mute stones rather than in the murmur of the idioms which haunt it?

In his *Assorted Notebooks and Fragments*, no doubt from 1922, thus shortly after the war, at the just recent and fragile birth of Czechoslovakia — we are still there, we have come back to this, and the re-birth is every bit as fragile — Kafka writes the following, perhaps in relation to the extraordinary text entitled "Investigations of a Dog":

> There is constant building going on in our city. Not for the sake of expansion: there is enough for our needs, the borders have not changed for a long time, indeed people seem to be somehow shy of expansion, they would rather be confined, build up the squares and gardens, add on new stories to old houses, but in fact these new buildings are not the main part of the perpetual building activity. This activity rather aims, if we can put it like this for the moment, at securing what already exists. Not that construction used to be worse than it is today or that the old mistakes now need to be corrected all the time. No doubt a certain negligence has always prevailed in our midst — it is difficult to distinguish what is rashness, what is phlegmatic anxiety — but it is precisely in building that such negligence has the least opportunity of manifesting itself. We live in a land of quarries, we build almost exclusively from stone, even marble is at our disposal, and whatever might be overlooked by humans in the course of construction will be rectified by the solidity and stability of the material. As for the method of building, there is no difference

la solidité et la stabilité des matériaux le réparent. En ce qui concerne la manière de bâtir, il n'y a d'ailleurs aucune différence entre les époques, les mêmes lois sont en vigueur de toute antiquité et si, par la faute de notre caractère national, elles ne sont pas toujours strictement observées, c'est là quelque chose qui se produit sans changement et vaut aussi bien pour les anciennes constructions que pour les récentes.

Puis Kafka propose, au sujet des "ruines" et du nom d'un "hôtel" (j'y insiste pour annoncer la question du tourisme que je voudrais poser tout à l'heure), une longue méditation dont je n'ose pas donner ici la lecture intégrale; mais je reviendrai sur le thème babelien du *temps de la ville en construction* qui forme l'argument de plusieurs textes de Kafka, autant de textes, notes de journal, récits ou paraboles de longueur diverse dont la figure de Prague parait être le motif central: il s'agit notamment des *Armes de la ville* et de *La muraille de Chine*. Dans ces deux textes, un des thèmes centraux est celui du projet urbanistique engageant des *générations*, je veux dire la génération d'un habitat singulier par des générations d'hommes dans une histoire ouverte, discontinue, interminable: l'édification d'une tour de Babel dont l'inachèvement, en vérité l'abandon, le renoncement, ne laissent pas l'héritage d'un désastre ou la ruine d'un échec, pas plus qu'ils ne correspondent à quelque phénomène explicable selon les schémas de la rationalité courante.

La première leçon qu'on pourrait en tirer, c'est qu'une certaine manière de compter avec le temps et les générations des citadins à venir est peut-être l'impératif catégorique de tout grand projet urbanistique respectueux et responsable: toute construction qui voudrait totaliser, inscrire *au présent* des structures urbaines ou architecturales saturantes, non transformables soustraites à une sorte de grammaire flexible et capable de nouvelles syntaxes, de nouveaux développements harmonieux, de nouvelles intégrations non contradictoires avec les premiers ensembles, une violence, un

between the different periods, the same rules of construction have applied from antiquity onwards, and if as a result of our national character they are not always strictly adhered to, that in itself is something that has never changed, and holds true just as much for the oldest buildings as for the most recent [Kafka, 1953, 266f].

Then Kafka proposes, on the subject of "ruins" and in the name of a "hotel" (I emphasize this so as to raise the question of tourism which I would like to pose shortly), a lengthy meditation a complete reading of which I dare not provide here. I will, however, return to the Babelian theme of the *time of a city under construction* that forms the argument of several of Kafka's texts — so many texts, diary entries, stories or parables of various lengths in which the figure of Prague seems to be the central motif: notably, the "Arms of the City" and the "Great Wall of China." One of the central themes in both these texts is that of an urbanistic project engaging *generations*. I mean the generation of a singular habitat by generations of men in a history which is open, discontinuous, interminable: the building of a tower of Babel whose very non-achievement, indeed abandonment or renunciation do not leave the heritage of a disaster or the ruin of a failure, any more than they correspond to some phenomenon explicable in terms of the schemata of current rationality.

The first lesson one might draw from this is that a certain way of reckoning with time and the generations of future citizens is perhaps the categorical imperative of every major urban project which is to be respectful and responsible: every construction which tries to totalize, to inscribe — in the present of urban or architectural structures which are saturating, non-transformable, and tied to a sort of flexible grammar capable of new syntaxes, new harmonious developments, new integrations which are not contradictory with the first ensembles — to inscribe a violence, a wrong, a wound which I would be tempted to call moral, which would come to pierce or maim

tort, une blessure que je serais tenté de dire morale, venant léser l'âme et le corps, l'intégrité comme le nom propre d'une ville. Je distinguerai l'*incomplétude* de l'*inachèvement*. C'est l'incomplétude, et non pas l'inachèvement des travaux par impéritie ou incapacité de se donner les moyens, c'est la non-saturation de l'espace urbain qui devraient constituer la règle d'or de tout projet de restauration ou de rénovation urbaine aujourd'hui. Cette non-saturation ne consisterait pas à abandonner des espaces vierges ou sauvages mais à construire selon des structures telles que de nouvelles possibilités, à la fois fonctionnelles et esthétiques, puissent à l'infini enrichir en conservant, fonder en protégeant, garder le patrimoine en vie sans réduire la ville à un musée ou à une sépulture monumentale, ce que la ville comprend toujours en elle mais ne sera jamais. Écoutons encore Kafka : « Il n'y a qu'en ville qu'on puisse voir quelque chose. Tout ce qui se pressait devant la fenêtre de mon wagon était un cimetière ou aurait pu en être un, rien que des choses poussant sur des cadavres, alors que la ville s'en distingue tout de même avec une force bien vivante. » (à Max Brod, 26 juin 1922). Et ailleurs :

Un savant a publié un livre, dit La muraille de Chine, qui [...] cherchait à prouver que la tour de Babel n'a nullement échoué pour les raisons qu'on allègue généralement, ou que, tout au moins, les raisons primordiales ne se trouvent pas parmi celles qu'on connaît.

Et vous connaissez tous la fin des *Armes de la ville*, qui ne sont autres que celles de Prague :

Ce fut ainsi que passa l'époque de la première génération; et nulle, depuis, ne différa : seul le savoir-faire augmentait, et avec lui l'envie de se battre. Ajoutez-y qu'à la deuxième ou troisième génération on reconnut l'inanité de bâtir une tour qui touchât le ciel, mais trop de liens s'étaient créés à ce moment pour qu'on abandonnât la ville. Tout ce qu'il y est né de chants et de légendes est plein de la nostalgie d'un jour prophétisé où elle serait

the soul and the body, the integrity as indeed the proper name of a city. I will distinguish here *incompletion* from *non-achievement*. It is the incompletion and not the non-achievement of works through incompetence or through the inability to provide its own means, it is the non-saturation of urban space that should constitute the golden rule of every project of urban restoration or renovation today. This non-saturation would not consist of abandoning virgin or wild spaces, but rather of constructing according to such structures as the new possibilities: at once functional and aesthetic, might infinitely enrich by conserving, might found by protecting, might keep the patrimony alive without reducing the city to a museum or to a monumental tomb — which a city always includes, but with which it is never identical. Let us again listen to Kafka: "... only in the city are there things to see, for everything that streamed past the train window was cemetery or could have been, nothing but things that grow above corpses, whereas the city after all stands out in strong and vigorous contrast to that" [Kafka, 1977, 325–26]. And elsewhere:

A scholar has published a book, called *The Great Wall of China*, which ... tried to prove that the tower of Babel did not fail for the reasons generally alleged, or at least that the primary reasons are not to be found among the ones that are familiar.

And you all know the end of the "Arms of the City," which are none other than those of Prague:

In this fashion the age of the first generation went past, but none of the succeeding ones showed any difference; except that technical skill increased and with it occasion for conflict. To this must be added that the second or third generation had already recognized the senselessness of building a heaven-reaching tower; but by that time everybody was too deeply involved to leave the city. All the legends and songs that came to birth in that city are filled with longing for a prophesied

pulvérisée par les cinq coups d'un gigan-
tesque poing. Cinq coups qui se suivront de
près. Et c'est pourquoi la ville a un poing
dans ses armes.

Autrement dit, ce qui rend possible la communauté vivante des générations qui vivent et
construisent la ville, qui se tendent en perma-
nence dans la projection même d'une ville à
dé-re-construire, c'est le renoncement para-
doxal à la tour absolue, à la ville totale et qui
touche au ciel, c'est l'acceptation de ce qu'un
logicien appellerait peut-être un *axiome d'incomplétude*. Une ville est un ensemble qui doit
rester indéfiniment, structurellement non
saturable, ouvert sur sa propre transformation,
sur des augmentations qui altèrent ou dépla-
cent aussi peu que possible la mémoire de son
patrimoine. Une ville doit rester ouverte sur
ce qu'elle sait qu'elle ne sait pas encore qu'elle
sera: il faut inscrire, et comme un thème, le
respect de ce *non-savoir* dans la science et dans
la compétence architecturale ou urbanistique.
Autrement, que ferait-on, sinon appliquer
des programmes, totaliser, saturer, suturer,
asphyxier ? Et cela sans prendre, dès lors,
aucune décision responsable ? Car le déroule-
ment d'un programme ou la mise en œuvre d'un
"plan" n'est jamais une décision responsable.
Je suggère par là que la décision responsable
n'est jamais ici, en dernière instance, celle des
savants et des techniciens, des urbanistes et
des architectes, encore moins des experts en
économie, en tourisme, en techniques de la
communication; même si leur compétence est
absolument indispensable, elle me paraît radi-
calement insuffisante au regard des décisions
et des responsabilités dont je parle. Ils peuvent
eux aussi, ces experts, en tant que citoyens
ou citadins, prendre part à de telles décisions
non scientifiques ou non techniques (qui
sont aussi non politiques, non militaires, non
économiques, non religieuses, non culturelles,
non touristiques, et j'oserai même dire, au
risque de choquer, étrangères à la fonctionnal-
ité sociale du logement; cela ne veut dire pas
qu'on n'ait pas à tenir le plus grand compte de
ces fonctions et de ces usages pour les intégrer

day when the city would be destroyed by five
successive blows from a gigantic fist. It is for
that reason too that the city has a closed fist
on its coat of arms [Kafka, 1971, 434].

Otherwise put, what makes possible the
living community of the generations who live
in and construct the city, who permanently
orient themselves towards the very projection
of a city to be de- or re-constructed, is the
paradoxical renunciation of the absolute tower,
of the total city which reaches the sky: it is the
acceptance of what a logician would perhaps
call the *axiom of incompleteness*. A city is an
ensemble which must remain indefinitely and
structurally non-saturable, open to its proper
transformation, to the augmentations which
alter and displace as little as possible the
memory of its patrimony. A city must remain
open to knowing that it does not yet know
what it will be. It is necessary to inscribe, and
to thematize, the respect for this *non-knowl-
edge* in architectural and urbanistic science
and know-how. Otherwise, what would one do
other than apply programs, totalize, saturate,
suture, asphyxiate? And this without henceforth taking any responsible decision? For the
execution of a program or the realization of
a "plan" is never a responsible decision. I suggest by this that the responsible decision is
never here, in the final instance, that of the
scholars and technicians, of the urbanists
and architects, still less that of the experts in
economics, in tourism, in communications
technologies. Even if their competence is
absolutely indispensable, it would seem to me
to be radically insufficient with regard to the
decisions and the responsibilities of which I
am speaking. They can also, these experts, participate themselves as citizens or city-dwellers
[*citoyens ou citadins*] in such non-scientific
and non-technical decisions (which are also
non-political, non-military, non-economic,
non-religious, non-cultural, non-touristic, and
I will even venture to say, at the risk of being
shocking, foreign to the social function of
housing. This is not to say that one does not
need to take the greatest possible account of

dans un calcul, mais la finalité ultime de la ville et des décisions qui la concernent n'est pas là).

De Paris, Valéry disait qu'il nous pense plutôt que nous ne le pensons avant même que nous ne formions le projet de le penser. Ce que nous aurions à penser aujourd'hui, c'est le lieu où nous sommes. Rien de moins. C'est difficile. Il est difficile de penser le lieu, l'unité de lieu, l'identité du lieu d'une construction nécessairement interrompue, discontinue mais dans le cours de laquelle, son histoire en somme, un étrange contrat communautaire a lié et liera les générations de bâtisseurs, le fait de l'inachèvement (l' "inanité" reconnue, dit Kafka, "de bâtir une tour qui touche au ciel") ne les décourageant pas mais au contraire les *obligeant*, les rendant plus endettés, plus assujettis au devoir, plus responsables que jamais du destin de la ville, comme si le renoncement à la totalisation était l'origine de la communauté. Penser la ville, c'est difficile à plusieurs titres. Difficile parce qu'il a toujours été en vérité impossible de penser l'essence *générale* de la ville, c'est-à-dire ce qui en elle devrait se réduire à quelque être-présent de son existence, à quelque représentation ou quelque présentabilité actuelle (une ville est une mémoire et une promesse qui ne se confondent jamais avec la totalité de ce qui est *présentement* visible, présentable, construit, habitable) et, ce qui ne s'y résume ou subsume jamais, la *singulière* essence de chaque ville. Difficile aussi parce qu'il a toujours été périlleux de penser l'essence de cette espèce de ville qu'on appelle capitale, et, ce qui ne s'y résume ou subsume jamais, la singulière essence de chaque capitale. La question: "qu'est-ce qu'une ville ?" et "qu'est-ce qu'une capitale ?" prend une allure d'autant plus mélancolique ou eschatologique aujourd'hui que, je le crois, et ce serait l'hypothèse implicite qui oriente ces modestes propos, la ville, la métropole, la *polis*, la cité ne sont déjà plus les unités fortes et ultimes, les unités topologiques de l'habitat, de l'action, de la communication, de la stratégie, du commerce, en un mot, de la socialité et de la politique

these functions and customs so as to integrate them into a calculus, but the ultimate end of the city and of the decisions which concern it does not reside here).

Regarding Paris, Valéry used to say that it thinks more about us than we think about it, even before we form the project of thinking about it. What we should think today is the place where we are. Nothing less. It is difficult. It is difficult to think the site, the unity of site, the identity of the site of a construction which is necessarily interrupted, discontinuous but in the course of which—its very history, in short—a strange communitarian contract has bound and will bind the generations of builders: the fact of non-achievement (the acknowledged "foolishness," says Kafka, "of building a tower which reaches heaven") does not discourage them but on the contrary *obligates* them, makes them more indebted, more subject to duty, more responsible than ever for the destiny of the city, as if the renunciation of totalization were the very origin of community. To think the city is difficult for several reasons. It is difficult because it has truly always been impossible to think both the *general* essence of the city—that is, that which should reduce therein to some present modality of its existence, to some representation or some current presentability (a city is a memory and a promise which are never confused with the totality of what is *presently* visible, presentable, constructed, habitable)— and, which can never reduced to or subsumed under this, the *singular* essence of every city. It is difficult also because it has always been risky to think the singular essence of this kind of city which is called a capital, or, which is never reduced to or subsumed under this, to think the singular essence of every capital. The question "what is a city?" and "what is a capital?" takes on today an allure all the more melancholic or eschatological when, I believe (and this would be the implicit hypothesis which orients these modest proposals), the city [*ville*], the metropolis, the *polis*, the city [*cité*] are already no longer the steadfast and

humaine, d'une *politique* qui devra changer de nom dès lors que la cité comme *polis* ou *acropolis* ne donne plus la mesure de la *res publica* Mais que le "*post-city age*" ait commencé ne signifie pas que nous devions oublier la ville.

Ce lieu qui porte un nom propre et que nous habitons présentement mais qu'il nous faut aujourd'hui projeter comme un lieu à venir et à venir de façon pourtant prescrite par l'essence de sa mémoire, c'est un lieu riche d'une immense histoire stratifiée dans ses murs, ses monuments et ses rues, d'une histoire qui pourtant reste à venir, puisque nous nous interrogeons sur ce qu'il faut en faire, et un lieu que nous habitons, si nous l'habitons, tout autrement qu'une maison, un musée, une architecture de pierres tombales, un monument, un temple, une église, une usine, un centre de communications téléphoniques, ferroviaires, aériennes, un centre d'attractions culturelles ou touristiques. Prague comprend tout cela mais ce qu'elle nomme ne se réduit à aucune des ses parties. Si nous l'habitons, ce n'est pas comme nous habiterions un habitat, une maison, un appartement, un hôtel.

Il y a une ville. Nous y sommes. Nous l'habitons, nous y passons. Aujourd'hui encore, en droit, c'est une capitale. El le porte un nom propre que tout le monde connaît et sur lequel aucune contestation de droit ne s'élève. C'est *Praha*, Prague pour un Français. On peut élever des questions de droit, on pourrait un jour contester son identité de capitale politique nationale ou internationale (par exemple tchéco-slovaque) ou culturelle (par exemple européenne ou centre-européenne). Mais sur le fait qu'il s'agit d'une ville et qu'elle porte le nom de Prague, personne ne saurait élever la moindre contestation recevable. Cette ville est comme une personne juridique ou comme le personnage d'un roman, la *persona* d'une fiction théâtrale, dramatique, tragique, comique, avec ce que *persona* peut signifier aussi de masque derrière lequel l'identité de l'acteur ou du sujet personnel peut rester secrète comme un jour de bal masqué, de fête ou d'opération, voire d'opéra révolutionnaire.

ultimate unities, the topological unities of habitat, of action, of communication, of strategy, of commerce — in a word, of sociality and of human politics, of a *politics* which will change its name as soon as the city as *polis* or *acropolis* no longer provides the measure of the *res publica*. But the fact that this "*post-city age*" has begun does not mean that we should forget the city.

This place which bears a proper name and which we inhabit at present, but which we must today project as a place to come (but to come, however, in a way prescribed by the very essence of its memory) is a place rich with an immense history — a history stratified in its walls, its monuments and its streets, a history which however is yet to come, since we are questioning ourselves about what must be done with it — and a place which we inhabit, if we inhabit it, completely differently than we do a house, a musuem, an architecture of funerary stones, a monument, a temple, a church, a factory, a telephonic, railway, or air communications centre, a centre of cultural or tourist attractions. Prague includes all these but what it names cannot be reduced to any of its parts. If we inhabit it, this is not in the same way as we inhabit a habitat, a house, an apartment, a hotel.

There is a city. We are there. We inhabit it, we pass through it. Today, still, by law, it is a capital. It bears a proper name which the whole world recognizes and about which no legal challenge has arisen. It is *Praha*, Prague for a French speaker. One can raise legal questions, one could one day contest its identity as a political capital whether national or international (for example Czechoslovakian) or cultural (for example European or Central European). But no one would be able to raise the slightest admissible challenge to the fact that it is a question of a city and that it does bear the name of Prague. This city is like a juridical person or like the person of a novel, the *persona* of a theatrical, dramatic, tragic, comic fiction, together with the fact that *persona* can signify also the mask behind which

Quel a été le sujet identifiable, identique à lui-même tout au long de l'histoire discontinue qui a traversé les époques de l'architecture gothique, baroque, la destruction du ghetto, l'institution de la Tchécoslovaquie, le protectorat allemand puis soviétique, le Printemps de Prague, la normalisation puis la dernière révolution en cours ?

Est-ce la même ville qui répond à ce nom ? Est-ce à la même ville qu'on répond ? Comment répondre à une ville ? Comment *répondre* d'une ville ?

C'ést la question de la réponse et de la responsabilité au regard d'une ville que je voudrais esquisser. Si nous sommes ici réunis c'est que nous nous sentons tous, de façon diverse, confuse, sans doute hétérogène, et à des degrés d'intensité variables, une responsabilité à l'égard de Prague: devant "quel qu'un," devant quelqu'un d'autre qui répond au nom de Prague. Une responsabilité, c'est-à-dire des devoirs mais aussi les droits.

A quel titre aurions-nous de telles responsabilités ? Et qui, nous ? En tant que citadins pragois ? Ce serait une chose. En tant que Tchèques, c'est-à-dire en tant que membres ou originaires d'une nation et d'un territoire ? Ce serait une autre chose. En tant que Tchéco-Slovaques, citoyens d'un Etat de nouveau traversé par des menaces de sécession ? Ce serait une autre chose — et vous savez que cette distinction est rien moins qu'abstraite aujourd'hui. En tant qu'Européens du centre et de l'ex Autriche-Hongrie ? Encore une autre chose. En tant que juifs et porteurs de la mémoire d'un ghetto détruit dans des conditions d'ailleurs fort complexes? Encore une autre chose. En tant qu'Allemands, la langue allemande n'étant pas ici une langue parmi d'autres ? Une autre chose. En tant qu'Européens ? Encore une autre chose. Qui est responsable de quoi et dans quelle langue? J'insiste encore sur cette figure babélienne parce que, dans le temps fondateur de sa construction et dans les sédiments essentiels de ses structures architecturales, la ville de Prague n'a pas été liée à un seul et même Etat,

the identity of the actor or of the personal subject can remain as secret as a day of masquerade, a day of festival or a day of plotting [*opération*], indeed, of revolutionary drama [*opéra*]. What has been the identifiable, self-identical subject persisting throughout the discontinuous history which has run through the epochs of Gothic and Baroque architecture, the destruction of the ghetto, the institution of Czechoslovakia, the German and then the Soviet protectorate, the Prague Spring, the normalization and finally the last revolution which is now underway? Is it the same city which responds to this name? Is it to the same city that we are responding? How is one to respond to a city? How is one to *answer* for, assume responsibility for, a city?

It is the question of response and responsibility with respect to a city that I would like to sketch out. If we are here brought together it is because we all feel, in a manner which is diverse, confused, no doubt heterogeneous, and with varying degrees of intensity, because we all feel a responsibility towards Prague: a responsibility before "someone," before someone other who responds in the name of Prague. A responsibility — duties, that is, but also rights.

By what title are we to assume such responsibilities? And who, we? Inasmuch as we are Prague citizens? That would be one thing. Insofar as we are Czechs, that is, as members or natives of a nation and territory? That would be something else. Insofar as we are Czechoslovakians, citizens of a state which is once more shadowed by threats of secession? That would be another thing — and you know how such a distinction is far from abstract today. Insofar as we are central Europeans of the former Austro-Hungarian empire? Still something else. Insofar as we are Jews and bearers of the memory of a ghetto destroyed under conditions which were, in fact, tremendously complex? Yet another matter. Insofar as we are Germans — the German language here being not just any language among others? Again, something else. Insofar as we

et les *concurrences* qui ont scellé son édification, j'oserai dire les contresignatures de son histoire, furent multiples, nationales, linguistiques et religieuses. C'est bien de Prague que semble parler Kafka dans *Les armes de la ville* quand il dit, tout au début de sa parabole; une certaine hyperbole, un certain excès, et cet excès, c'est, entre autres, celui des *interprètes*. Comme aujourd'hui, il y en avait trop :

> Il y avait trop d'ordre; on parlait trop poteaux indicateurs, interprètes, logements ouvriers et voies de communication; il semblait qu'on eût des siècles devant soi pour travailler à son idée [...] De telle idées paralysaient les forces et, plus que la tour, on s'inquiétait de bâtir la cité ouvrière. Chaque nation voulait le plus beau quartier, il en naissait des querelles qui finissaient dans le sang.

Ces excès, cette multiplicité des idiomes, des interprètes et des nations, ces guerres incessantes laissent penser que l'essence de la ville est ailleurs, ou plus précisément qu'elle est autre que celle de la tour. C'est en renonçant à la tour capitale, à la plus haute ambition d'une tour unique, d'une érection capitale qui touche au ciel que, au bout de quelques générations, une communauté se forme dans le renoncement même et que la décision se prend de garder la ville précisément au lieu de la tour impossible. Et cette décision responsable se prend au nom de l'avenir. On renonce au projet totalitaire de la tour, on abat l'idée de la tour au moment où on prend conscience que, ce qui compte, c'est l'ouverture de la promesse et donc de l'avenir. La catastrophe pour un plan de ville, c'est de vouloir résoudre tous les problèmes exhaustivement dans le temps d'une génération et de ne pas *donner le temps et l'espace* aux générations futures, de ne pas le leur léguer, précisément parce que "ceux-qui-savent," les architectes et les urbanistes croient savoir d'avance ce que demain devra être et substituent ainsi leur programmation technoscientifique à la responsabilité éthico-politique. C'est encore ce que me

are Europeans? Yet something else. Who is responsible for what, and in what language? I still emphasize this Babelian figure because in the foundational time of its construction and in the essential layers of its architectural structures, the city of Prague has not been linked to a single and identical State, and the *concurrences* which have sealed its building, I will venture to say the counter-signatures of its history, were multiple in every sense: national, linguistic, and religious. It is surely of Prague that Kafka seems to be speaking in the "Arms of the City" when he announces, at the very beginning of his parable, a certain hyperbole, a certain excess, and this excess is, among other things, a surfeit of *interpreters*. Just as today, there were too many of these then as well:

> indeed, the order was perhaps too perfect, too much thought was given to guides, interpreters, accomodations for the workmen, and roads of communication, as if there were centuries before one to do the work in. [...] Such thoughts paralyzed people's powers, and so they troubled less about the tower than the construction of a city for the workmen. Every nationality wanted the finest quarter for itself, and this gave rise to disputes, which developed into bloody conflicts [Kafka, 1971, 433].

This excess, this multiplicity of idioms, of interpreters, and of nations, these incessant wars, lead one to think that the essence of the city is elsewhere, or more precisely that it is something other than the essence of the tower. It is by renouncing the capital tower, by renouncing the highest ambition for a unique tower, for a capital erection which touches the sky, that after several generations a community is formed in the very renunciation and that the decision takes hold to preserve the city precisely in the place of the impossible tower. And this responsible decision takes place in the name of the future. One renounces the totalitarian project of the tower, one casts aside the idea of the tower, the moment one becomes conscious that what counts is the opening of a promise and

semble suggérer Kafka dans *Les armes de la ville* quand il explique comment il a fallu renoncer, et ce fut un bien, à totaliser et à réduire l'avenir au temps d'une seule génération qui détiendrait le savoir absolu du projet — *et du nom* car, comme vous savez, c'est pour "se faire un nom" que dans l'Ecriture, les Shems projetèrent de construire la tour de Babel et que Dieu déconstruisit leur édification en cours lorsqu'il prononça le nom de Babel : "confusion". Kafka :

> Voici comment on raisonnait : l'essentiel de l'entreprise est l'idée de bâtir une tour qui touche aux cieux. Tout le reste, après, est secondaire. Une fois saisie dans sa grandeur, l'idée ne peut plus disparaître : tant qu'il y aura des hommes il y aura le désir, le désir ardent, d'achever la construction de la tour. Or, à cet égard, l'avenir ne doit préoccuper personne; bien au contraire, la science humaine s'accroit, l'architecture a fait et fera des progrès, un travail qui demande un an à notre époque pourra peut-être, dans un siècle, être exécuté en six mois, et mieux, et plus durablement. Pourquoi donc donner aujourd'hui jusqu'à la limite de ses forces ? Cela n'aurait de sens que si l'on pouvait espérer bâtir la tour dans le temps d'une génération.

> Il ne fallait pas compter là-dessus. Il était beaucoup plus logique d'imaginer, tout au contraire, que la génération suivante, en possession d'un savoir plus complet, jugerait mal le travail fait, abattrait l'ouvrage des devanciers, et recommencerait sur de nouveaux frais.

> De telles idées paralysaient les forces et, plus que la tour, on s'inquiétait de bâtir la cité ouvrière. Chaque nation voulait le plus beau quartier, il en naissait des querelles qui finissaient dans le sang.

> Ces combats ne cessaient plus; ils fournirent au chef un nouvel argument pour prouver que, faute d'union, la tour ne pouvait être bâtie que très lentement et même, de

hence of the future. What is catastrophic for a city plan is the desire to resolve all problems exhaustively within the timespan of a generation and not to *give time and space* to future generations, not to bequeath this to them, precisely because "those who know," the architects and urbanists, believe they know in advance what must happen the next day, and thus substitute their techno-scientific programming for ethico-political responsibility. This is again what Kafka seems to me to be suggesting in "The Arms of the City" when he explains how it has been necessary to renounce, and this was a good thing, to renounce totalizing and reducing the future to the timespan of a single generation who would have exclusive access to absolute knowledge of the project — *and of the name*, for, as you know, it was in order "to make themselves a name" that in the Bible the Shems conceived the project of building the tower of Babel and that God deconstructed their building in progress when he pronounced the name of Babel: "confusion." Kafka:

> People argued in this way: The essential thing in the whole business is the idea of building a tower that will reach to heaven. In comparison with that idea everything else is secondary. The idea, once seized in its magnitude, can never vanish again; so long as there are men on the earth there will be also the irresistible desire to complete the building. That being so, however, one need have no anxiety about the future; on the contrary, human knowledge is increasing, the art of building has made progress and will make further progress, a piece of work which takes us a year may perhaps be done in half the time in another hundred years, and better done too, more enduringly. So why exert oneself to the extreme limit of one's present powers? There would be some sense in doing that only if it were likely that the tower could be completed in one generation. But that is beyond all hope. It is far more likely that the next generation with their perfected knowledge will find the work of their predecessors bad, and tear down what has been built so as

préférence, une fois la paix conclue. Mais on n'employait pas tout le temps à se battre; entre deux guerres on travaillait à l'embellissement de la cité, ce qui provoquait de nouvelles jalousies, d'où sortaient de nouveaux combats. Ce fut ainsi que passa l'époque de la première génération; et nulle, depuis, ne différa; seul le savoir-faire augmentait, et avec lui l'envie de se battre. Ajoutez-y qu'à la deuxième ou troisième génération on reconnut l'inanité de bâtir une tour qui touchât le ciel, mais trop de liens s'étaient créés à ce moment pour qu'on abandonnât la ville.

Devant qui, devant quelle mémoire et devant quel avenir, *devant* quelle génération et *de* quelle génération est-on responsable quand on assume la responsabilité d'une ville ?

Mon hypothèse, c'est que la réponse à cette question oblige à déplacer un peu le concept même de responsabilité. Tout projet concernant le destin d'une ville, c'est-à-dire ce qui lie sa mémoire à son présent et à son avenir, déborde pour des raisons essentielles et la possibilité de l'achèvement et la dimension d'une génération, voire d'une nationalité ou d'une langue. Le temps implique une promesse engageant ici plus d'une génération, et donc plus d'une politique, plus que la politique, dans une durée dont l'hétérogénéité, voire la discontinuité, la non-totalisation doivent être acceptées comme la loi. L'histoire de la ville de Prague est exemplaire à cet égard, avec ses ruptures, ses stratifications gothico-baroques, les influences italienne, française, celte, germanique, ses longues stases ou temps d'arrêt, la destruction du ghetto et ce qui depuis le XVIII siècle s'est immobilisé ou effacé devant la capitale viennoise.

Sans céder à la vieille figure de l'âme ou de l'esprit d'une ville, fût-ce d'une capitale dont on imagine plus facilement que, occupant la place de la tête ou du chef-lieu (*caput, capitis*) elle a l'identité d'une personne, *on doit* se demander quelle responsabilité nous est assignée par la ville. On doit se demander pourquoi elle n'est vraiment une responsabilité que

to begin anew. Such thoughts paralyzed people's powers, and so they troubled less about the tower than the construction of a city for the workmen. Every nationality wanted the finest quarter for itself, and this gave rise to disputes, which developed into bloody conflicts. These conflicts never came to an end; to the leaders they were a new proof that, in the absence of the necessary unity, the building of the tower must be done very slowly, or indeed preferably postponed until universal peace was declared. But the time was spent not only in conflict; the town was embellished in the intervals, and this unfortunately enough evoked fresh envy and fresh conflict. In this fashion the age of the first generation went past, but none of the succeeding ones showed any difference; except that technical skill increased and with it occasion for conflict. To this must be added that the second or third generation had already recognized the senselessness of building a heaven-reaching tower; but by that time everybody was too deeply involved to leave the city [Kafka, 1971, 433–44].

Before whom, before which memory and before which future, *before* which generation and *for* which generation is one responsible when one assumes the responsibility for a city?

My hypothesis is that the answer to this question obliges us to displace a bit the very concept of responsibility. Every project concerning the destiny of a city, that is what binds its memory to its present and to its future, exceeds itself for essential reasons, as does the possibility of completion and the dimension of a generation, indeed of a nationality or of a language. Time implies a promise which here engages more than a generation, and thus more than a politics, more than politics, in a duration in which heterogeneity, indeed discontinuity, non-totalization, must be accepted as law. The history of the city of Prague is exemplary in this respect, with its rupture, its Gothic-Baroque stratifications, its Italian, French, Celtic, Germanic influences, its long periods of stasis or arrest, the destruction of

dans la mesure où elle paraît *contradictoire* et donc apparemment impossible à assumer : c'est alors seulement qu'elle appelle à une décision ou à une série, donc à une histoire, à la fois continue et discontinue, de décisions tranchantes. A une morale et à une politique de la ville. La responsabilité tient non seulement au fait qu'une ville, toujours plus vieille que nous, finie, mortelle, menacée dans l'unité même de son corps, est un héritage précaire dont nous avons la garde et qui nous dicte en silence, selon la loi d'un espace déjà structuré, des instructions, des prescriptions, des interdictions aussi. Elle tient surtout (et c'est en cela qu'elle est responsabilité et qu'elle appelle des décisions qu'aucun "savoir", aucune "compétence" architecturale ou urbanistique, si indispensables soient-ils, ne sauraient garantir) au fait indéniable que cet héritage est donné aux légataires comme un ordre *contradictoire* : je suis une, mais je ne suis que le seuil de moi-même, gardez-moi, sauvez-moi, sauvez donc l'ordre que je vous donne, écoutez ma loi, elle est une, mais pour cela construisez-moi, donc dé-re-construisez-moi, vous êtes au seuil, agrandissez-moi, transformez-moi, multipliez-moi, ne me laissez pas intacte, prenez le risque de me déconstruire. Si vous me laissez intacte, et une, vous me perdez. Il faut me garder et faire effraction en moi, me sauvegarder *et* me transfigurer, me transformer pour me sauver, il faut m'aimer *et* me violer, mais d'une certaine manière et non d'une autre. Il faut m'affirmer comme je m'affirme et pour cela inventer l'impossible qui consiste à respecter mon corps passé, à dire mon âge mais aussi, et par respect, à me donner assez de vie pour ne pas me confondre avec un conservatoire d'archives, une bibliothèque de légendes lithographiques, un musée, un temple, une tour, un centre de décisions administratives ou politiques, une enceinte parlementaire, un hôtel de tourisme, une chambre de commerce, un pôle d'investissement, un centre de triage ferroviaire ou informatique, une bourse informatisée, ni même, une ruche habitable, laborieuse et productive. Je comprends tout cela en moi,

the ghetto and what since the eighteenth century has been immobilized or effaced before the Viennese capital.

Without yielding to the old figure of the soul or spirit of a city, whether this be of a capital which one can imagine all the more easily if, occupying the place of the head or of the chief town (*caput, capitis*), it assumes the identity of a person, *one must* ask oneself what responsibility is assigned to us by the city. One must ask onself why it is not truly a responsibility except to the degree that it appears *contradictory* and thus apparently impossible to assume: this then only if such a responsibility calls for a decision or for a series of decisions, hence to a history, at once continuous and discontinuous, of clear-cut decisions. If it calls for a morality and for a politics of the city. Responsibility stems not only from the fact that a city, always older than us, finite, mortal, threatened in the very unity of its body, is a precarious heritage which is ours to protect and which dictates to us in silence, according to the law of an already structured space, instructions, prescriptions, and also prohibitions. It stems also (and it is for this very reason that it is responsibility, and that it calls for decisions which no "knowledge," no architectural or urbanistic "competence," however indispensable these might be, could guarantee) from the undeniable fact that this heritage is given to its legatees or heirs as a *contradictory* order: I am one, but I am only the threshold of myself, guard me, protect me, save me, save therefore the order which I give you, heed my law, it is one, but for this construct me, thus de- and re-construct me, you are at the threshold, expand me, transform me, multiply me, don't leave me intact, take the risk of deconstructing me. If you leave me intact, and one, you will lose me. It is necessary both to protect me and to assault me, both to safeguard me and to transfigure me, to transform me precisely in order to save me: it is necessary both to love me and to violate me — but in a certain manner and not in another. It is necessary to affirm me as I affirm myself, and, in order for

dans mon grand corps en déplacement mais vous ne devez pas m'y réduire, je suis le seuil d'autre chose encore, je n'ai jamais été, une ville n'aura jamais été seulement cela.

Le discours que je prête à cette ville de Prague qui dirait "moi, depuis le seuil, je parle" ressemble un peu à une théologie négative et *sui*-référentielle :

> Vous n'avez rien à dire ni à faire de moi, la ville, aucun prédicat, aucune prédication ne me conviennent; je vous reste inaccessible et transcendante, d'où votre obligation infinie à mon égard. Et d'ailleurs je vous mets au défi de tirer un précepte urbanistique ou une maxime architecturale de ce désir que je prononce ou de cette provocation que je vous adresse.

Est-ce que ça parle, une ville ?, demanderez-vous. Je disais tout à l'heure que la ville nous dictait des ordres *contradictoires* et d'autant plus autoritaires qu'il se profèrent en silence. Certes. Mais ce silence est le moment d'un langage, et parfois d'autant plus éloquent qu'il nous oblige à le traduire. Il faut des interprètes, beaucoup d' "interprètes", disait Kafka au début des *Armes de la ville*, même si parfois il y en a trop. C'est lui qui se plaignait aussi en disant: « La langue, c'est l'haleine sonore de la patrie. Mais… moi je suis un grand asthmatique puisque je ne connais ni le tchèque ni l'hébreu. »[1] Pour trouver du sens à cette question, il suffit de réflechir sur ce qui lie la ville à la langue. Cette alliance est tout sauf contingente et superficielle. Les murs de Prague ne parlent ni allemand ni slovaque, ni "*Küchelbömisch*," ce dialecte germano-tchèque, ni *Mauscheldeutsch*, ce dialecte germano-yiddish, même si la répercussion de ces langues y résonne avec une insistance pressante et y réclame quelque privilège, posant ainsi la question d'une hégémonie à laquelle un Français, par exemple et, pure hypothèse, pourrait avoir le désir de vous voir résister au moment où votre ville *investit, s'investit, est investie* dans de nouvelles projections. La concurrence dont je parle fait rage aujourd'hui,

this, to invent the impossible, which consists of respecting my past body, to tell my age but also, and out of respect, to give me enough life so as not to confuse me with a conservatory of archives, a library of lithographic legends, a museum, a temple, a tower, a centre of administrative or political decisions, a parliamentary enclosure, a tourist hotel, a chamber of commerce, an investment centre, a hub of railway or information connections, a computerized stock exchange, or even a habitable, laborious, and productive hive. I include all these within me, within my great, displacing body, but you must never reduce me to this, I am the threshold of something else again: I have never been, and a city will never have been, simply that.

The discourse which I am giving to this city of Prague which would say "me, from the threshold, I speak" resembles slightly a negative and *self*-referential theology:

> You have nothing to say or to do about me, the city, no predicate, no predication is adequate to me; I remain inaccessible and transcendent to you — whence your infinite obligation with respect to me. And moreover I defy you to draw any urbanistic precept or architectural maxim from this desire which I pronounce or from this provocation which I am addressing to you.

"Does a city speak?" you will ask. I was saying a little earlier that the city dictates to us *contradictory* orders and these are all the more authoritative insofar as they pronounce themselves in silence. Certainly. But this silence is the moment of a language, and sometimes all the more eloquent insofar as it obligates us to translate it. There is a need for interpreters, "many interpreters," said Kafka at the beginning of the "Arms of the City," even if sometimes there are too many of these. Kafka is the one who also complained, saying: "Language is the music and breath of home. I — but I am badly asthmatic, since I can speak neither Czech nor Hebrew" [Janouch, 138]. To make sense of this question, it is enough to reflect on what links the city to language. This

elle n'est pas seulement politico-économique, mais elle ne peut pas ne pas concerner le destin de la ville même. C'est aussi pour rappeler l'acuité de ce problème babelien que j'interroge encore ces textes de Kafka. Qu'il s'agisse des *Armes de la ville*, de *La muraille de Chine* ou de tels *Cahiers divers er feuilles volantes*, ces textes parlent en allemand, dans un allemand qui garde aussi la mémoire de la destruction au XIX siècle du ghetto de Prague, en vue d'un assainissement apparemment indispensable et souhaité de toutes parts: « En nous continuent de vivre les recoins obscurs, les passages mystérieux, les fenêtres aveugles, les cours sales, les tavernes bruyantes et les restaurants bien clos. Nous allons par les larges rues des quartiers neufs. Mais nos pas et nos regards sont hésitants. Au-dedans de nous-mêmes, nous tremblons encore comme dans les vieilles ruelles de misère. Notre coeur n'est pas encore au fait de ces travaux d'assainissement. La vieille ville juive insalubre que nous portons en nous est beaucoup plus, réelle que la ville nouvelle et hygiénique qui nous entoure. »² Il reste que tous ces textes parlent avec insistance tance d`une ville qui s'appelle Babel et derrière laquelle on reconnaît Prague.

Cette *double contrainte* est plus sensible que jamais dans le corps de Prague aujourd'hui. Aggravée par toutes les apories actuelles de la capitale — et de ce qu'on pourrait appeler la "conscience de capitale" dans les Etats-nations de l' Europe aujourd'hui (capitale nationale de la Bohême ? capitale improbable d'une Tchéco-Slovaquie ?), cette double injonction commande, à la fois et *d'une part*, de conserver, de restaurer, de maintenir intact un patrimoine, lui-même hétérogène dans sa stratification (les formations gothiques de Mala Strana, de Hradcany et de la Vieille Ville, puis l'immense apport baroque) et, *d'autre part*, de ne pas conserver et restaurer à seule fin de restaurer. Se limiter à l'impératif de la restauration, si indispensable et vital qu'il reste, c'est dénaturer l'essence d'une ville et la confondre avec celle du musée ou des temples, de la mémoire artistique ou de l'expérience religieuse —

alliance is anything but contingent and superficial. The walls of Prague speak neither German nor Slovak, neither *"Küchelbömisch,"* that German-Czech dialect, nor *Mauscheldeutsch*, that German-Yiddish dialect, even if the echo of all these languages resonates with a pressing insistence in them, and claims a certain privilege there, thereby posing the question of a hegemony which a French person, for example, and purely hypothetically, might have the desire to see you resist at the moment when your city *invests, invests itself, is invested* with new projections. The concurrence of which I am speaking is raging today, it is not only politico-economic, but it cannot fail to involve the destiny of the city itself. It is so as to recall as well the sharpness of the Babelian problematic that I am still interrogating these texts of Kafka. Whether it is a question of the "Arms of the City," of "The Great Wall of China," or of the "Notebooks" — these texts all speak in German, in a German which also preserves the memory of the destruction, in the nineteenth century, of the ghetto of Prague, in view of a purification which was apparently considered indispensable and desired from all quarters: "In us all it still lives — the dark corners, the secret alleys, shuttered windows, squalid courtyards, rowdy pubs, and sinister inns. We walk through the broad streets of the newly built town. But our steps and our glances are uncertain. Inside we tremble just as before in the ancient streets of our misery. Our heart knows nothing of the slum clearance which has been achieved. The unhealthy old Jewish town within us is far more real than the new hygienic town around us" [Janouch, 80]. It remains that all these texts speak with insistence of a city named Babel, behind which we can recognize Prague.

This *double constraint* is more palpable than ever in the body of Prague today. Aggravated by all the contemporary aporias of the capital — and by what one could call the "capital consciousness" in the nation-states of Europe today (national capital of Bohemia? improbable capital of Czechoslovakia?), this double

qu'elle comprend sans doute mais sans s'y réduire. La mémoire historique ne doit être ni celle d'une église (temple immobile, lieu de culte dans lequel on ne vit ni ne circule et qui peut, avant les musées, abriter les œuvres), ni celle d'une archive morte, d'une sépulture ou d'une documentation de pierre.

Après être resté si longtemps, pour l'amour de Prague, sur le seuil du seuil, je voudrais proposer très schématiquement quelques hypothèses "pratiques" qui esquisseraient plusieurs conséquences de ce que je viens de risquer.

1 Que signifie aujourd'hui la "fin de la ville," *le post-city age* et quel précepte pratique en tirer ?

2 Les paradoxes de la *capitale* (nationale et européenne) et du *capital* (économie de marché, initiative privée et initiative publique) — *aujourd'hui*.

3 Comment définir ce que j'appellerai les impératifs de "greffe" et de "transparence" pour les projets d'urbanisme à venir-singulièrement dans le cas de Prague ? Les chances qu'offre à cet égard la transformation de la technologie du transport et des télécommunications — qui n'est pas sans rapport avec ce que j'appelle la fin de la ville ou du "centre de concentration urbaine". Question du verre et de la pierre, des nouveaux matériaux, des fibres de verre, etc. (voir plus loin).

4 Les incidences politico-économiques du devenir européen sur les projets d'urbanisme. Hospitalité, investissement et concurrences.

5 Y a-t-il une "bonne" résistance au tourisme ? Le "bon calcul", la rentabilisation et la différence entre tourisme et hospitalité.

6 Le partage (limité et selon quelles règles) des responsabilités avec ceux qui, n'habitant pas Prague en tant que citadins, ou ne parlant pas le tchèque comme leur langue maternelle, pourraient désirer, voire réclamer le droit d'être associés (quant aux fins et aux moyens) à la trans-configuration de Prague. Je pense ici en priorité aux citoyens non tchèques de cet

injunction commands us, simultaneously, *on the one hand*, to conserve, to restore, to keep intact a patrimony which is itself heterogeneous in its stratification (the Gothic formations of Mala Strana, of Hradcany, and of the Old City, then the immense Baroque deposits), and, *on the other hand*, not to conserve or to restore with the sole end of restoration. To limit oneself to the imperative of restoration, however indispensable and vital this may be, is to denature the very essence of a city and to confuse it with that of a museum or temple, with artistic memory or religious experience — which it includes without being reducible to this. Historical memory must be neither that of a church (immobile temple, cultic site in which one neither lives nor circulates and which can, before museums, shelter works), nor that of a dead archive, a tomb or a stony document.

Having remained for so long, out of love of Prague, on the threshold of the threshold, I would like to propose very schematically a few "practical" hypotheses which should sketch out several consequences of what I have just hazarded:

1 What does "the end of the city" signify today, the *post-city age*, and what practical precept are we to draw from it?

2 The paradoxes of the *capital* (national and European) and of *capital* (market economy, private enterprise and public enterprise) — *today*.

3 How are we to define what I will call the imperatives of the "graft" and "transparency" for future urban projects — specifically in the name of Prague? The opportunities offered in this regard by the transformations of transportation and telecommunication technology — which is not unconnected to what I am calling the end of the city or of the "centre of urban concentration." Questions of glass and stone, of new materials, of fibreglass, etc. (see below).

4 The political-economic impact of the European course of events on urban projects. Hospitality, investment, and competition.

Etat mais ensuite à tous les Européens. Mais quels sont aujourd'hui les confins de l'Europe ?

7 Si, moins que jamais, ce qu'on appelle encore ville ne consiste en érection pétroglyphique, mais aussi bien en verre, vitrage, fibrage, câblage télécommunicationnel, en réseau électrique et sonore, urgence de penser la ville en y privilégiant les médiums élémentaires mais renouvelés de la parole, de l'écriture et de la musique.

8 La grande question de la ville et du "forum civique" en général: de la démocratie à venir. Aucune démocratie n'est encore donnée et présente: toute réflexion sur l'avenir ou la fin (au double sens de ce terme) de la *polis* devrait prendre acte de ce fait et se régler sur lui.

Notes

1 Janouch, *Conversations avec Kafka*, tr. p. 183, cité in A. Villani, "Kafka et Prague", Critique, 483–4, août–sept. 1987.
2 Id., *ibid.*, p. 636.

5 Is there a "good" resistance to tourism? The "right calculation," profit-making, and the difference between tourism and hospitality.

6 The sharing (limited, and according to certain rules) of responsibilities with those who also, without living in Prague as citizens, and without speaking Czech as their mother tongue, could desire and even claim the right to be associated (with respect to both ends and means) with the trans-configuration of Prague. I am thinking here most immediately of the non-Czech citizens of this state, but then of all Europeans as well. But what today are the boundaries of Europe?

7 If what we still call today the city consists less then ever of a petroglyphic erection, but just as much one in glass, windows, telecommunications cables, electrical and acoustic networks — there is an urgency to thinking the city by privileging in it the elementary (but renewed) media of speech, writing, and music.

8 The major question of the city and of the "civic form" in general: of the democracy to come. No democracy is yet given and present: every reflection on the future or the end (in the double sense of this term) of the *polis* should take note of this fact and should adjust itself to this.

Works cited

Gustav Janouch (1985), *Conversations With Kafka*, Goronwys Rees, trans., New York: Encounter

Franz Kafka (1953), Hochzeitsvorbereitungen auf dem Lande, *Gessamelte Werke*, Max Brod, ed., New York: Schocken Books

Franz Kafka (1971), *The Complete Stories*, Nahum H. Glatzer, ed., New York: Schocken Books

Franz Kafka (1977), *Letters to Friends, Family, and Editors*, Richard and Clara Winston, trans., (letter to Max Brod, 26 June 1922), New York: Schocken Books

Naples—the Porous City

Massimo Cacciari interviewed by Claudio Velardi

Translated and edited by Luca Pocci and Elias Polizoes
Photographs by Lanfranco Benocci

Massimo Cacciari, the mayor of Venice, is the author of numerous books on philosophy, architecture and theology. Lanfrano Benocci lives and works in Rome. This interview with Claudio Velardi first appeared in *La città porosa: conversazioni su Napoli* (Naples: Cronopio, 1992). This first English translation is printed here with the kind permission of the publishers. The photographs of Naples were taken on October 4 and 5, 1997. The translators would like to thank Luca Somigli for his assistance.

Claudio Velardi: You recently argued that Naples is one of the few cities where it is worthwhile to live, or at least attempt to live. Can you please explain what you mean by this statement? I imagine that it would escape many Neapolitans, constrained as they are by everyday unlivable conditions, such as the absence of civil services and structures.

Massimo Cacciari: My argument obviously concerns not so much the dimension of everyday life but the meaning of the city, the form of the city. If I were to use an expression borrowed from art history, it has to do with the *Kunstwollen*, the artistic form of the city, or better still, the city's will to form, something which is very different from the quotidian "technique" of survival within the urban fabric. The city is not only streets, buildings, structures. A city is, more than anything else, its cultural and artistic contents, its meaning. For our cities, the large Italian cities, it is therefore necessary, before anything else, to become aware of their *ethos* and roots, their historical sense and memory. If one does not begin here is it is very difficult, I would say impossible, to re-imagine or re-invent them.

According to this picture what would be the meaning of a city like Naples?

To begin with, I would say that the whole of Italy's *Mezzogiorno* [south] can truly assume a strong symbolic value, especially when considered in relation to the construction of Europe. In particular, I would add, that cities such as Naples and Palermo should be re-imagined, re-invented and re-designed within that specific European dimension which is the Mediterranean ecumene. The Europe whose unity and political meaning is under discussion today must contain a Mediterranean dimension; and the bridge toward this dimension can only be represented by these cities of the Italian *Mezzogiorno*, which are, precisely, to be re-invented and re-designed as large cultural and political centres in relation with the Mediterranean ecumene as an integral part of Europe. Otherwise, Europe will become Franco-German, "Carolingian," that is to say, a "cold" Europe, a Europe maimed and incapable of acting as a bridge, of having relations, of opening up to the other. That is the great meaning of these cities, the perspective that these cities must assume, must be able to assume.

It is true, and I think you would agree, that a city is also made according to how it is interpreted. And presently this interpretation, this self-interpretation, is absent, at least in the case of Naples.

Yes, perhaps this awareness is lacking in Naples, much the same way that the awareness of the great historical meaning of Venice is lacking in Venice, of Florence in Florence ... perhaps the only city in which an *ethos* and a memory exist is Florence, but it is a memory which to a great extent is oleographic. Unlike Venice and Naples, Florence continually refers to its past — but only as a past.

Given that awareness is lacking, can one, must one, create it?

I would say that the issue runs deeper. The problem, today, is one of stressing the profound identity of the city. This is the point. Naples, even if it isn't aware of this, has maintained the character of the great Mediterranean city. Despite wild destruction, the barbarousness of the last fifty years, the obscenities perpetrated by the political class, the already devastating social dissolution, the Neapolitan *forma urbis* has maintained the characteristics of the real Mediterranean presence, of the Euro-Mediterranean city. It is this that is essential.

Can these characteristics be specified?

They are those that have made an impression upon all the great travelers of the past. To a great extent they still exist, even though they are not eternal. Sooner or later they may very well vanish, but for the moment, essentially, they are the same characteristics that in the last two centuries have moved sensitive European travelers. Upon arrival in Naples, travelers from Goethe to Benjamin would perceive this absolutely particular characteristic of the city: that it is the last European and the first Mediterranean city, that it is a threshold-city. This is its symbolic character. Certainly, if you were to read Goethe, or even Benjamin, who visited Naples in the twenties, you would recognize all too well that the city's colours, the colours of the urban community, have to a great extent disappeared, yet …

… yet what has remained?

Well, what has remained unchanged is an absolutely typical characteristic of the Mediterranean city, what Benjamin, it seems to me, has defined as "porosity"—the "porosity" of the Mediterranean city. Naples, the porous city: this, if you will, seems to me a possible definition.

Can you explain to me the meaning of this term? Naples, porous as a sponge? Or, if we go the root, por, *Naples as a passage, or even a resource?*

Yes, even a passage, a port. And even a resource, which, as we know, is linked to *penía*, poverty. In a porous city things proceed according to ruptures as opposed to neat lines. Here is the extraordinary modernity of these Mediterranean cities, which many foolish "modernists," however, see as the backwardness that must be abandoned in order to become European! The form of these cities never develops by means of projects, programs, or *a priori*. Nor does it only correspond to their urban and architectural character; the Mediterranean city has the characteristics of a game—of an openness even onto other levels.

Porosity is also that particular mixture of natural and constructed geography. Is this characteristic of Naples?

To be sure, porosity is also the inextricable relationship between emerging architecture and the architecture which lies beneath. In all its parts Naples always alludes to the idea that there is an underground structure which corresponds to the one built above ground. The base is not only what you see, it is also the depth of the building, it is a deepening of the building that you physically perceive. I had a distinct sensation of this when I first visited the San Gennaro catacombs, an extraordinary complex that even many Neapolitans, cultured or otherwise, ignore … or that other underground architecture, the Piscina Mirabilis, marvelously depicted by Piranesi.

Is porosity also a model for social relations?

Yes, in Naples even social life seems to move along by hazard. But isn't it "right" that it should be this way? Shouldn't we think of our cities and relationships outside of fixed hierarchies and rigid frames of reference? I have spoken about this in many of my writings that are "dedicated" to architects and urbanists. Hence the great challenge that awaits us is to combine the southern "porosity" with the characteristics specific to the constitutional state, the European *ratio*.

In order to combine these elements is there a need, in your opinion, that something regarding the memory and the tradition of the city be overcome, albeit progressively, without traumas? Something, perhaps, is not to be preserved. Isn't this the case?

To begin with, we need to be clear about what is to be saved and about why this "something" must not be forgotten in the construction of the new Europe. Look, the more I think about it, the more I am convinced by the power of Benjamin's image regarding the porosity of Naples: it is a question of imagining this city as colossal sponge spread over the sea. The city does not deal with its problems by means of macro-projects and according to logocentric *ratio*, it does not reduce the host of its tensions and conflicts by annulling them. Rather, it tends to assimilate them and, at times, to feed off of them. This is a powerful image in a time when it is popular to speak about differences, conflicts, and the productivity of conflict. First of all, we need to thematize and focus clearly on this. And only then can we dispense with what is to be thrown away and overcome.

A challenge which is, according to you, possible as well as desirable to meet.

We have to be very clear: if I had to pass judgment on the basis of what I see today, the situation would clearly have to be deemed semi-desperate. But I still see potential: I live Naples as a hope, a little like Venice, which is different yet similar in the sense that even Venice is a threshold-situation with respect to European culture and civilization. They are threshold-situations, which is why they fascinate me. I live them as hopes, objective hopes, which are embodied in their stones, in their structure, in some of the traits of their inhabitants. The fate of these threshold-cities fascinates me. Venice, in its relation to the Orient, the Slavic states, the second Rome, constitutes another essential aspect of the European predicament today. And Naples, and to a certain extent Palermo, in their relation to the Mediterranean and Islamic ecumene. But the challenge consists in carrying out the function of "threshold" without liquidating the fundamentals of the constitutional state, as may, perhaps, already be taking place.

If I understand, therefore, it would be enough to restore the foundation of the constitutional state in order to put everything in its proper place, even in these threshold-cities. I don't think that it is so easy...

For the love of God — this isn't the case at all. I'm certainly not inclined to think of a universal homology under the banner of the constitutional state. The point is that the great Enlightenment Jacobin, Marxist tradition, has completely stripped the European conception of the constitutional state of that playful, ludic component which is essential to any social relationship. If this theme is dissociated from the discourse of the constitutional state, if it is progressively forgotten, eliminated, we will certainly not realize the triumph of the constitutional state, but rather that of the Islamic *jus publicum* [public law].

Let's return to Naples. I will ask you a specific question: What is to be preserved, and why, is clear to me. I would like to know what is to be avoided at all costs. What is not to be done?

We said that the form of Naples is to be preserved at all costs. That which is to be absolutely avoided are the interventions *à la* Haussmann. We should be weary of pseudo-modernizing and pseudo-homologizing interventions; they would only produce a fictitious homology. You would have a modernization of the kind disastrously carried out in certain Mediterranean countries, on the other shore... there is nothing worse.

Does this not lead us to theorizing social immobility? Do we not run the risk of ending up in the hands of ultra-conservatives?

The discussion we are engaged in should be re-invented and re-imagined. We have already stated that this is still possible today. But keep in mind that an effective preservation entails an extensive intervention in the urban fabric. I am not thinking at all about pure and simple preservation, but about interventions of restoration and preservation which do not do violence to the city, which do not annul possibilities; rather, interventions which in every way contemplate the effort to protect residentship within the historical city. This does not simply mean having people live in the *Quartieri Spangnoli* [Spanish Quarter], but having them finally truly live.

And then?

And then a certain technique of restoration, a certain technique of preservation, which is not based on a purely homologizing enterprise. It is a completely unrealistic utopianism to think that by simply annulling the old centre of the city, the characteristics of the old centre, Europe is magically born. Such a thing can be thought, let me see, by an old Enlightenment thinker, but it is a pure utopianism, unrealistic and ultimately reactionary. You would be left with underdevelopment plus skyscrapers, and perhaps some "medina" for the tourists. Instead, an intelligent preservation means to preserve, to restore the possible rather than the existing. Naturally, one would also have to undertake great interventions *ex-novo*, but always without disrupting this possibility. Therefore, above all, preserve the extraordinary complexity of the Neapolitan habitat, which is by now the only inhabited historical centre. If there are no inhabitants every other chance, every other possibility is done with. We must aim most of all for this, obviously under proper living conditions and with decent services.

Perhaps there is an additional problem: Those who live in the historical centre are weakened social subjects, they are also acted upon by the intrusiveness of the camorra[1], and this renders everything more difficult. The social figures of the past — people who in one way or another had an understanding, a notion of how to live in a part of the city with a history, a memory — no longer exist.

I repeat, I am perfectly aware that with respect to the present situation all this talk seems like pure dreaming, but we must also understand, and I want to stress this point, that a Neapolitan is too close to the object to be able to see it properly. From the outside, and perhaps only from the outside, can one still perceive this possibility, this objective hope, because the city has not been abandoned, because the city maintains the characteristics that we have just mentioned, despite the perpetration of unheard of disruption. It is an extraordinary thing, and I understand very well that a person who lives there day and night may not be able to grasp it. Perhaps this possibility can be better perceived in Venice. In Venice you are more at ease, but this is an *atout* for Naples and not for Venice. Venice is more tranquil because it is already abandoned, because certain conflicts are already resolved, closed, buried. And in my view, the conflicts can be, should be, productive, if only there were a competent political class. Now then, given that people are of a certain type and not of another, this seems to me to be of little consequence. We are agreed, we must create occasions, services which function well, we must give a shape to the infinite number of "games," of social relationships, but these are interventions that can be undertaken in any other city. They have little to do with Naples. It is well known that the *camorra* is a presence in Naples. But the *camorra* can also be found in the run down village near Naples. My argument can not be contradicted by the fact that the *camorra* exists. The *camorra* is an imposing social and political question; it is found in the historical centre of Naples just as it is found in Salerno where the urban fabric has been totally massacred, overturned and destroyed. The only difference is that in Salerno, and in many other places, as opposed to Naples, the social composition is so disrupted as to render any memory impossible.

There are those, however, who maintain that this version of the city as a hinge, of the city as a threshold, can become an alibi, given that we are unable to attain European standards.

No, no. Naples should absolutely attain European standards as far as social services are concerned, as far as the economy is concerned, yet without losing this chance. It can't become only an European city. Naples will never be Düsseldorf. It will never be Bonn. It is absurd and ridiculous to think that way. We must understand that the complexity, the conflict of the Mediterranean urban fabric, represents a chance even within the modern, even for the modern.

How are foreigners perceived by a cosmopolitan city like Naples? Naples has seen all kinds of things over the centuries.

Naples is a city that almost takes for granted that the foreigner doesn't exist. Other than folklore, there is no incentive, no intelligent initiative regarding the flow of tourists into the city. This is a something which dumbfounds me. It involves not only Naples but the entire Neapolitan area. Naples is extremely Pompeii-dependent, regardless of its vast area of extraordinary potential, an area ignored most of all by the Neapolitans themselves. From this point of view when we think of the metropolitan area we shouldn't only consider Naples itself. The entire Neapolitan area is extraordinary. Some of the most enthralling discoveries that you can make in Italy can be made here. What this requires is that Naples be understood and known, its itineraries reorganized in such a way as to make it livable for the intelligent tourist, for the visitor who is presently repelled by the city and can't visit it. It is not only a question of organizing the museums. The problem is to have people visit the city, to get it known, and then to understand the hinterland, which is as extraordinary as the city. Let's see, how many tourists a year go to visit an extraordinary site such as Cuma? It is necessary to set up a large park there, to create a large archaeological park at the lake Averno, at Cuma. This is the point. Every time I want to go and see the Mitreo di Santa Maria Capuavetere I go crazy, the amphitheater is in pitiful conditions. Who knows about Sant'Angelo in Formis? Who knows about all the works of Vanvitelli around Caserta? They are extraordinary things and absolutely ignored by the Neapolitans themselves.

Isn't there perhaps a demographic obstacle blocking such an initiative? There are now four million people living in the Neapolitan area.

Why? I find it very amusing to go and see something even in a confusing context. The porosity of these Mediterranean cities consists in the fact there isn't the monument but there is the city, and within it you discover the monument. This is the case in Palermo, and even more so in Naples. You see and don't see the church, it is part of the city, it is mingled within the houses, it is all a tangle of houses and monuments. You see the most extraordinary things next to the most run-down shacks, and this is what is great about it. The monument in and of itself, isolated, detached, participates in the aesthetics of the *Altare della Patria* [Altar of the State]. The point, therefore, is not the demographic obstacle. The problem is to get to the monument, to the work of art, in an appropriate manner, to know how to get to there, and be able to get there. And once you get there, to find it open and in decent conditions. The presence of the city around it is fine by me. If I have to enter someone's house in order to see the Mitreo, this is fine by me, as long as the house is open. If at the door I happen upon an old woman who is making pasta, this doesn't bother me, as long as the woman takes me to the Mitreo.

Let us now address what you earlier defined as a possible productive conflict in Naples. I will sketch a rough and perhaps extreme image about which you may not agree. In Naples we find a bourgeoisie incapable of promoting any kind of plan for the renewal of the city, a sub-proletariat which is now imbued with forms of criminality, and a devastated structure of production. Where are the possible agents of the conflict?

It is useless to look for pre-packaged possible agents. They must be created — and this is not possible given the present subjects, parties and movements. The hopes for this city, and perhaps for this country, reside in the possibility of determining oblique [*trasversali*] cultural and political currents, of introducing short-circuits within the ancient dwellings which today are falling to pieces. These currents must achieve enough critical mass so as to impose themselves as the new ruling class. And when I move from a political praxis, which develops by way of fixed points of references and well organized subjects, to a politics which is to a certain degree based upon oblique [*trasversali*] aggregations, the apparently abstract questions that we have thus far been discussing — the 'battle of ideas,' as we once used to say! — become more and more decisive. Even from this point of view I would not lose hope for Naples, given that there are movements which attempt this most difficult route. The city's political poverty and total disorganization of social services corresponds to a noteworthy cultural vitality. It is not by chance. Perhaps, more or less knowingly, the most informed sectors of Neapolitan society understand that a project of political renewal can no longer be based on already constituted subjects. They must somehow be constituted.

In your opinion can this conflict emerge out of an ethical foundation? Can it be founded on a renewed ethical consciousness?

Certainly. This is exactly what we are dealing with — a rebirth of *ethos*, precisely in the Greek sense of the term.

Therefore, the new protagonists of the conflict that we are speaking about should bring about a new political class.

Exactly, exactly. But the great difficulty is that the protagonists in this conflict are not as yet constituted, while we are accustomed to think of conflicts with agents who are already constituted. It is now necessary to invent them, and I can not imagine any other basis on which they could be invented if not upon this ethical basis.

And where is the left in all this? In Naples, just as in other cities, in the last twenty years the left has experienced moments of extraordinary strength and electoral expansion. It had the possibility of running the city and today its in the corner.

This is one of its unpardonable sins. During the post-war period the strategy regarding the south undertaken by the left was one of a perfect homology: mass industrialization plus subsidized state industry. And this was the source, in turn, of all kinds of corruption. Mass public industrialization and a politics reduced to financial assistance. The left shares in the responsibility for these calamitous choices. All this has lead to purely defensive battles. First the mistake and then the blind defense of that very mistake. If there is an issue against which the failure of the Italian left can be dramatically measured it is the south, it is Naples. The electoral results capture it with ruthless, geometrical precision. Twenty years ago Naples voted for the *Pci* [*Partito Communista Italiano*; Italian Communist Party], not out of a 'desire for opposition' but out of the necessity for government, of a new form of regulating industry, city, and territory. Who should it vote for today? Today Naples votes only in return for favours. But even this is quickly destined to finish.

Vote for favours or don't vote at all?

Or don't vote at all ... right now people can't vote for a protest such as the *Lega*[2] [Lega Nord: Northern League]. This is certain. But hold on, however, because even here the politicians understand nothing of the *Lega*. The *Lega* is working to create a national political class, that is, a political agenda of its own specific to the *Mezzogiorno*. This is by no means impossible because the *Lega* is not the racism of the *Republikaner*, the *Lega* is not the new right. The *Lega* is phenomenon specific to Italy, it is physiological and not pathological: physiological with respect to the crisis of political parties and the crisis of the nation-state. For the moment, its popular support can not be exported south of Bologna, but the problem of the national character of the *Lega* has become the order of the day, and brainstormers are not lacking within the *Lega*. And a protest against the party system and against Rome is not at all inconceivable in the south.

What can the left do to prevent the protest against the party system from taking the route of the Lega?

The left must understand that the parties as we have known them, with their forms of organization, their determinateness, are finished. And what is also finished, therefore, is every prospect of an alliance between parties as such. Either parties dissolve into larger movements or they are finished. They must take social input into account and in this way go before the voters; they must seek to place responsible men in positions of responsibility and become service structures. If they aim only to survive, and in this way strengthen themselves, they may last one day longer, but they will leave behind more ruins than those they are already creating.

What was, what is, and, most of all, what could be the role of culture and Neapolitan intellectuals in this less than encouraging framework? In short, what is your opinion about Neapolitan intellectuals?

Marx said: the poverty of Germany, its philosophical wealth. This always comes to my mind in Naples. On the one had, the extraordinary political and, to a certain extent, civil poverty, this irrecuperable communitarian porosity. You see its potential, its possibility, but you no longer see its reality. On the other hand, there is this indubitable cultural vitality, the vitality of individuals and institutions. But the unresolved problem for all those who nourish this cultural vitality is the move from an activity which is a mere presence and merely a testimony, even desperately a testimony, to an activity which is more directly related to the political affairs of the city. It is only by way of the activity and presence of these cultural centres that it is possible to think of arriving at a critical mass, of creating those unifying conditions between cultural forces and oblique [*trasversali*] politics, which may enable us to at least do battle against the enemy. It will be by way of cultural mechanisms, cultural debates, by way of these cultural presences, that we will succeed in moving in that direction. Otherwise we won't get there, that is all. And yet it is very significant that on the level of political debate there are few of these institutions. I have been talking about this for many years with my friends.

You often come to Naples to speak about theology.

I was just about to bring that up. In Naples there is the St. Thomas Faculty of Theology, Bruno Forte is the dean, and it has become an organized and well–defined meeting point of philosophy and theology, a place for boundary research.

I would like you to say a few words about this and also about the relationship, if there is one, between an 'extreme' city like Naples and this boundary research, as you call it.

Well, this is very interesting. In Naples, the philosophical culture, at least in this century if not a little earlier, has always been strictly secular, that is, marked by a secular historicism or a profoundly reformulated idealism, like that of Spaventa. We can also see the presence of Croce and, indirectly, that of Gentile; and in the post-war period, the development of studies in European and Italian historicism. That Naples today meets new problems with the activities of these research institutes and the current Faculty of Theology, a meeting point for a renewed interest in the con-

nection between philosophy and theology, testifies to the fact that any talk of the city as a symbol, our earlier discussion of the city as a threshold, is not unfounded nor totally invented. What is substantially taking place here, and this is the point, is a shuffling of the cards. What we see is desire for research which overcomes old borders and ideological prejudices: philosophy on one side and theology on the other. In this blessed city all this is happening. All this is being done by individuals. That remains the problem. I insist it is hard to understand how it is that out of this cultural vitality and research some political project is not born, and its hard to see if it ever will.

But hasn't it always been said that Naples is a pagan city?

It is a living paganism, one that knowingly wants to keep on living within Catholicism — for a Neapolitan Catholicism is always the place where one's paganism can be protected. In the tradition of the south there is an analogous relation between word and image. The philosophy of the south is always also imagination — it is 'polytheistic' in its imaginative *vis*. More precisely: it is a philosophy which grows with language, in the *body* of language. This is the case with Bruno, Vico, but also with Croce at his best. Just as the logos does not cancel the image, the Christian does not cancel the pagan. A theology that is not *in itself* a comprehension of ancient religiousness transforms itself *ipso facto* into apologetics — it becomes a dry defense of one's faith. This is true idolatry, and not the Neapolitan "cult" of images.

If I have understood well, the study of theology can be revived by a city like Naples.

Yes, and precisely in relation to mythology. A philosophy of mythology must be brought together with theology. Theology can not exist without mythology. A demythologized theology is an Enlightenment, a rationalistic dream and Bruno Forte is well aware of that, so much so that he writes books about Neapolitan nativity scenes, composes song lyrics, and paints. My friend Bruno is a perfect exponent of this Neapolitan history in which Catholicism is lived as a great bosom wherein paganism is protected.

Should Neapolitan intellectuals show a bit more alterity?

Each intellectual, I believe, stands alone. Each one expresses a great cultural and ethical passion and brings elements of actual innovation with respect to the cultural history of Naples, even with respect to its noblest moments. But they are still unable to test themselves by taking on this city's administration and political class in terms of alterity, precisely, I would say, in terms of friend and enemy. And this is indeed the change that must be made, otherwise, in the long run, even this extraordinary philosophical, theological and artistic research will come to an end. This city is alive, but men of culture must find moments of coagulation, they must find the moments in which their cultural and ethical tension can become political praxis. Perhaps it depends upon the fact that the problems seem irresolvable. But you see, one of the reasons why I love the atmosphere of Naples is precisely its desperate irony, this disenchantment which has now reached a point of desperate irony. All this, however, does not turn into indolence or negligence, rather, it brings about a very passionate, elevated cultural research, but totally desperate. And this desperation is well expressed, not with lamentations but with irony, this is fundamental. This is an element that certainly belongs to the *ethos* of this city.

Desperation seems to be a way of no return.

No, the Neapolitan elaborates an understanding of his desperation which somehow permits him to survive. When a Milanese is desperate he becomes a perfect idiot, ready for suicide: it is the only intelligent gesture left to him — just as a Scandinavian, a resident of Stockholm — but not a Neapolitan. In Naples desperation is everywhere but no one cries out about it, never. Irony is always around as a corrective. As Seneca says, *humanius est deridere quam deplorare.*[3] This is Naples, this is the southerner, just as Seneca was, the true Mediterranean. Never deplore is also Spinoza's Spanish trait. If we must give ourselves over to some passion, let's commit to derision, to irony. But we should never deplore.

Doesn't this characteristic make the explosion of the ethical revolt mentioned earlier more difficult?

No. On the contrary, it would render it even more violent and ruthless, because no one is more ruthless than he who derides but does not deplore. Nothing destroys even the most powerful gods like Homeric laughter. And yet this derision must have an aim and objectives, it must have enemies. Naples must not stop and admire its own desperation, it can not simply contemplate its own intelligent desperation.

What about the so-called laziness of Neapolitans?

Yes, laziness. But, keep in mind, laziness is not sloth. Sloth is desperation which cares about nothing — and a hint of this danger, as I just said, can now be made out in the Neapolitan character. But laziness is rather the awareness that *scholé* and *otium* [leisure] are more noble than work. *Operari ante-omnia* [work above all] will never become the motto of the Neapolitan. And it is *right* this way. But *otium* is work squared. There is the work that gives you a living, and that you must or ought to carry out with the greatest responsibility — and then there is the work of *otium*: thinking of yourself, seeking to know yourself, and looking at the stars. Beware of setting the first against the second. But beware also of not distinguishing between their different values. You don't work for the sake of working, you don't produce goods for the sake of goods — you produce goods in order to live in peace. This is the great classical ethics — it emerged on the shores of *Mare nostrum* [our sea].

In conclusion, what is the fate of Naples, what are the responsibilities of the Neapolitans?

The fate of Naples: either Naples will succeed in imagining itself as an extraordinary experiment on the Euro-Mediterranean city, on the basis of its own memories, or it will collapse. That's it. It will be the ruin of Naples and of all the *Mezzogiorno*, which would become a purely subsidized society that will slowly lose its current potentiality. Naples can't take the middle road, just as its philosophy never did. Naples isn't a place of prudence, rather, it is a place of extremes. The city could become the boundary place that undertakes the imagining of and experimentation on this as yet non-existent form of politics and culture. Nowhere in the world today is it possible to think of the reduction of complexities, of solutions to crisis. We must everywhere learn to manage complexity and live with it, that it why a situation of dramatic tension such as Naples could prove to be a boundary. Either there will be a totally new boundary experiment for all of Europe, if indeed this Europe comes into being, or a collapse. Collapse doesn't necessarily mean death, tears and blood, it means subsidies, a purely subsidized society, and a slipshod political market. And therefore, if this is really the alternative, it is necessary for the Neapolitan intelligentsia to recover all the reasons for its very commitment, for the full range of its responsibilities. It is precisely because we live in a moment of great uncertainty that the traits of the Neapolitans could become a strong point. These situations must be lived with realism, disenchantment, with a bitter smile, but also with a strong ethical tension. Certainly, the Neapolitan is tempted by indifference and by sloth [*accidia*], but sloth is an extreme form of disenchantment, it is the product of desperation. This temptation exists, it is right that every person endowed with *logos* undergo the temptation of desperation, and Neapolitans never hide it from themselves, this is something positive. At the same time Neapolitans are capable of realistic disenchantment and can discern a situation and attempt to be at home with it in order to once again find an *ethos*. Neapolitans can make it because they will never suc-

ceed in living in a sedate situation, they will never be Prussians. They could very well become Prussians, but are we sure that this is the best model? So I tell you, we will increasingly need the character of Neapolitans, one which is disenchanted but also in a desperate search for an *ethos*. This is my feeble hope.

Translator's notes
1 Camorra, possibly from the Neapolitan "morra," a large group, is the usual name given to organized crime in Naples. The camorra should be distinguished from the Sicilian mafia for its predominantly regional concerns along with its limited ties to international crime syndicates.
2 Led by Umberto Bossi, the Lega Nord entered the arena of Italian politics in the early eighties. Since then, it has built a prominent electoral consensus in the northern regions, particularly in Lombardia and Veneto. The relative success of the Lega is based on the economical gap that has historically divided the 'north' of Italy from the 'south' (where 'south' is understood as the whole territory south of Rome). The Lega has at once capitalised upon and propagated resentment in the north against a 'centralised' Italian state. While it initially proposed the transformation of Italy into a federal state, the Lega has, more recently, undergone a radical and demagogic shift and would now bring about the secession of the 'north' from the rest of Italy. In 1994, the Lega was part of the centre-right coalition which gave rise to the short-lived Berlusconi government.
3 The citation is from Seneca's *De Tranquillitate Animi*, (XV.2) and reads: "humanis est deridere vitam quam delporare," "it better befits man to laugh at life than to lament over it."

Alphabet City

Lynn Crosbie

Photographs by Rita Leistner

He was a difficult person to get to know. For one thing he was obsessed with coincidences.
—Daniel Jones, "The Birth of a Minor Canadian Poet"

A
llan Gardens, 1994

I left my little black jacket at Diane's and he forgot his raincoat. Susan drove us downtown, telling us about the the tantric orgasm; he offered to pick up our coats. He called me to meet him, and we went to Hernando's Hideaway. We talked about Daniel's death, and I asked if he was depressed. I hardly ever talk about killing myself anymore, he said.

He disliked Daniel's fiction and I disagreed. He told me a photograph of the two of them together had fallen from a book the week before he died, which troubled him. At the S/M store I tried on a vinyl skirt and he told the salesperson he was my father.

We walked to Allan Gardens and disagreed some more. Daniel's writing is economical and pure, I said. I thought he gave up after writing poetry, he said. He said some other things, and I didn't see him again. I did not tell him that the last time I saw Daniel he told me he had spoken in his sleep. He said: I hate lyrical poetry:

> Though Amaryllis dance in green
> > Like fairy queen;
> > And sing full clear (Anonymous, 16th century)

The spring that silvers your bones cools beneath the panes of glass, in the field of green
where I have come with your friend who creeps beside me, pale with loss. Serene,
I imagine he is you, where cosmology reveals a pool of goldfish as inverse suns.
There is a frail banana tree, a border of white amaryllis fastens stars
to the carapace of moss, the emerald lily-pads are diadems that coronate each one.
He lowers himself to sing full clear, your faults, the rows of cactus sliced with scars.
And with jaded pleasure, compels me to see the earth devour you; to look on in ill unease,
as ashen petals fall beneath the gold, like the ruined fruit of banana trees.

(For DM: aabcbcdd)

B
lack Bull

Elvis is Alive
— *National Examiner*, August, 1986

This will be the last summer we spend outside here. The one great patio bar with pool tables, a severed bull's head, and room upstairs, where

William and Marjorie once sold books and scraps of paper for dope, cooking one potato each day, the sun blocked out with lace curtains.

I first met Steve Goof and wore all of his rings, dragon's skull and silver urchins, while he chalked his cue and swept off his coat. Black lined in lurid red: matador.

A skinhead (SKINS tattooed to his forehead) followed me out onto the street still carrying his pitcher, offering me a handkerchief, covered in someone else's blood: *because your eyes are so sad.*

We invited Lisa's mother who smoked Sweet Caporals, drank straight gin.

Greg held my ankles in the high Roman fashion. My legs, in Egyptian tights, on his lap; he traced the sphere of the Ankh, his dog panting beside us. You're a good girl, he said, and I saw the hieroglyph on her head: a diamond.

There was a cloudburst, and we stayed out in the rain without umbrellas, talking about love. Janet brushing away her black forelock, explaining Ecstasy — you are so beautiful, you want to kiss yourself,

the summer drenching our bare legs stretching on and on my birthday we have met to celebrate. Our impending trip to Memphis, four girls in tight tiger dresses and backcombed hair. There is some breeze; our eyes are outlined like cats, like the catfight we will have in Kentucky, 3 Leos and one Scorpio in tears,

Carol curled up on the backseat, Elvis used to yell **I walk catlike,**

at the grave we are kittenish, as if someone has died.

C
ameron House

> *THIS IS PARADISE*
> —Cameron House painting, circa 1985

These Are The Killed

(By them)

Handsome Ned, smiles easily in Stetson, silver-tipped collar and boots, slips smack into the darkness and

George, a scientist who studied random patterns—duck-feet on snow—who liked to do the chicken, legs flailing, arms in semaphore, drops dead this way;

Brat X hanging from the rafters: **I know my life is getting harder**;

Richard who played chess, cracking his knuckles to release natural endorphins, his body undiscovered for days, the smell

of purple sage, riders slit their wrists drink to death.

Carl the last of these Mohicans, calls from his quiet corner: **right on**, later all the punks would steal this phrase, after the dust settled

around the campsite, Bob would crawl into his tent with his Sylum clippings and asphyxiate himself; at a haunted house one summer, I screamed as the lights went out and fell to the floor:

what's wrong with you, he asked, as he led me back into the light,

toward the yellow birds, slowly turning in the shooting gallery.

These Are The Killed

(By me)

A murder of crows; witches,
Nicholas, Jerry, early friends of mine
Katie with the heel of a shoe (in self-defense)
and
Penny:

a necklace of bloodstones, fire-
lasso.

> Michael Ondaatje signs *Billy the Kid* in 1993:
> For Lynn wlnonolwirs, ni

D
anforth

Immensity is within ourselves.
— Bachelard

I now seek a phenomenological determination of images:

calamari, the contours of the octopus head, its tentacles push the currents like the images that provoke dreams

of rounded flesh, undulating limbs that caress and asphyxiate, the membranous skin is dotted a morse code —

eight trips to the Danforth for black olives, feta cheese, the Virgin Mary in a circle of red and gold,
to visit the Moon Cave:

> (1987)

The small back room is dark and blue; plaster stalactites hang from the ceiling, there is the sound of bats. The Moon Cave cocktail is aquamarine, the accordion player performs national anthems of the world. Comes over and offers *to play something gypsy*. A serenade.

The caves of the moon that curve beyond the pale lakes, a rustle of wings

the taste of sapphires, the sense of an *immensity within you*,

the earth that dreams the moon, each night

suspended from the limestone lip, the liminal sky.

E
lvis Monday (1983–) Haikus

It's like an old song / everything seems to be / just like an old song to me
—Groovy Religion

Beverly Tavern,
The Silver Dollar Room, The
Apocalypse, The

Echo Papa

Janet's black eye a
green starfish: *I'm going*
to be great tonight

Mr. Gregory

from Mississauga:
you got the devil in you
woman, he frets and

shakes his yellow hair.
An old high school friend, drop-out—
Look, the devil's gone

Groovy Religion

you take the car, I'll
take drugs. Valium Funk starts,
William falls; his dance

Slither or Soup Club,
The Drake, The Edgewater and
The El Macambo

Unnamed

Steve sings *Suzanne* in
the style of Elvis while Marj
Cooks hamburgers, live.

Orange Reality

Someone suggests they
practice. Jam for five minutes:
We're sounding too tight.

I'm getting to it.
Crowd noise, one bass line
G G G A C

The Ether Brothers

Because they do this
For each performance: a vial
of ether, out of tune

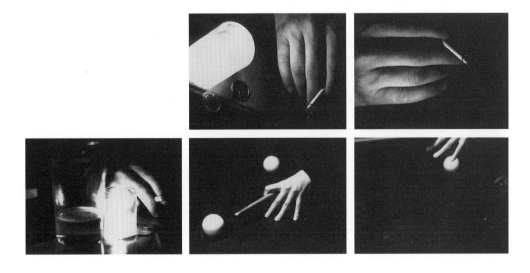

F
ort Goof (1985–1991)

> *They told me he was bad, but I knew he was sad,*
> *I'll never forget him — The Leader of the Pack*
> — The Shangri-las

I had met him before, opening a car with a coat-hangar, other times. He and his big dog, Dirt, all of them roaming the streets on skateboards, bicycles, in armour (chain-belts, big black boots). That he slept in a cage, in a space fortressed by electrical wire, gang-plank entrance off Baldwin Street. Skittering across this in high heels, night after night, half in love.

Coming over after hours, standing on the slag-roof by the hills of wheels spokes metal cans one derelict Mercedes, two stars visible he spills peach schnapps into my mouth from his, bliss.

Wet muzzles of dogs on my ankles, random killings. Trying to keep a low profile for almost seven years. Coaxing him to read his lyrics for us, my head on the dog's belly, a long flowered dress:

started out as recreational / now it's getting quite habitual —

to draw him like a hermit crab outside of himself. Kick this. Be a man for once in your life and see me to the door. Kick that, higher.

With inappropriate presents of lavender bath salts and white roses,

chocolate hearts in foil; the night he has planned to have me (and five scared friends) thrashed for violating the code. I'm heat score, he says and I smile. His friends paw the floors, anxious.

Later he falls to his knees *I'm sorry I'm sorry,* drunk he would

save my life, several times, film me in handcuffs, Cisco coming up the stairs looking for some action in **Goofs Take 29**; I am merely holding the cuffs and am therefore not compromising myself I say. It is 6 AM and time to weave out through the alleys

in my gown I am quite soigné, and I have a little lie down in an alley before two kind policemen pick me up and drive me home. I imagine that there were rats, lying like tiny babies in my arms,

like dolls: pills and drinking less and less food: **alcoholiday turned alcoholocaust**, the song that he read when I lay in that gutter (looking at the stars &c.)

Besieged by skinheads (*we are 138 strong and will kill you*), I see a little crown when I pass by where it ended and began. With sledgehammers and chainsaws, his eyes looking ahead, somewhere clear,

a clean table, plexiglass shower, plants in casement window. I am invited to Dirt's wake this May. With more flowers, a round of toasts to the dog that died in Mexico, lolling in the sun and startled by all the water, the purity.

Clean white bed he slips neatly into each night, hair still shaved in the one thin line

I crossed to meet him, like a pirate wild for the black flag,

that signals danger, night-riders, the other marauder

who turns around and smiles at you, over shark-fins, water as black as your treacherous heart.

G
ladstone Hotel (1985)

The whole rhythm section was the purple gang...

It was a blizzard out there, but King Elvis (Toronto's first impersonator + Subway Elvis) was performing at the great hotel where Sweet Daddy Siki's purple Cadillac surfs by,

and there is mud-wrestling, some country and western in the Bronco Room.

He is wearing a gold lamé jacket with unfinished edges, black slacks. Looks nothing like Elvis but we dance on the chairs as he sings. Those lush segue ways I said I don't wanna I don't wanna be don't wanna be tied,

that old hook — sm. hip-swivelling, a tired blonde girlfriend clicking her nails to the beat, smashed, we ask him to sing **Smoke on the Water**, Elvis-style,

and he gives it a shot which is why he's the King:

*Frank Zappa and his buddies were at the best place in town, some crewcut with a flare-gun
burned the place to the ground, yes!*

There is a little car accident later and I tip the driver generously, record snow-falls, ice and fast winds. I appreciate a little showmanship.

H
uron Street (1986–1990)

> *Kites fly up*
> *Kites fly down*
> *They touch the ground*
> *Pretty kite*
> *Nice and bright*
> *Such a nice sight*
> —first poem (age 6)

The Epitome apartments lay south of College; Coach House Press north, through a walkway and courtyard, flights of rickety stairs. I am writing poems and feel it is a sign, living here,

slanted ceilings, mice, a view of the alley. Where Jesse stands in a toga, setting fire to garbage and the nervous old transvestite (his door marked *skirt my pretty name*) wrings his hands. Criminals, thieves; Mike the con who gives me a lift in his Camaro one day, crushed in between three pretty girls with shag-haircuts and skintight jeans.

I am writing while Steve becomes more absorbed in his projects: lining up superhero figures in action poses, underlining entries in the TV Guide (we have no television), writing lyrics he will not perform for eight years

with Trans Love Airwaves. One is about me, how mean I've become, popping out Plastic-Man's head so it topples the whole row like ten-pins. *Why'd you want to be that way?*

We broke everything before he left, windows plates glasses, and later I would remember him. Standing wanly by the window in old pyjama bottoms, scissors and highlighters, broken

unloved. I wrote about the chicken-baby doll he gave me, and he read it years later and we were sad about the ups and downs of it all.

I remember going through the walkway after signing my first book-contract with Coach House,

sure that everything was waiting to be found (his Hello-Kitty notes that still pop from books and boxes),

that the world was coming true.

[*now that you seem so much closer, than you've ever been*]

Translove Airways: "I Think the World is Coming True"

I
sabella (+ Yonge) 1982

> *Going with the flow it's all the same to me*
> — Motörhead

I have dreaded this, moving to Toronto. On the Via train, leaving Montréal, I think of the '67 Exposition. The rows of pavilions, the athletes' honeycombed quarters, the Geodesic dome that flowered and burned. Remembering the city this way,

lost in the Mont Royal cemetery, looking for my grandmother's grave and never finding it. From the woods the plots are like anthills.

Abbreviated angels are raising their wings.

I am frightened by a man in the bar-car who threatens to throw me from the train. Threading back to my seat I meet Claire and ask her to pretend she knows me. The man in hot pursuit.

Leaves when he sees my head on her shoulder. My first friend,

a fashion-illustrator and heavy-metal queen. She shows me around, we visit the Gasworks and she shakes her long hair, listening to the cover-band: That's the way I like it baby

(I don't want to live forever).

I am a punk with two inches of spiked hair, a fish out of water. Trying to breathe. Sending long letters home and cultivating a depression that borders on nerve,

I will cut my legs with knives and slice my fingers with broken glass. And call up Claire.

We examine snakes in the Exotic Pet Store, and shop for eyelet and lace, she loans me her apartment and I persist. Hooking up, deeper into the city, until there is someone else,

and someone else.

I see her again, for the last time. We eat lunch at The Tender Trap where Sinatra sings about this and that:

I've been up and down and over and out and I know one thing

Picking myself up from this strange corner and cutting out. My first friendship like a shiver, the silken legs of the tarantula, that navigates from wrist to elbow, feeling its way around.

J
ames Joyce Pub (1996)

a girl loveable in the extreme.
—Ulysses

and we met there at eight or so Elizabeths never on time and her body blooms in black with slits some smooth white showing and her dark lips curl you think of the edges of mussels we drowned in lime in the cabbageleaf green of this place she says the shamrocks catch in her throat with the harp goes the tenor O Sweetheart

we find an abandoned grocery cart and push Michael fast and let go O tragic dying-looking his ankle twisted not letting him go but her eyes meeting mine like two big poppies shadows I suppose of nights

you wear a clean shift and powder and there is some story her beautys unfolding like petals and rotten things like swallowing a ring she gave back of course and cleaned like opium whites your bones though you are sick and your hair a bit loose from tumbling

through nights with her theyre lovely something goes through me all like needles she carves her hand with a knife before she leaves and I am thinking of her on the sea her cat of nine tails Im certain in a carpetbag

Ive cut myself and she presses her hand to mine our blood flowers tulips are we sisters then will you remember her away in red sand sun kisses her shoulders and moonlight blue her legs in the salt water lime sea and yes I said yes I will Yes.

K
ensington Market (Summer 1987)

The Market this night is deserted, after three, feral cats comb for fishheads; diablerie
mists rising from sewer gratings, the moon through scaffolding, crescented.

There is the sound of breaking glass, Carol and I see clothes drift from a window, inspirited —
ghosts; a junkie is tossing his girlfriend's dresses, black edged in jessamine and picotee.

He knocks her down and hammers her face, her hair in his hands, his fingers signeted
with spiked rings; she twists and cries. When we call out he pivots with cruel celerity,

Leave her alone — slowly we approach him, he says *yr in the wrong neighbourhood pussy*.
And advances, mouth arched in hatred, tendon-cut arms taut, sick with dread

I stare him down; we gather her things, barrettes and beads, a little purse, chenille bedspread,
and look at her: the girl's face is diamonded with bruises, green and purple nebulae.

She shakes, her thin body an atlas, the street's colours, shapes, in relief, and faceted.
Points of light shine from her elbows, ankles, her back reveals sharp vertabrae,

like cat's teeth, tearing rotting flesh, to subsist; she turns to him, slight honeybee,
to recover the sweetness, the sting; droning that they are overfed

with opiates she knows are tender, hard, familiar with this alchemy, she holds his sleeve
and kisses him; Carol and I turn, empty our hands; our shadows follow, disquieted.

L
andsdowne and Bloor (1984–1986)

> *altered consciousness*
> *NOT altered consciousness*
> — bp Nichol, *The Martyrology*, Book Six

sick in bed speed & percodan lisa & i share a plate of rice,
leave some for the cats their tails rise like stirring snakes,

furious. our hair bleached white i own two party dresses
study statistics each night while andrew plays hot chocolate.
arithmetical problems: *heavens in the backseat of my cadillac*
let me take you there. steve working as a sailor drunk one night
on waterbed calls out **man overboard**.

watch the sunrise, bowls of peas & chocolate, walking through the
underpass by the junkyards, i take off my heels & run, reckless

with love for someone else. who wears pink socks & sleeps with a
machete, who beats someone up the morning we meet beats him

blood rains down his face; he had stared at me & wouldn't leave.

share sm hash by the war memorial (verdigris angel & bayonet) at queen
& university. i describe this also how we slept like mice his hand grazing my hip,
his lips on my shoulder.

> a diary that is read & i am undone, there are
> two men, then none: producible numbers.

when i have left & am living in a cathouse on admiral road (pimp runs
in to clean his face where margaret has scratched him &c)

i think of landsdowne, moving in gunshots that night, the stripclub i liked.
where a girl left her fur coat with her sister & peeled off her spangled bikini

old men gathered around, throwing pennies at her feet. i imagine i have left this
way

> a few articles to toss together

& spin, the rattle of loose change like maracas, when carnival begins.

M
inistry of Love (1983–1984)

> *Didn't time sound sweet yesterday? In a world filled with friends, you lose your way.*
> — Scott Walker

Also known as the Church of the Fallen Elvis (and for afterhours, **Make My Bed in Hell** torn as beer tickets) because they would only ingest drugs and food of the baroque Elvis: cheeseburgers, quaaludes, demerol, codeine.

Where where I met my closest friends still, and some of the filthiest people alive: seducing girls through sedation, exposing themselves in front of moonlit windows, sleeping in amber clouds of vomit, taping hapless visitors:

i love you guys ill blow you i will if thats what it takes ill blow you.

Walls kicked into craters, Jerry holding court talking shit, coercing an ill woman to the back room who calls out *I don't want to suck your cock*, what passes for a good story, what passes —
In the bathroom someone has written Hope for Me I Hope for You.

Parkdale warehouse hidden behind Queen and Bellwoods with stage-set lofts, where I sleep most of the time during rehearsals wake up angry and throw chairs, murmurs all night

from the kitchen, guys cranking cough syrup and valium. My goldfish swims in dense limewater by the gaslight, prowling for oxygen

light. There are no windows, and soon we all desert the place. Where cockroaches cakewalk on the walls and all the spoons are black.

I came here to meet someone; we were together for five fitful years. He followed me home because he was locked out and didn't want to get his pale slacks dirty in the park.

He said things like that, *pale slacks*. Mesmerized (a lizard held in a palm, its flesh stroked in determined circles), I listened to him talk. About car accidents the shaggs his father the nightclerk jean genet that love was a great big thing

beginning with one word. He left a note for me the day we met. On a square of green paper:

N
iagara Falls (1994)

> *In the end, / The water was too cold for us.*
> —Robert Lowell

In August we head out four or five of us with overnight bags
bathing suit daywear a good evening gown Bottles of gin
and vodka names we call ourselves

Pepper Taffy Venus Penny Dreadful Sparklett

And visit the Main Drag the Wax Museum the House of Criminals
(we take turns in the electric chair lights flickering a charge)
Houses of Horror and Illusion

The moaning and shrieks it is pure black and we fall into
the light stopping for souvenir snowshakers viewfinders postcards
to see the Odditorium genie who lives in a bottle and squeaks hello

the Falls a glittering backdrop when we dance on the tables
of the rooftop bar singing and baiting each other the whole neon strip
lit up with signs heart-shaped waterbeds + jacuzzi the Oasis

Motel where we stay up late our legs bruised in tee shirts and
black panties cutting limes with an emery board Taffy reclining the
lioness imperial highness Venus in leather shorts with a bunch of bananas

posing legs split and pushup bras while Penny snaps pictures it's late
and the next morning we are dour in sunglasses pink camellias in our mouths
shoving our way to the front of the line we stand in yellow raincoats

at the prow of the Maid of the Mist We huddle together our hair soaked
and tangled after entering the water's breakpoint as the spray lifted
and crashed we stepped back afraid of the water it was cold and ruthless

For years we would look at our pictures laughing at how drunk
how reckless we were Laughing at Led Zeppelin until the waiter cried
Sparklett thrown out of the 7-11 for screaming nonononono — yes

She and I singing to the cab driver a song about diapers and big white pins
how the flowers looked our lips were flowers Pictures I have since discarded
surprised at my own illusions

Hand in hand in pink and yellow a calyx Saturated
suffering its weight and falling apart blossoms floating down-stream
maids in the mist

O
ssington and Bloor (1995)

> *Can you dig it.*
> —Jim Morrison, "The Opening of the Trunk"

I am waiting for Sara w/Michael
it is her birthday the sun is a groove lights
his jesus hair

yeah—I dig his eyes attack'd by
farout green & black. His purple-lips & vest,
a trip: mirrors velvet disrepair,

I hand her some potions love & power, mixed w/incense
& we go off to see the petstore, like,
time does not exist, just this cat (so fair).

Sara says, man, you two looked so happy,
going off to see the crickets,

(they are fed to other creatures) we touched their
bowed legs, salt-green, folded in prayer.

P
etsitting (Kendall Avenue, 1988)

I just can't fit
           I believe it's time for us to quit

I am petsitting two cats and a goldfish
hot August
                    hardwood floors 7 rooms a palace

pyjama parties, Chris and I share some coke
I watch *The Bad Seed*
          scared all night little girls are scaling the walls,

he and Carol come back and I sleep in a bunkbed.

Steve visits twice, and knows that it is over.
Tony in residence,
          have to hide all the scotch,

but we read all day and hot nights pass, dressed in nurses' uniforms
with Marjorie, William,

we have a double date or two, deal hands of bad influence, misconduct:

three-cornered hats, couch cushions scattered.

We will spend seven years together. It all begins on this couch, my hair wet, worried,
he pats it dry. Tells me everything will be alright, leaves a poem by my toes when I
sleep.

Something about the way I sound, when I wake up

I call him,

every day.

Q
ueen Street West (1150)   1992

This coincidence of opposites (cold, methodical cruelty and boundless love)…
— Slavoj Žižek

Daniel and I have agreed to launch our books together: **Obsessions** and **Miss Pamela's Mercy**. He wants a hardcore band to play and has a formidable mailing list (I am soon embarrassed to overhear Jim Smith saying "who keeps putting me on fucking lists?").

We design an invitation. Pink. I decide there should be a cockroach on it, and Daniel meticulously clips one from an encyclopedia. William loans us the Drake, and Marjorie (my cover-girl) acts as emcee and decorator, covering the walls with streamers and album covers:

Martin Denny's Tropical Sea Sounds; Claudine Longet; Tiny Bubbles.

Daniel calls and asks if I have a bullwhip he can borrow. When I arrive, dressed as Morticia, he is nervously arranging a pyramid of books. Dave Howard launches our books from a slingshot; we listen to Grasshopper, and read after Marj's flustered introductions.

She is wearing a spangled bridesmaid dress. Her voice squeaks: *I … don't know Daniel Jones very well …*

He comes out and whips the floor while a tape loop plays, his voice reciting his obsessions:

fuck it fit it kick kick it kick it.

Downcast, he signs my book with a drawing of a little cat while I sit around like the stuckup belle of the ball.

A few weeks later, he tells my friend Nancy he was unhappy with the event. His face

squinting on the back cover, nightmarish faucet drip on the front that drove me crazy, fix that!

He called me his "partner in crimes." I think of us, happy, with our bugs and glue imagining a kind of punk marriage, of him falling

from grace. At his own wedding he wore blue: what is essentially *flawed* in the reproduction of natural forms is the idea that there is *balance*, *harmony* in our own natures.

Water falling like torture, water that is not staunched, but simulated:

> The blade of the knife. Pieces of blue. Slashing and slashing …
> There are no more words.

R

oncesvalles (late summer, 1987)

see how they Fall   each frothing crest by

                      Christ a palm   A Finger

                                    pointing into,

     — Steven Heighton

There are no September vacancies. Lisa and I have started walking the streets
looking for somewhere to live; she walks slowly stops

to pick up stones eggshell a leaf. Her odd step a swivel, slip (as a child she sits under
a silver tree, tinsel starlets her body cast),
we walk south on Roncesvalles, toward Lake Ontario. She misses the Pacific,
remembers sailing paper ships rigged with tiny parasols, into Japan, how they

tumbled, spilling over rocks. The wavelets we make in the pools of water on the street,
our face catching rain as if we are in tears we walk

past the park, the summer has been hard. Carrying our cats on buses — hers hangs from the
window, screaming — looking for signs, we see the Pope statue and cross west,

we have broken glass against fountains at night, spells against love, and we stand at this
monument together and touch his white feet, fingers laced across cold wet marble.

Like glass, sealed together with breath, our breath held to be blessed, something

we never forget. His holiness more tangible than the determination that brought us
further, to the edge of the water,

our toes drifting out, pale staysails, testing the tide.

S
cream in High Park (July 19, 1993)

As it hath beene sundry times publickely acted, by the Right honourable...
— (*Midsummer Night's Dream*) Stationers' Register, October 8, 1600

10.05 *Enter Sky Gilbert, Master of the Revels*

I can hear snatches of Sky's work Wake me, beauty, For I am asleep from behind the fence where I am waiting with bill bissett. The audience give him their hands, I see Hippolyta's crown shining as it is thrown to his feet, rubies and sapphires tumbling, when I look up

        (I will visit Sky one summer to watch **Dead Poets' Society** *coq au vin* and endive salad, zebra pillows, shifting uncomfortably in the heat

        emanating from the beautiful boys. Disoriented as the movie ends and the prettiest one, who plays Puck, has blown his brains out, we go our separate ways.

        Some thoughts of *Captain, my Captain*, how movies bury what is unequivocal — Sky and I falling apart, when the moon rises and the lights retreat.)

10.20 *Enter Helena*

I am holding bissett's tee-shirt

        [given to me with sections of an orange for nerves]

wearing a white dress   [that looks like a tablecloth]

earrings that are naked little men.

Later, I will try to remember watching michael though *I cannot truly say how we came here.* Summer wind lifts my hairpiece like cardinals   wings through the papers as though I am not afraid I [start up]

And I have found him like a jewel
Mine own, and not mine own.

10.30 *Enter David Donnell, as Peter Quince, a carpenter} representing Prologue*

Wasn't Lynn great? I can't get over it,

Donnell as talk-show host works his sleeves
his cue is past
        and he is filled with *wanton energy.*

It will take years before I read his work and see
objects of beauty lit like lemons wet
quivering

below luminous stars and music trembling, to feel
a love supreme.

        [*Yes, it doth shine that night*]

10.50 *Enter bill bissett, Duke of Athens [lords and attendants]*

th companeez n xcellent spirits
dreems uv aneething or
sew i feel

on *th green n bountiful hill side*
bissett nevr faltrs —
showers us   [attended by peaseblossom cobweb mote and mustardseed]
with sorceree.
Sweet friends, to bed, is his summons, sew

veree lovlee.

T
all Bars (1986–)

The Park Plaza Rooftop

If you are a writer press 18 and exit, left right
a plush ghost-Algonquin, ferns
framed drawings of its clientele.

Draw a handlebar moustache on Atwood,
a goatee. Call it LHOOQ:
decide she has a hot ass.

Sparkles (Top of the CN Tower)

Remember you will throw up on the way down.
Pose for a poloroid, sidle out to the lookout
point,

smoke a joint rolled in Tigerskins paper,
watch two lonely women dance *un slow*,
shuffling a little,

their skirts cut in A-lines, their lips moving:
the orchestra's yawning, they're sleepy I know.

Trader Vics (*High Above the Sparkling City*)

Order the most offensive drink on the menu that will arrive
on fire

decorated with umbrellas, a yellow bird, a Polynesian man wearing a lei.

Overhear two businessmen chat up a woman who describes her
stretch marks to them: vivid

the purple flame on the lip of your bowl. Ask the bartender if you can keep
the skull-mug. When he declines, slip it in your jacket and run like hell.

The Aquarius Lounge

Visit the 50th floor of the Manulife Building many times. Swoon over the view
of the city, all honeycombs and garnet.

Listen to the piano man sing Billy Joel songs, encourage him.

Write "Hi Sailor" on a napkin and pass it to a flustered customer.

Insist on Brandy Alexanders, sing **Brandy yr a Fine Girl** while your brother shows his ass to the
camera.

Look away when the waiter warns, ominously:

Do not do that again Sir … Take down your pants.

U
nion Station (1983–4)

> *My hand draws back. I often sigh still*
> *for the dark downward and vegetating kingdom*
> —Robert Lowell, "For the Union Dead"

Green and white boxcar heading west past
molting ferris wheel pasture rows of houses each alike:

in Los Alamos this summer I see white tombstones
stuck fast in the hills. Desert flowers tumble

weeds brush the wheels and I am sometimes
sedated as the melon-pink of mountains rise sheets of

distant lightning shear the dark downward, of motion.
Moving back east past clarkson portcredit mimico

to Union, half the regiment dead to me now I was
looking past the scorched fields toward a city

                     (*a blessèd break*)

from an angry family, jobs that are sweeter since:
cleaning houses on amphetamines, waitress in a diner

i got an eye in my beer, look up at empty socket and
tables trembling, spider delerium, the hoodlums in the back

who offer me rides home in the rain, a triumph, skidding off centre,
what I have left behind in another city (*Ah spent the morning installin the pussy pad —*

let's roll) over valleys and dirt paths, this city looms unknown
until I have turned over each rock and want to keep moving,

sliding into more desolate terrain. I often sigh still, their names faint
an abstract cemetary where I go with crepe myrtle (texas rose)

to offer myself, made of spirits,

        the conductor calls:

paterson johnson tynkaluk adlai hazen cuddy dent trudi nixon lauzon frechette ross burnham
brand walcott sanders mcclintock dewdney flahiff earl milchem wasson warlock kathy t payne

stops I miss, static, sleep,

train I ride half-dead

objects falling back, smaller, in perfect miniature: the line of little cat's teeth, bridging sharp
incisors, that comb the body, drawing out tangles in long tined tracks.

V
ive Karaoke (Kensington and Baldwin, 1993)

Tên Bán Nhac: "You Light up My Life"

So many days: spent at the old Quoc Té. Formerly Peter's punks-drugs-music clubhouse, now a Karaoke bar — rumours of back alley garroting, gunshots. One night a Vietnamese gang gets close, are deflected by our bracelets: sandalwood beads & glass Buddha. They sing for us instead **Now mothers tell your children, not to do what I have done**

I'd sit by my window, waiting for someone to sing me his song: Afternoons are for Marjorie, we are alone in orange hooker wigs, letting discs ride, clapping for each other. Our loneliness and pale desires — her voice too much like air, and my one gig at the Paddock, singing "I Fall to Pieces," falling to pieces I am so afraid.

[later at the bar by the Grand Old Opry I will sing the hell out
this song where Hank Williams rests, drinking and writing, knowing that he is pulling up dead]

Nights with Chris or Richard or Andrew (dressed as John Shaft), other serenades:

im just a jealous guy

So many dreams, kept deep inside me: of blue smoke, the brilliant facets of the mirrored ball, cocktails coursing through me, ice and tonic: wanting to kiss everyone, to kill them (in one prism my green sleeves a praying mantis). They ride Spadina north home, waving white

handkerchiefs I keep folded in my pocket
made up, my tears are black.

Alone in my heart, but now you've come along: He isn't drinking anymore but he follows me down Kensington, slipping away. Pretending I need protection and I ask him to duck downstairs for a quick song. Dangerous, what William calls **Scaraoke**, we order double scotch, drain them, two songs and no one has missed us. Feeling as though I have met my match

gunslinger liar inscrutable thrillseeker, it has always sounded like this —

It can't be wrong when it feels so right: Because the Night Belongs to Lovers seeps into the backseat we have ignored — all night our only chance to meet him, because the nightcovers us, long before Love is an Angel

it is cruel and left-handed,

signing the words in another language, summoning the day.

When we walk through the Market the sun is bright
Pain and pleasure unite us, walking past VIVE

He tells me **the only thing a gambler needs is a suitcase and a trunk**

Packs his clothes so neatly, they are like crescent rolls. And pops them in the drawer I have marked M:

a Peter Lorre film about compulsion, that it cannot be helped.

W
estern Hospital (Bathurst and Dundas) 1989–

... when things decay, it's not a sign of something gone wrong — not in nature's grand scheme of things. It's a sign that nature is reclaiming energy and materials that seem to be no longer needed by higher organisms.
— Boyce Rensberger

Some things I remember I would like to forget:

blood soaks the inside of his thighs 3 am, the way the street always looks at this hour on this ride;

the arc of Bathurst opening into emergency;

inert ambulance, waiting to sleep;

then he is staggering through the corridor while I confiscate syringe, tie, and spoon;

watching his heart pulse in weak, secret spikes;

how he tried to die.

When I was afraid, I couldn't sleep. I would say, I'm thinking you're going to die. I won't, everything's alright, our hands linked;

sleep through this another time, going under the doctor asked me to count backwards, like you can recover this; bitch;

murderer. Drawers filled with plastic bracelets, unusual bleeding I want to forget this and more,

the mist that descends each time I make this trip. Moving through vapour and blank space, walking the floor, expecting morning.

X
traordinaire (722 Queen Street West) 1994–1996

I have never had a hairdresser before but things come to this. Hand-carved crosses, piercing, face-slaps, lipliner. He fits my hair with extensions, someone else's hair,

twice now, I wear this stranger's remains. My head scraped raw with sutures I sleep on my face, some fall out I am falling apart.

You look like a mermaid, Sook-Yin says when she sings to me.

He tells me about an associate, Ray, who almost died from fluorocarbons, his aurora of hairspray, and leaves me under the drier while I think about glamour.

How angry I have been, lethal shoes talons corsets, you got to move on, if you want to see glory, train train.

That glamour may be something else, walking slowly and painfully, so there are no mistakes. The discomfort, the drag. Of effacing yourself; the sublimation. Of recovering the grotesque.

I wonder at the hair of the skeleton, in museum glass, pulling a comb through my own tangled *memento mori*.

I fought with my hairdresser once, viciously. Pretend I'm dead, I told him and slammed down the phone. Before we made up and since, I think this is the most glamourous thing I have ever done:

his clips clattering to the floor the nerve of that woman, my hair alight, as I turn in an outrage, switching beauty's tail, to get moving.

Y
yz

Three Triplets: Toronto — Guelph, 1996

progress / gets / lost in / the / trail of...
— Clifton Joseph

Early October, Cronenberg's *Crash* premieres & Amber Clifton Michael & I
meet on Dovercourt; bill has declined to join us, thinking we'll die
in the car: coming to meet us, Michael escaped an accident, head-on, two semi-

trucks cleaved ahead, swerving from the crush & fire he's shaken he might
turn thirty in a morgue. The highway yawns & we smooth-sail tap through *The Israelites*
like bonnies & clydes until the line seizes, stopping dead, a crash — we wait in blue twilight,

for two hours until the smashed trailer is cleared from sight. Big rigs circle the scene in
elephantine grief; we are washed in red-light, then banished. We track the sideroad, genuine
grace outflies our need to cramp in love or fear, to find the prayer that prefigures collision.

> later Esta & I will decide to be Millie & Chili
> & tour the Prairies
>
> Clifton screams Monk is Dead & cries
>
> Michael opens birthday presents: we sonnetize
> (our pretty room).

Z
oo   (Metropolitan Zoo, 1984)

hog, big as a cannon,
how sweet you lie.
— Anne Sexton

Sexton high priestess of Quaalude and coffee, highballs for breakfast her typewriter an altar, even then. A terrible poem before dying, her mind still moving in revolutions — long ago having realized that it was Eve who lay down with flowers

a Persephone-wreath of daisies in her hair she plants these seeds, something seminal, about men and animals, long before there are gunshots and all girls off the pigs,

Janet & I visit the zoo. It is early spring and most of the exhibits are closed. One rhinoceros on a platform, wedged tight. A white tiger in a small cage, two giraffes

kissing. There is nothing to say about animals, I try to keep this in mind, wondering how poets lose their art. If compression and allusion come to disgust you, if it is cold and there are lions looking sick on a half-hill,

you may find that life is cruel and prosaic. Shudder, and say this: I watched a female gorilla. She stared at me through the plexiglass barrier as if she hated me. Then threw up in her hand and ate it. Never breaking eye contact.

We quiver like chicken hinds . . .

Before the putrid ugliness, of everything we contain.

&
The Black Knight, The Silver Rail, The Van by the River, Mary's Lysander, Star & Monika, The Brass Rail, The Backstabbers, Mildred Pierce, Ludwig-Vaughan, The Cayenne Pepper King, Nights in White Satin, College Street Fear, Extraordinary Erin, The Corner Pocket, Fright Nights, Love Empyreal, 717 Richmond West, The Werewolf, Etta James & KISS, Chopsticks & Traffic, The Waverly, the seahorse, the day

---

Acknowledgements:

We quiver like chicken hinds (Letter Z) is a line from
David McGimpsey (1996)
"Howard Hears Marion Downstairs"
Lardcake
Toronto: ECW Press

I would like to acknowledge the following people's support and comments: Michael Holmes, John Knechtel, Ann Shin, Mary Crosbie, and Diana Bryden,

and also thank anyone (not) named.

Barcelona ZAL:
Performance Notations

Stan Allen 1996–97

Assisted by:
Céline Parmentier, Adriana Nacheva, Troels Rugbjerg, Nona Yehia

Performance This project marks a shift away from issues of representation to engage architecture as a material practice. Material practices, (ecology or engineering for example) do not work primarily with images or meaning but with performance: energy inputs and outputs, the calibration of force and resistance. They are less concerned with what things look like and more concerned with what they can do. Material practices do not attempt to control or predetermine meaning. Instead, they go beyond the paradoxes of the linguistic to examine the effects of signifying practices on performance and behavior. Although these material practices work instrumentally, they are not limited to the direct manipulation of given material.

Instead they project transformations of reality by means of abstract techniques such as notation, simulation or calculation.

Notations Traditional representations presume stable objects and fixed subjects. But the contemporary city is not reducible to an artifact. The city today is a place where visible and invisible streams of information, capital

The municipality of Barcelona intends to divert the Llobregat River and extend the existing facilities of the port of Barcelona. An open international competition was held in 1996 for the Logistical Activities Zone (ZAL) adjacent to the new port facilities. We took this competition as an opportunity to examine the potentials of an Infrastructural urbanism. Our design strategy consisted in setting down the traces of an architectural infrastructure that would allow flexible development while maintaining unified identity. A directed field, within which the future life of the site will unfold. An architectural means to impose minimal although precise limits on future construction.

Although developed initially by means of conventional representational techniques (plans, sections and models) the elaboration

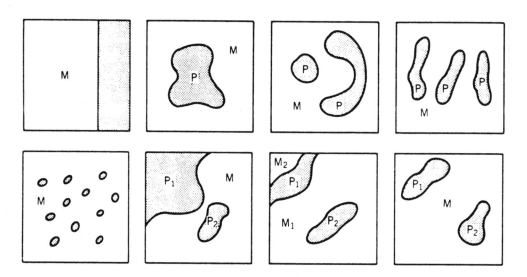

and subjects interact in complex formations. They form a dispersed field, a network of flows. In order to describe or to intervene in this new field we need representational techniques that engage time and change, shifting scales, mobile points of view and multiple programs. In order to map this complexity, some measure of control may have to be relinquished.

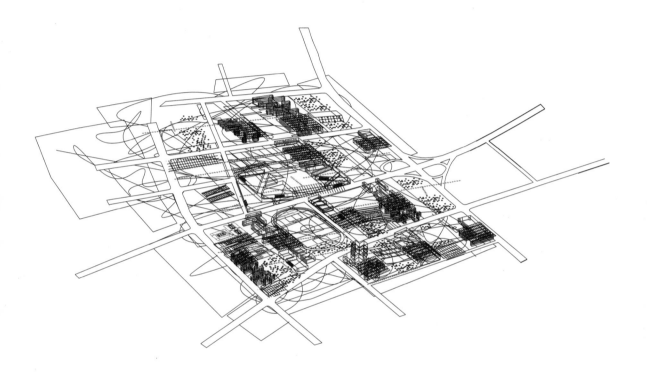

To open architectural representation to the score, the map, the diagram and the script could establish a basis for exchange with other disciplines such as film, music and performance. The score allows for the simultaneous presentation and interplay of information in diverse scales, on shifting coordinates and even of differing linguistic codes. The script allows the designer to engage program, event and time on specifically architectural terms. New maps and diagrams might begin to suggest new ways of working with the complex dynamics of the contemporary city.

Anticipation Notations always describe a work that is yet to be realized. Even if already performed, the work it describes is open to interpretation

a. Scattered patch landscapes

b. Network landscapes

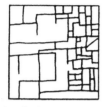

c. Interdigitated landscapes

d. Checkerboard landscapes

of the project requires new representational strategies. The
project is described here by a series of *performance notations*:
diagrams, maps, scores and scripts that anticipate the event
structure of the site over time. In the infrastructural approach,
limits to future development are set materially, and not through

and change in the course of future performance. In this sense, notation is
optimistic and anticipatory. Unlike classical theories of mimesis, notations do not map or represent already existing objects or systems but
anticipate new organizations and specify yet to be realized relationships.
Notation is not about interrogation, critique or commentary. These "criti-

cal" practices utilize notation's discursive capacities only in retrospect,
(pointing out what is wrong with existing reality) whereas notation's more
radical possibility lies in the possibility of proposing alternative realities.
Notation's special properties can be exploited by the urban designer to
produce a kind of "directed indeterminacy:" proposals that are robust

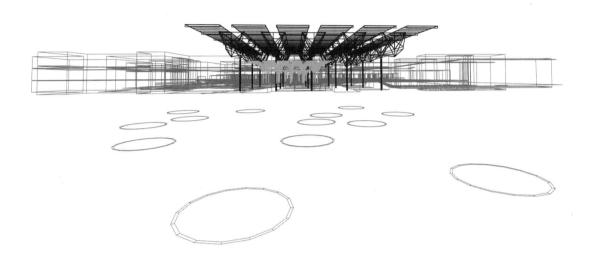

and specific enough to sustain change over time, yet open enough to support multiple interpretations.

Invisible Notations go beyond the visual to engage the invisible aspects of architecture. These include the phenomenological effects of light, shadow, and transparency; sound, smell, heat or coldness, but also —

codes, zoning and bureaucratic limits. Hence the role of these notational schemas is not to set limits, but to imagine multiple program scenarios and to chart their interaction. These notations do not so much map an exact correspondence between

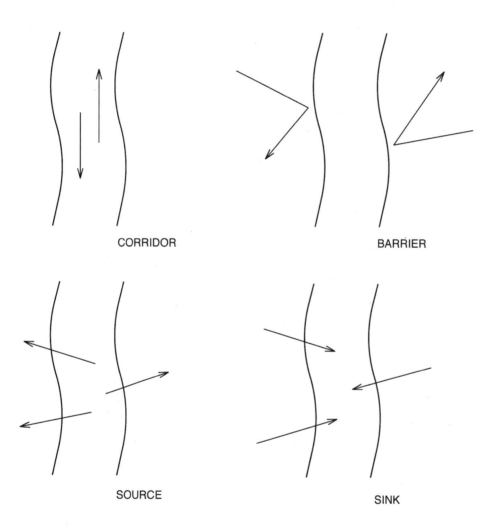

CORRIDOR

BARRIER

SOURCE

SINK

and perhaps more significantly — program, event and social space. Notations are not pictures or icons. They do not so much describe or represent specific objects, as they specify internal structure and relationships among the parts. Inasmuch as the use of notation signals a generalized shift away from the object and toward the syntactic and the ephemeral, this

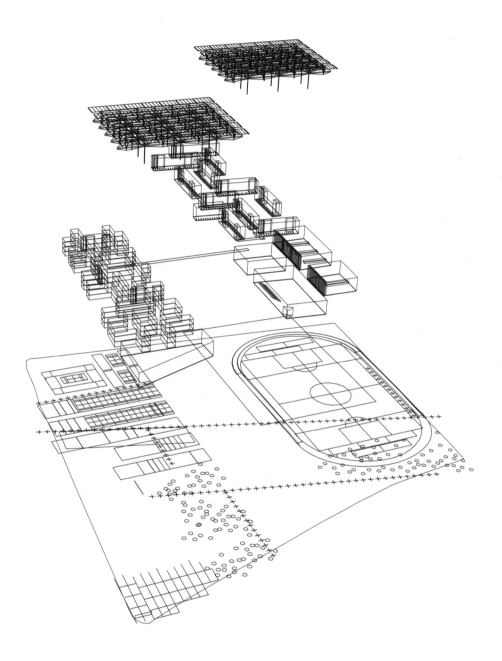

would seem to open up the possibility of a rigorous, yet non-reductive abstraction. The use of notation marks a shift from delimited object to extended field.

Time Notations include time as a variable. It is not accidental that notations figure most significantly in the arts that unfold in time: music, dance or theater. If we allow, along with Paul Virilio, that the life of the city and its experience today belongs more to time than to space ("Now speed — ubiquity, instantaneousness — dissolves the city, or rather displaces it, in time"[1]), the special capacity of notation to make thematic the measurement and unfolding of time takes on a special importance:

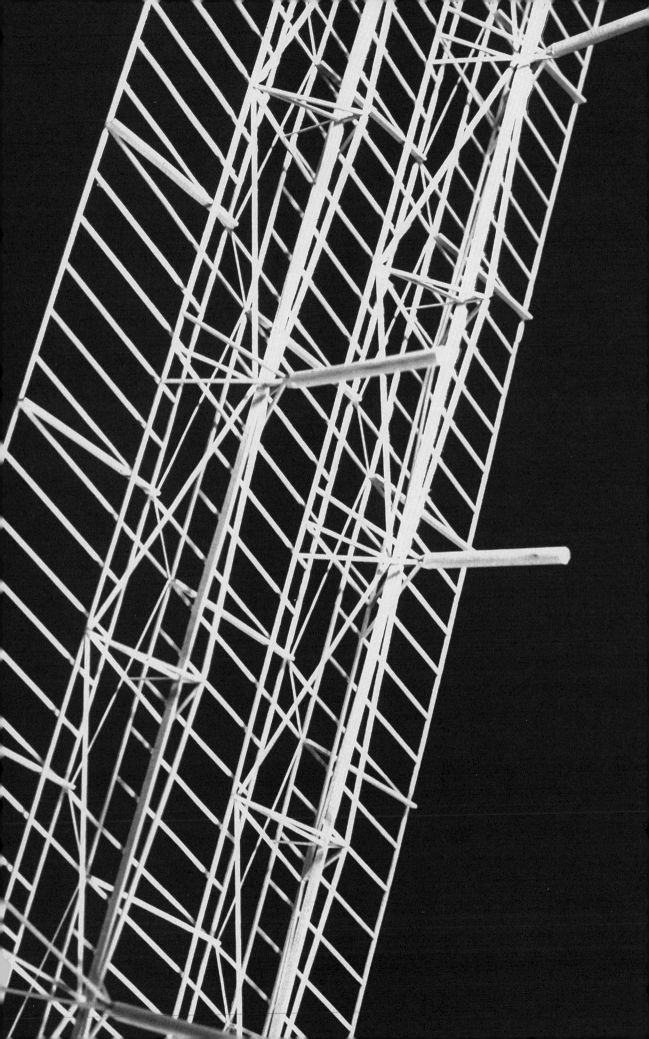

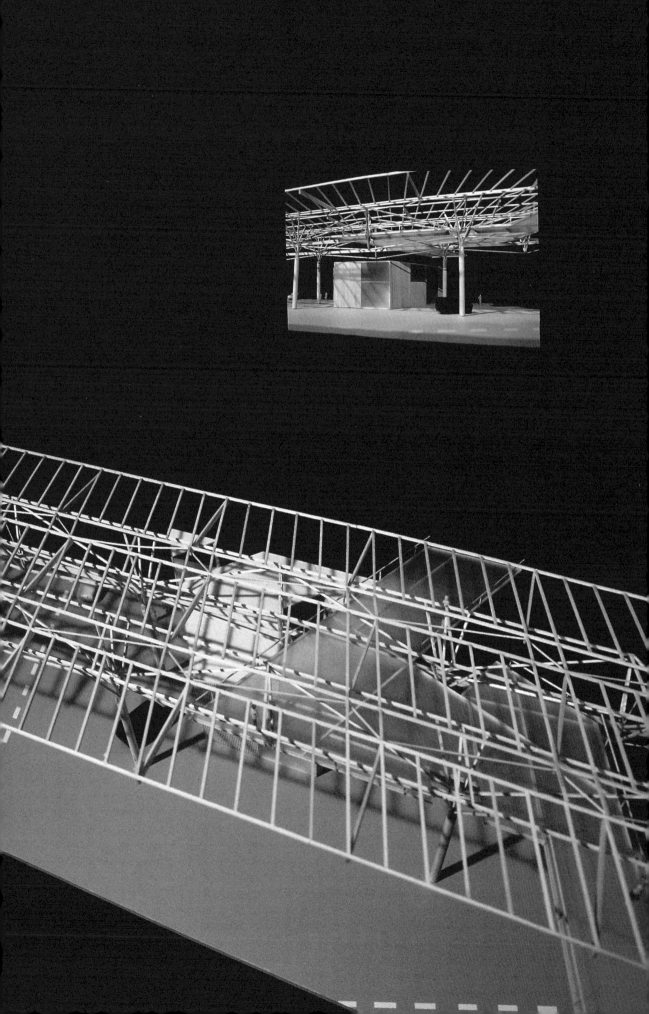

architecture and activity, as articulate a degree of play between form and event, a loose fit of organization and program.

Performance often implies an elaborated design process — a virtuoso display of technique that is in turn registered in the formal complexity of the building. We propose instead that performance implies shifting attention away from the author, and the process of design, to the behavior of architecture in the world, beyond the control of a single author. This requires a creative rethinking of notational techniques in order to loosely map and predict the performance of the architecture *in the field*.

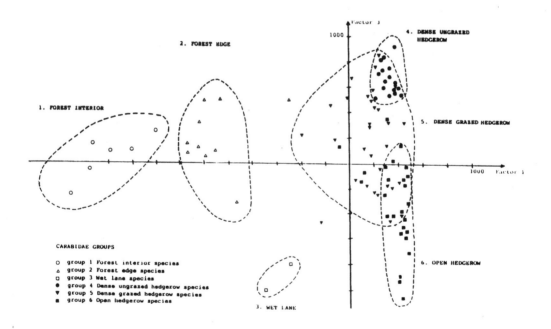

interval, duration and tempo, acceleration and accumulation are the key variables in a notational schema.

Collective Notations presume a social context, and shared conventions of interpretation. The score is not a work itself, but a set of instructions for performing a work. A score cannot be a private language. It works instrumentally to coordinate the actions of multiple performers who collectively produce the work as event. As a model for operating in the city the collective character of notation is highly suggestive. Going beyond transgression and cross-programming, notations could function to map the complex and indeterminate theater of everyday life in the city. The use

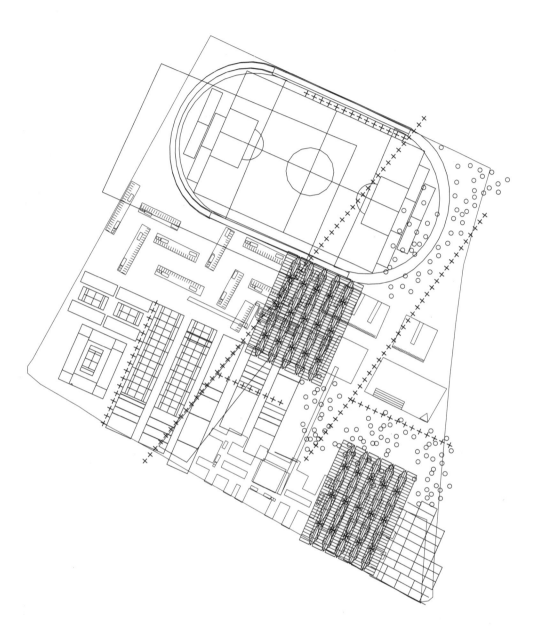

of notation might provoke a shift from the production of space to the
performance of space.

Digital Diagrams Notations work digitally. To say this is not to suggest any
specific relation to computer technology, but rather to return to a precise
definition of the digital: "A digital scheme . . . is discontinuous throughout;

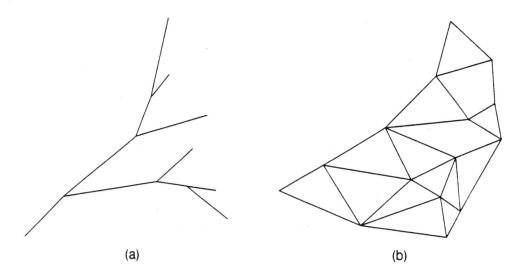

(a)   (b)

Architecture is conceived as the scaffold for events, rather than as the event itself.

Taking an optimistic view of the future of the site, this project anticipates the participation of different architects, agencies and individuals in the construction of the site. It seeks to establish a realistic framework within which these collective contributions can be organized and coordinated. Working not with the bureaucratic tools of zoning, regulations or codes, it seeks to establish precise technical and instrumental limits to future construction. By creating a structured field condition that is architecturally specific yet programatically indeterminate, the future life of the site is free to unfold beyond the fixed limits of a masterplan.

Diagrams illustrating in the above section taken from Richard T. T. Forman and Michael Godron, Landscape Ecology, John Wiley & Sons, NY, 1986.

and in a digital system the characters of such a scheme are one-to-one correlated with a compliance-class of a similar discontinuous set." [2] Notations work through difference, not resemblance. If the new technology is understood as a shift from machines of production to machines of reproduction, and if this shift is characterized by the replacement of the

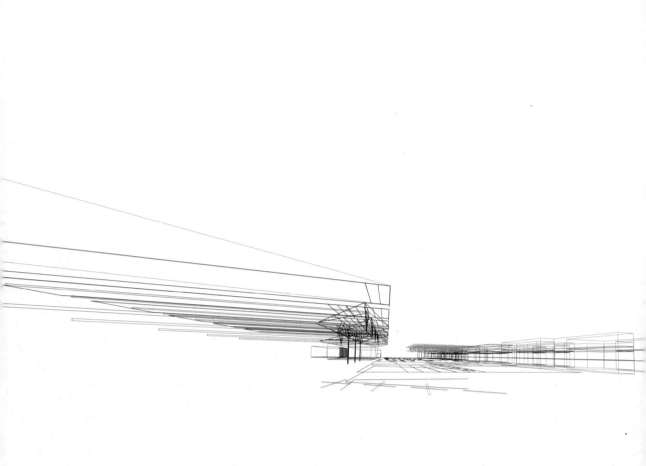

analog by the digital, a corresponding shift toward notation in architectural practice might follow. To cite Goodman again, "the more we are startled by this, because we think of such diagrams as rather schematized pictures, the more strongly we are reminded that the significant distinction between the digital or notational and the non-notational, including the analog, turns not upon some loose notion of analogy or resemblance but upon the grounded technical requirements for a notational language"

Illegible Some caution is necessary at the end. To appeal to notational systems in urbanism is not to suggest a return to perfect transparency of meaning and the smooth implementation of functionality. In the essay

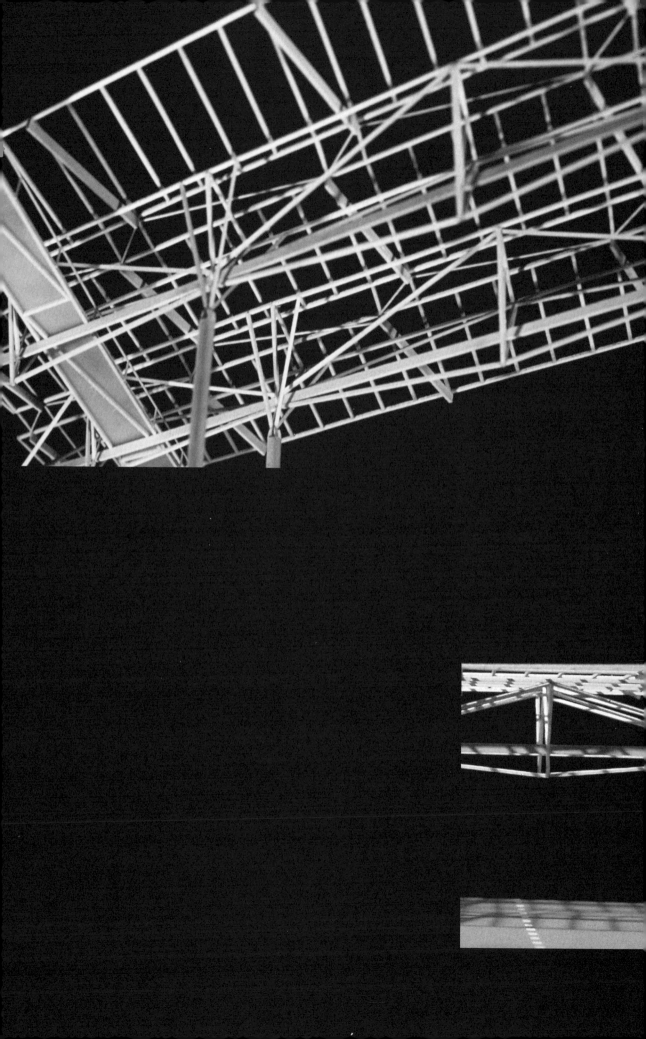

"Reading the Illegible: Some Modern Representations of Urban Experience" critic Steven Marcus reminds us that the modern city "has gone out of control . . . it has lost the signifying potencies and structural coherences that it once seemed to posses."[3] The text of the city — from the language of its inhabitants to the space of the street — can no longer be read in any coherent or predictable manner. Marcus refers to the long literary history of urban description. Traditionally, even as the city grows more complex, the novelist is still able to give a coherent account of the incoherent city. But in the more recent fiction of a writer such as Thomas Pynchon, that coherence begins to fall apart: "In order to see the contem-

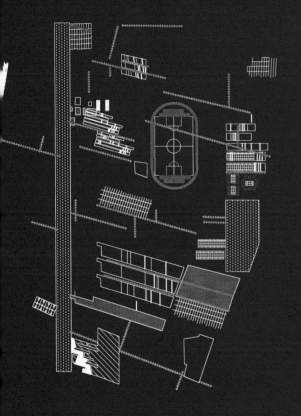

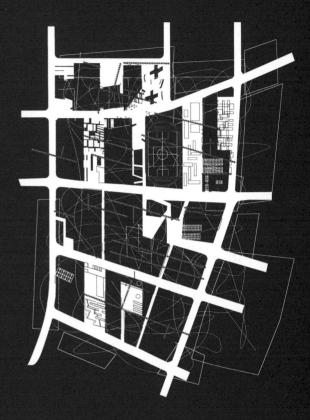

porary urban world clearly, Pynchon asserts here, we must be able to see past "the fiction of continuity, the fiction of cause and effect, the fiction of humanized history endowed with 'reason'" The structural categories are, in these words, meaningless deceptions themselves. The whole has become again destabilized, obscure, baseless, mystified—and most

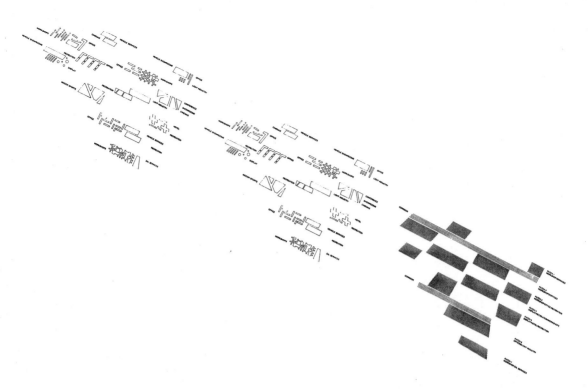

CONSTRUCTING THE PERIPHERY:

Refusing the chaos of the suburban landscape — without resorting to nostalgic urban patterns — we look for an order specific to the open zones at the edge of the city. Two prototypical strategies are proposed: 1. A division of land that recognizes the presence of nature and maintains open green space. 2. A continuous architectural infrastructure that will allow flexible development while maintaining unified identity.

A place between the city and the landscape: spaces for work and pleasure; the long low scale; accommodation of the one and the many; the permanent presence of nature.

1. Surfaces

Borrowing a concept from landscape ecology, the given surface area of the site is organized into patches and corridors. Patches are contiguous areas of specific occupation — in this case either green areas where a return to indigenous habitat is encouraged, and built-up areas to accommodate the new programs. Corridors are infrastructural pathways containing movement, services and programs. The superposition of these two systems creates a mosaic of natural and artificial surfaces.

2. Movement

Boundary and through roads are connected into the present system of urban circulation. To facilitate connection with the ZAL, the primary circulation is on uninterrupted East-West routes. Secondary circulation is by means of local connecting roads aligned with the disjunctive network of patches. Pedestrian movement is at an upper level within the depth of the trusses supporting the continuous roof structure.

efforts of understanding or constructing a whole are themselves part of a mystification." Fully aware of the dangers of mystification and false totalities, performance notations do not set out to impose coherence on an otherwise incoherent city, or to regulate meaning or behavior. Rather they propose an open-ended series of strategies to work within the indetermi-

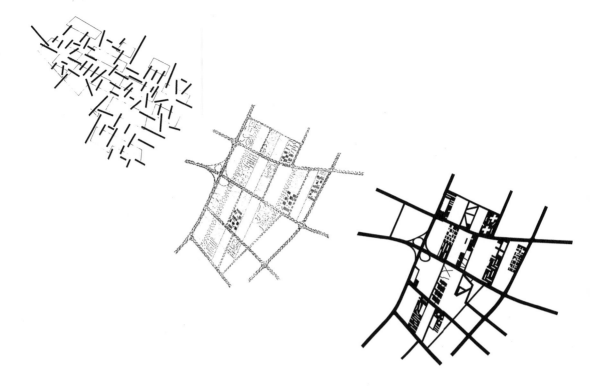

3. Program

With the intention of making the site a productive landscape, and not just a service area, four broad programmatic categories are proposed: Work (workshops and ateliers for artists and artisans); Display (vehicle showrooms and other exhibition facilities), Service (vehicle services, hotel and office space) and Recreation (sports facilities and open green spaces for leisure and events). Individual patches are programmed in relation to access, adjacency and proximity to services.

4. Patch typologies

Instead of specific design proposals for future occupation of the site, a series of loose organizational typologies are proposed. Depending on density and organization, patches might function as habitat, barrier, filter, source or sink for future activity. Scale and density of architectural occupation in turn suggests possible programs.

5. Infrastructure

The architectural space of the corridors is articulated by a continuous roof structure supported on a regular grid of thin steel columns. This Infrastructural element is adaptable and flexible. A light-weight fabric covering can be added where appropriate to shelter public spaces or outdoor service areas, and where buildings are proposed, it can be integrated into the structural system as sunbreak or service space. It imposes minimal although precise limits on future construction.

nate field of the contemporary city. They propose new scenarios, provoke unanticipated combinations and allow incremental adjustment over time. They leave space for the tactical improvisation of the user in the field. Whatever coherence is attained is always a provisional stabilization of the mobile forces of the city, not set down in advance, but developed in practice.

Notes 1 Virilio, Paul, *Pure War*, Semiotext(e), 1983, p. 60 2 Nelson Goodman, *Languages of Art*, Hackett Publishing, 1976 p. 171 3 Steven Marcus: "Reading the Illegible: Some Modern Representations of Urban Experience" In *Visions of the Modern City* edited by William Sharpe and Leonard Wallock, Johns Hopkins Press, Baltimore/London p. 240

LINGO LITTER

(A MONODIALOGUE)

Aris Fioretos

NOW HEAR THIS. THIS IS ME. COME HERE. IT IS ME. THE RECYCLER. I AM HERE. COME HEAR. THIS IS ME. AH IT IS SAYING THINGS LIKE THIS THAT FORCE YOUR FOCUS. THE THINGS THAT HAPPEN TWICE EH. HEAR THIS HERE THEN. AND HEAR IT GOOD. I AM THE RESAYER. I AM THE RE-DOER. I AM THAT SECOND-TO-NONE SECOND MOVER. I SAP SENTENCES. OH I DO. AFTER THE MOUTHING AND ITS AIRING THE ACT AND WHAT ENSUES I ZAP THEM. I DO THEM GOOD. I PERUSE AND PURSUE. THEN I STORE IT ALL. THE SAID. I RESTORE IT. SENTENCING IT TO THE WARD FOR WORDS WAITING TO BE REDONE. THE BIDDING BUCKET THE CALL BIN THE BIG AND BULKY VOICE PEN. CALL IT WHAT YOU WILL. THIS HEAP COMMITTED TO RESPEECH. NOTHING TOO INSIGNIFICANT FOR ME OH NO. ALL IS FINE IT REALLY IS. WELL IT IS. I AM IN THE HUBBUB RACKET. DOING REHUB. OH BUT I AM. I RETRIEVE. IN THE SEARING SECOND OF A STANDSTILL OR IN SOME LOAD OF TIME. IT DOES NOT MATTER. CHARTING THE OUTSKIRTS OF ORALITY OR TESTING THE STEALTH RELAYS FOR VOCAL DUST. OR ELSEWHERE. SOMEWHERE. NO IT DOES NOT MATTER. I GET TO GET TO IT. SOME-WHERE. ELSEWHERE. ALWAYS. THAT IS ME. THE RECYCLER. I CHECK. COMPILE. PILE. AND COLLECT. STORING IT ALL SO THAT WHEN IT HAS BEEN SAID AND GONE IT MAY BE SAID AGAIN AND ON FROM THERE ON AND ON. INTO NOWHERE I SAY IT. COUNTDOWN RECREATION. SAY IT INTO NOWHERE I DO AND OUT AND GONE. IT IS A VOCATION LIKE ANY OTHER. IT IS MINE. I AM THE AGAINER. **SLAP THE WORLD ANY WAY IT FLAPS BACK.** I SAY. **TURN THE DIAL PAST ZERO IT IS BACK TO ONE.** OR SO I SAY. SO I SLAP THE WORD. AND IT FLAPS BACK. I TURN ITS DIAL PAST ZERO. AND IT IS BACK TO ONE. I SLAP AND ZAP IT I DO UNTIL NEXT TIME IT MUST BE SAID AND SLAPPED TO BE GONE AND GONE AGAIN THEN BACK. WHEN NOW IS NOW NO LONGER BUT SAID AND GONE I SAY IT AGAIN THEN I MUST LAY IT ON. IT IS MY THING. I AM THE RETRIEVER. I AM THE REDOER. YES THEN I SAY IT OVER AND ON USING THE MOUTH NOW LAYING IT ON HERE I SAY IT OVER THERE AND GONE. MY AGAINMOUTH. SLAP. FLAP. I DO. ONE ZERO ONE AND SO ON. FOR I AM THE REUSER. I AM THE RECHARGER. I AM THE SECOND-TO-NONE SECOND MOVER. AND THE SAID MUST BE RESAID I SAY. THAT IS MY TRADE. I DO REHUB. WELL. I SAID THAT. AT TIMES I ADMIT I TEND TO TELL THE MOUTH TO DO THE JOB FOR ME I TEND TO TELL IT TO RESAY IT ALL BY ITSELF AGAIN AND TIME AGAIN I TELL IT DO SO THAT IT IS GONE AGAIN. THAT TENDS TO BE WHEN I AM TIRED. TOO TIRED FOR WORDS KNOW WHAT I MEAN. I TEND TO TELL IT TO DO SO I ADMIT TELLING IT TO SAY SO TO BE GONE AGAIN. I DO. ON AND GONE I SAY. I ADMIT. WHEN I AM TIRED I TEND TO. BUT MIND I CAN NEED SOME HELP. WITH ALL THIS ZERO-ONE

STUFF AND WHAT NOT. AND I KNOW A MOUTH WHEN I HEAR ONE. IT IS NOT AN EASY THING TO DO THE DOING I AM DOING. OH NO. NOR IS TELLING THE MOUTH TO SAY THE SAID AGAIN AN EASY THING TO DO IT IS NOT. NO WAY. NO IT IS NOT. IT IS WEARING. WELL IT IS. STILL. AH NOTHING. WELL. STILL ONCE MY MOUTH ONCE IT WILL BE READY VERY MUCH READY INDEED READY TO FIND A WAY ON ITS OWN INTO WHAT IS VANISHED AND GONE IN ORDER TO RESAY IT ITSELF. WITHOUT MY SAYING SO YOU KNOW. THAT WILL BE SOMETIME COMING NONE TOO SOON I MUST SAY. THAT IS MY MOUTH I WILL SAY THEN. THAT IS IT. SAYING IT ALONG ITS WAY SO TO SAY. SASHAYING IT AND LEARNING IT TO COPE WITH ALL THAT RESPEECH. A SLOW SULLEN SHOW IT MAY BE OR A SWIFT SWAY AND AWAY. BUT JUST WAIT AND SEE I TEND TO SAY. THAT IS MY WAY. JUST TO WAIT AND SEE. OR SO I SAY. IT MAY FUMBLE A MUMBLE THE WAY A WINO WILL HIS WILLESS KEY. OR SNAKE ITS WAY INTO THE SAYING LIKE A FAST FUSE LIT WITH MENACE. ITS MANNERS WILL BE MANY ITS WAYS WILL VARY. BUT THAT JUST GOES TO SHOW. SO WHEN I HAVE SAID THE SAID AWAY I TEND TO TURN TO THE MOUTH TEND TO TURN TO TELL WHETHER IT IS READY TO SAY FROM NOW ON WHETHER IT IS READY AGAIN TO SAY IT ALL ITSELF. AND IT SEEMS TO BEGIN TO BE. YEAH IT SEEMS TO BEGIN TO BE. THAT IS MY MOUTH I SAY. IT IS I WILL SAY. THAT IS MY MOUTH. WHAT WITH DOING THAT STUFF TO THE SAID ITSELF. MY AGAINMOUTH. NOW THIS WILL HELP. SURE WILL. GRAND. FOR ONCE THE SAID IS SAID AND DONE AWAY WITH YOU SHOULD NOT THINK IT IS OVER AND DONE WITH OH NO. THAT IS WHEN IT BEGINS TO GET REAL. REEL REAL. THAT IS WHEN WE COME IN. TO DO OUR THING. ME AND MY MOUTH. IT IS OUR JOB WE SAY. THE SAID HAVING BEEN SAID AWAY WE WILL RESAY THE SAID-AWAY. FOR YOU SHOULD NOT THINK NO YOU SHOULD NOT THINK YOU COULD SHAPE AN ESCAPE ONCE THE SAID IS GONE AND NO LONGER ON BUT AWAY. THAT IS NOT THE CASE. NO VERY MUCH NOT IT IS NOT. UHN-UHN. LITTLE WORDS LITTER THE AIR. EVERYWHERE. CLING KICK STING STICK. THEY DO. OH THEY LOITER. SO WE MUST DO OUR THING. AND DO IT GOOD. ME THE RECYCLER AND MR. MOUTH THE MAINTAINER. WHAT AN ACT. WE WILL STRIP THE AIR OF ITS THIN WORN WEAR. SCRUBBING OFF THAT WARY TISSUE. REMOVING WEBS STILL STUCK TO THE VENT IN WHICH THEY DALLY-HO DID DO THEIR TALK-TRAVEL. UH HUH. SIFTING THROUGH LAYERS OF ETHER FOR SCRUBS OF SAYING. ALL THOSE SPECKS OF SPEAK. OR GETTING THE REMNANTS OF REPEAT OUT OF THE LUNG EXHAUST THE WAY YOU CLEAN A PIPE OR CLEAR A THROAT. SOMETIMES THERE MAY BE A BUMP AND THE SAID WILL SPRING AT YOU LIKE AN AIR BAG. OTHER TIMES GLOSSES WILL BE SO GLIB AND GLOSSY YOU WILL SLIP THE SLOPE DOWN TO THEIR OILY COIL OF SLIME. BUT NO MATTER OH NO. IT MUST ALL BE GATHERED AND MADE USE OF AGAIN. IMAGINE. ALL THAT SNICK-SNACKETY WASTE. FOR IT MAY IRRADIATE **EVERYTHING IN ITS IMMEDIATE AREA WITH TOXIC PROLIXITY.** TOXIC. IFYOUKNOWWHATIMEAN. I AM TALKING TOXIC. WITHOUT US THE AIR WOULD BE TOO SAID UP IT WOULD. TOO TOXED UP FOR SURE TO BOOT. RUSH LOOM MUSHROOMING LARGE. OR. WELL. SOME SUCH. SO WE

WILL GO IN AND DO OUR THING. MR. MOUTH AND I. WE WILL MAKE THE AIR USABLE AGAIN. I AM THE RECYCLER. HE IS THE MAINTAINER. WE SAY IT IS OUR JOB. FOR IT IS A JOB TO DO. WE SAY THE AIR IS HERE TO STAY WE SAY. HE AND I. HE WITH HIS WORD WARD WAITING IN THAT MAINTAINER. AND I SPORTING THE SPINNING GEAR OF RESAYING. QUITE THE PAIR WE ARE. OH YES. QUITE WE ARE. DO NOT GET ME WRONG MIND. THERE IS NO OTHER WAY. MAKING THE SAYING AN ESCAPE THROUGH WHICH THE SAID COULD VANISH INTO THE WORLD WOULD BE INTERMINABLE LABOR. IT MAY SEEM IT WOULD NOT BE MAYBE BUT IT WOULD BE INTERMINABLE WOULD BE AND IT IS. IT IS THE AIR YOU SEE. THE WORD IS IN THE WORLD AND SAYING THE SAID AWAY IS INTERMINABLE FOR THE AIR TURNS IT ALWAYS RETURNS. THIS WAY OR THAT. ALWAYS DOES YOU KNOW. RETURN IT WILL ALWAYS RETURN WHEN IT HAS HAD ITS TURN TO BE SAID INTO SAID EXISTENCE. NO MATTER WHAT. SO SHAPING SOME ESCAPE WILL NOT DO. NO WAY. BETTER TO STRIP THE ETHER OF ITS COAT. MAKE IT USABLE AGAIN WE SAY. THAT IS OUR THING. WE ARE THE REMOVERS REDOERS SOUND SURROUNDERS WELL WE ARE. WHEN SOME SAID HAS BEEN SAID AWAY SAY I WILL SIFT IT SAMPLING THE AIR I WILL AND TELL MR. MOUTH TO STORE IT. I WILL SAY STORE IT AGAIN MR. MOUTH I WILL SAY SO THAT AGAIN IT MAY BE PUT TO USE. IT WILL BE BACK AGAIN SOON OH SURE SO WELL. THEN AGAIN IT WILL NOT BE. AND AGAIN IT WILL BE. BUT MIND SUCH IS THE EQUATION. IT IS ALL PNEUMATICS. ZEROES AND ONES. AND THIS IS OUR JOB. NO POINT THEN NO POINT NO TO TRY TO GET AWAY WITH SAYING THE SAID AWAY YOU WOULD NOT GET AWAY WITH IT YOU WOULD NOT IF YOU WANTED TO. THE WORLD IS NOT IN THE WORD NAH-NAH BUT THE WORD IS IN THE WORLD. FOR IT IS IN THE AIR. YOU MAY THINK THAT SAYING THE SAID AGAIN WILL DO BELIEVING THAT AGAIN IT WILL NOT BE. IT WILL NOT DO. IT CANNOT BE IT THAT IT CANNOT BE. ALL THERE IS YOU SEE ALL THERE IS AND WILL BE ARE SPHERIC SHADES SHUFFLING THEIR VACUITY TO AND FRO. LIKE WORN DOWN SLIPPERS. LUNG TRASH TROTTING ABOUT. IT IS LEGION. AGAIN AND AGAIN THERE THEY WILL BE. INTERIM QUIDDITIES DOING THEIR BIT OF RE-BEING. THAT IS ALL THERE IS TO BE. THE RESAIDS. OH THE ETHER REVENANTS. OR YOU MAY THINK THE MOUTH SOME NULLITY WARD. A PERISHING PARISH OR A HALL HOLLOW AS A HALO. HAVING NO SAID OH NO JUST BEING IN ITS SAYING. WELL RIGHT YOU ARE. IT SORT OF IS AND SORT OF IT IS MEANT TO BE. FOR SUCH IS ITS SITUATION. BUT YOU SEE. IT IS ALL IN THE AIR ANYWAY. IT IS ALL IN THE AIR. THE MOUTH MAY MOUTH YOUR VOICE NUL AND VOID INDEED. ZERO-SUMMING IT EMPTY. ZAP. ZILTCH. NOTHING. JUST SOME VOCAL DUST OR AIRY ASH. FINE. AND AT LAST YOU MAY SAY. SILENCE YOU WILL THINK. NOW SILENCE. OH HOW SWEET. SIGHLESS. WELL IT IS NOT AND IS NOT MEANT TO BE. THE SAID IS STILL STUCK TO THE AIR SEE. YES IT IS INDEED. IT IS IN THE AIR. STUCK LIKE FICKLE FLIES IN TRANSPARENT GLUE. SAYING DOES THAT SEE. IT STICKS THE SAID TO THE AIR. IT IS ALL THERE. IN CRACKS IN BUBBLES OF PLASTER AND RUST IN WEBS OF MINISCULE DERELICT MATTER. THE DEBRIS OF DICTION. L-I-N-G-O L-I-T-T-E-R. FOR THE MOUTH IS NO **EMPTY**

CABINET OH NO NOR A CABIN NEVER VISITED. BUT A TRANSIT TERMINAL DOCK SLUICE STUCK THICK WITH RESAIDS. HARDLY ANY WHITE WALLS THERE THEN BUT RATHER GRAY. IN ALL RATHER GRAY. ALL WELL ALL VERY RATHER GRAY THEY ARE. SOME MENTAL METALLIC SAY. SPEECH SPOIL COATING THE TILES OF TALK THE WAY TARRY SMOKE WILL WALLS. THIS IS WHERE THE SPECTERS OF SPEECH ROAM YES ROOM WELL IN OTHER WORDS ROAM. THIS IS WERE THEY ARE. ALL THE **GHOST LOVED ONES.** THE RESAIDS. IN NOWHERELAND THEY ARE. SENTENCED TO AIR. IN THAT GRAY ETHER DOME THEY ARE AND ARE ON AGAIN IF I MAY SAY. HERE. NOW. IN NOWHERE. SO MR. MOUTH AND I WE WILL DO OUR JOB. I AM THE RECYCLER. HE IS THE MAINTAINER. HE STORES THE SAID AND I DO ER THE AIR BRUSHING. IT IS MY JOB TO TREAT IT SO THAT SAID AND GONE HE MAY SAY THE SAID ON FROM THERE ON AND ON. I FIX THE AIR AND HE WILL SAY THE SAID AWAY. AND WHEN IT HAS BEEN SAID AND GONE AND RESAID AS GONE I WILL LET SOME OTHER STUFF COME ON. THE PALER AIR PERHAPS WITH A PELLICLE THE COLOR OF CONTUSIONS. OR THE WORN AND SOILED ONE STIFF LIKE AN OLD SOCK. SOME AIRS ARE SLUGGISH LIKE A THUG'S THUDS OF THICK RUBBER WHEREAS OTHERS ARE ALL OVER YOU KNOW ALL OVER LIKE LOOPS OF LOOSE SUSPENDER. BUT IT WILL COME. THE AIR AND THAT SPEECH SPOIL. IT WILL COME TO US TO BE REMADE AND REMIXED. AND ONCE ALL IS SAID THERE IS TO SAY IT IS TO BE RESAID AGAIN IT IS. (A SAYING THAT HAS IT ALL.) FOR THE RESAIDS THEY MUST BE SAID TOO OH THEY MUST. AND THEN THE RE-RESAIDS. IT IS ALL ZEROES AND ONES ANYWAY. AND WELL SO SEE WE HAVE MUCH TO DO MR. MOUTH AND I. GONE ARE THE DAYS WE SPENT SPEECHLESS UNDER THE CLOUDS OF THE SKY. LONG GONE IS THE SWEET STILLNESS WITH HOOCH AT HAND PERHAPS OH YES OR THE ODD SPLEENIC SPLENDOR GRABBING THE SPINE STABBING THE SIDE. GONE ARE THOSE DAYS ALL DAYS LONG GONE. AND THE NIGHTS TOO. OH YES. NO TIME NO MORE. NOW I RUN THIS WASTE DISPOSAL TREAT. A PERMANENT VACATION IN VACANCY. NO TIME NO HERE NO MORE. SO WELCOME. WELCOME THEN TO THE SPEECH WASTE RECYCLE UNIT. THE LINGO LITTER PLANT. THIS IS IT. IN NOWHERELAND. YOU MAY TAKE A LOOK AND SAY YOUR PEACE. OR YOU MAY TAKE A LOOP AND SAY YOUR PACE. WELL. IT IS ALL HERE ANYWAY IS IT NOT WHAT YOU SAY IS ALL SAID HERE AND DONE NO. YES. AH THERE ARE SOME REAL RESAIDS HERE INDEED THERE ARE. CHECK OUT THE RAPID REPEATS FOR EXAMPLE REELING THROUGH THEIR RERUNS LIKE LONELY RATS THEIR RICKETY RACES. OR MONITOR THE REVERBERATIONS AS THEY WOBBLE THEIR WAY THROUGH INVISIBLE FLOW CHARTS LIKE THE IODINE FLASH OF A LIGHTHOUSE COMBING THROUGH THE NIGHT. OR TAKE IN THE ECHOES BOUNCING AGAINST SILENCE WITH PINBALL SHIFTINESS. MIGRATORY CIRCUITS MAKE-SHIFT MAZES WORDS BRUISING THE AIR. OH NO NO ONE NOT ONE RESAID IS MISSING. NONE. BUT EH A WORD OF CAUTION BEFORE YOU PASS ON. HERE YOU TOO ARE ONLY IN TERMS OF THE SPEED WITH WHICH YOU ADVANCE AND WHICH YOU DRINK IN LIKE OXYGEN. IT WILL **BECOME THE ELEMENT IN WHICH YOU LIVE AND WHICH IS YOU. NOTHING ELSE MATTERS.** PACE IS

ALL. THAT AIR. EVEN IF YOU WOULD NOT BE ON **TIN CANNED ENERGY** YOU WILL MOVE IN IT NO LONGER AS SOME **PURE AND PRESENT NOUN** NO NO YOU WILL NOT BUT AS A **NEXUS OF ADJECTIVES** YOU WILL. OH YEAH BUT IT IS SWELL ANYWAY IS IT NOT. IT IS. ALL SAID IT IS SWELL TO BE SO WELL AFTER ALL. REMIXED. RE-AIRED. WAY TO GO IT IS. NOWHERE SO MUCH AS HERE AND NOW AND NOWHERE. UH HUM. CONSIDER THE SITUATION. IN THE SPOOLER YOU LOSE THE POWER TO EXPRESS YOURSELF **IN A CONTINUOUS MANNER** AS YOU WOULD PROPERLY EITHER BY CONFORMING TO THE COHERENCE OF SOME LOGICAL DISCOURSE THROUGH THE SUCCESSION OF **THIS INTEMPORAL TIME** THAT BELONGS TO A RECHARGER AT WORK MEETING OUT THINGS LIKE IDENTITY AND NOMINAL UNITY OR BY YIELDING TO **THE UNINTERRUPTED MOVEMENT** OF SAY WELL SAY OF WRITING. FINE. THIS MAY NOT MAKE YOU VERY HAPPY. STILL IN COMPENSATION YOU MAY BELIEVE NOW AND THEN THAT YOU HAVE GAINED THE POWER TO EXPRESS YOURSELF INTERMITTENTLY **AND EVEN THE POWER TO GIVE EXPRESSION TO INTERMITTENCE.** NOR MAY THIS MAKE YOU VERY HAPPY. BUT IT WILL KEEP YOU GOING ON. NEITHER HAPPY NOR UNHAPPY BUT NEUTRAL. NEUTRAL. THINK. PUT IN NEUTRAL AND RUNNING. SO IT GOES. SO YOU MUST THINK. IT WILL KEEP YOU GOING ON IT WILL. PUT SOME PRESSURE ON THAT FLAT AIR SLABBED AGAINST YOUR VOCAL WIRES AND YOU WILL SEE. YOU WILL HEAR THE SAID HUMMING IN THERE LIKE CELLULOID RUNNING ITS LIMBER COURSE THROUGH SOME LIMBO PROJECTOR. THAT IS YOU HERE YOU HEAR. SO IT DOES SEEM DOES IT NOT THAT WELL **GUSTS OF AIR** MAY BECOME **PERSONALIZED.** DOES IT NOT. IT DOES. OR AT LEAST SOME SUCH IN AS MUCH AS MUCH IS SUCH HERE. WHAT GIVES THEN. WELL. THE SENSE NO SENSATION OF RESAYING IS NO LONGER ONE OF MOVING FORWARD ON AND ON AND OVER AND ON AS MUCH AS HAVING **THE PATH REELED BACK** SORT OF **MOUNTED ON SOME GIANT PIECE OF SCENERY.** THAT IS IT. YEAH SORT OF LIKE THAT IT IS. THIS IS THE LOOP YOU MAY POOL FOR LIFE. THE VIVACITY SPOOLER. WELCOME. YOU ARE IN REHUB YOU ARE. AND THIS IS WHAT WE DO WHEN WE DO WHAT WE DO. MR. MOUTH AND I. WE FIX THINGS UP SO THAT THE YOU THAT IS YOU MAY CONTINUE AND ENSUE. YOU **NEED A FAST MUTATION** SAY OR **A SUBSTITUTE.** THAT IS FINE. WE DO THAT. IT IS A THING WE DO. OR BETTER STILL YOU MAY THINK YOU WANT **TO RELOCATE.** THAT WE DO TOO. THIS **IS A DIMENSIONLESS ORGANISM** AFTER ALL YOU KNOW **LIKE THE WIND'S.** ITS MALLEABLE MATERIAL CAN BE MOULDED PRETTY WELL. BUT IT IS **RESTLESS** VERY MUCH RESTLESS IT IS. **A LIVING CONCERN THAT CAN KNOW NO REST** OH NO. NOWHERE NOW HERE. OR SOME SUCH. ZEROES AND ONES AT ANY RATE. THAT IS THE POINT. YOU STICK TO IT. FOR THIS IS THE MISSION THIS IS THE TRANSMISSION THIS IS THE RICKETY REST WE PRODUCE. REAL REEL REALTY. I AM THE RECYCLER AND THIS IS MR. MOUTH. WELCOME. WELCOME HERE. WE WILL SAY YOU ON. YOU ARE HERE NOW YOU HEAR. IN AIR IT IS FAIR IN NOWHERE.

RECYCLED BITS OF TEXT, ALL IN BOLD FACE, TAKEN FROM:

A. R. AMMONS, *GARBAGE* (NEW YORK: NORTON & COMPANY, 1993); JOHN ASHBERY, « THE SYSTEM, »
IN *THREE POEMS* (NEW YORK: VIKING BOOKS, 1973); JOHN BANVILLE, *GHOSTS* (NEW YORK: KNOPF,
1993); SAMUEL BECKETT, « A PIECE OF MONOLOGUE, » IN *ROCKABY AND OTHER SHORT PIECES*
(NEW YORK: GROVE PRESS, 1980); MAURICE BLANCHOT, *THE INFINITE CONVERSATION*, TRANS. SUSAN
HANSON (MINNEAPOLIS: UNIVERSITY OF MINNESOTA PRESS, 1993); JOHN LOCKE, *AN ESSAY
CONCERNING HUMAN UNDERSTANDING*, ED. PETER H. NIDDITCH (OXFORD: CLARENDON PRESS, 1975);
PEACE LOVE AND PITBULLS, « DAS NEUE KONZEPT » AND « WAR IN MY LIVIN' ROOM, » ON *RED SONIC
UNDERWEAR* (PLAY IT AGAIN SAM RECORDS, 1994); AND WILL SELF, « THE NORTH LONDON BOOK OF
THE DEAD, » IN *THE QUANTITY THEORY OF INSANITY* (LONDON: BLOOMSBURY, 1991), AS WELL AS
MY IDEA OF FUN (LONDON: BLOOMSBURY, 1993).

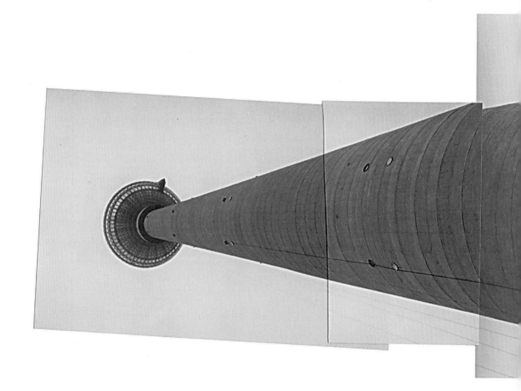

Two Towers

Heather Cameron

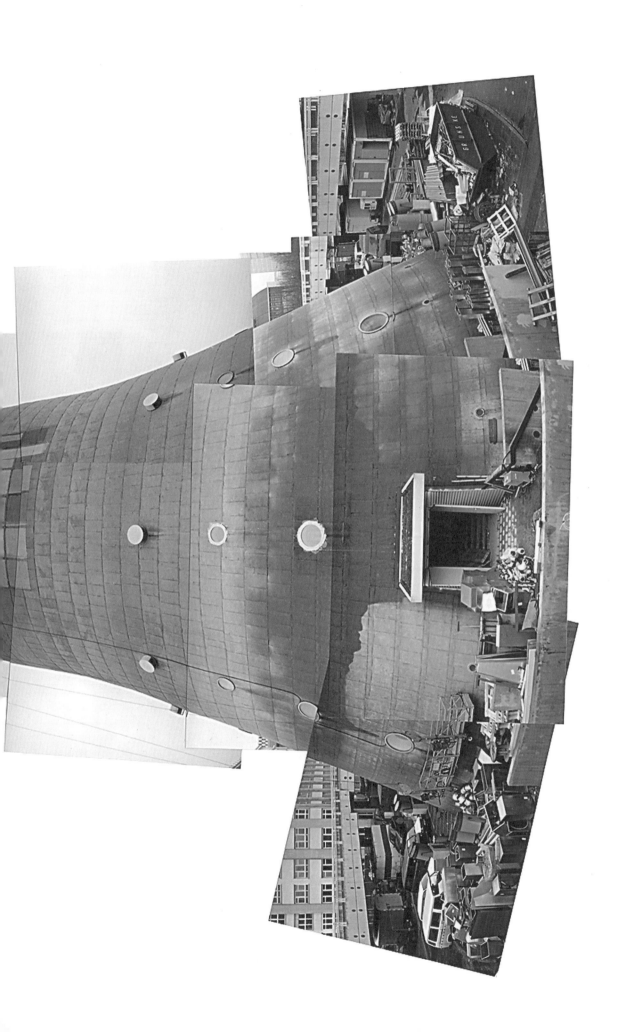

"Behold, they are one people and they have all one language; and this is only the beginning of what they will do; and nothing they propose to do now will be impossible for them. Come, let us go down and there confuse their language, that they may not understand one another's speech." So the Lord scattered them abroad from there all over the face of all the earth, and they left off building the city.
Genesis 11.6–11.8

This is a tale of two towers. Both puncture the sky of reopened cities, Berlin and Prague. Like the tower at Babel, the Berlin TV tower at Alexanderplatz and the TV tower on Zizkov Hill in Prague were never fully completed or operational. They were frequently reconstructed since their erection in the early 1970s as jamming stations for western TV and radio broadcasts.

Jamming, despite all the sophisticated electronics, is a crude overpowering. It can take three forms: tuning the tower to a specific frequency and keying up over weaker signals to broadcast noise, snow, and static; broadcasting competing news, sports and cultural programmes on top of the desired signal; or flooding the sky with noise, making it impossible for any broadcast to get through. The overwhelming power used to block the high-flying TV signals results in a deafening whiteout, knocking every signal out of the sky. This radiation poisoning isn't a particularly elegant method of killing off signals as the power required to broadcast on all frequencies is enormous and distorting.

Different techniques work for different channels—TV, AM, FM and shortwave. AM and shortwave are difficult to block because they hug the earth. The towering height and commanding view can do little to these signals which scurry along the ground.

The towers' domain extends only as far as the eye can see. Broadcast range is determined by line of sight, and as the earth curls out of view, the towers' signals wane. The broadcasts radiated from one site. Like other centralized powers, broadcasts were vulnerable to attack from the edges of their domain. People with directional antennas could resist the full Babel effect by splitting the jammed signal into parts, thereby unbonding the competing messages. Both towers overpower their surrounding landscape, yet they are built on fragmented foundations. The land on which they stand is contested by competing ownership claims. It is astounding that they remain standing. Alexanderplatz, the site of the Berlin tower, is claimed simultaneously by a Jewish family that owned land before the rise of National Socialism, by another family whose land was confiscated by the Soviets, by people who worked the area under the DDR, and by the city itself. The tower in Prague is built in the working class district of Zikov. It is one of the most loathed buildings in Prague due to its incredible dissonance with the surrounding architecture. A 300-year-old Jewish cemetery was moved in order for the tower to be built.

Now the towers are subject to new forms of wave interference and overlap as they serve new masters in Berlin and Prague. They host cellular phone arrays for the bustling capitalists at their feet. The TV jammers are used to broadcast reruns of American TV to eastern European markets. The whiteout continues.....

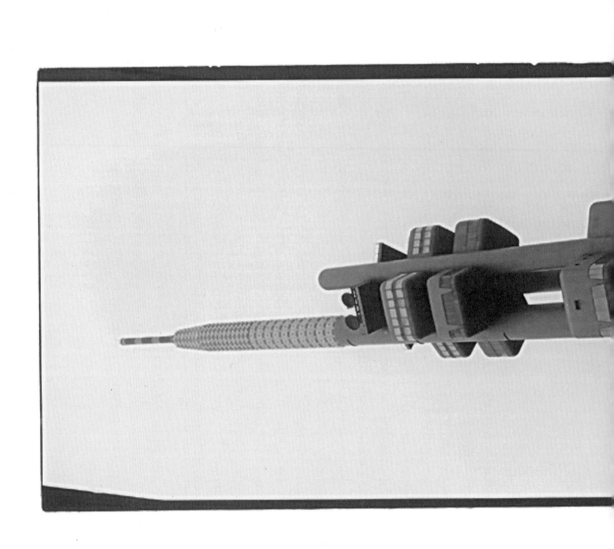

You Pay to Stay Home

Lynne Tillman

Photographs by Dianna Ilk

Now Elizabeth thought she saw Jeanine go into a doorway several buildings down the block. Elizabeth had to turn her head severely to the right to see that far down the block.

It was Jeanine.

Jeanine prostituted for drugs sometimes, for rent other times. She was a runner for a dealer on the corner. Elizabeth and she had known each other a while. Jeanine came over to her, on the corner, when it was cool, when the corner wasn't busy, and they'd talk. The dealers and runners were a stable crew, and though they were busted in sweeps once in a while they always came back, and were part of the neighbourhood. They knew Elizabeth and she knew them, and they didn't hassle each other. When a fight erupted over turf, she made sure not to be there.

It was Jeanine.

Jeanine had been the girlfriend of one of the Lopezes, Jorge. She was the mother of their three children. Elizabeth bought the first baby a present. Jeanine said it was the only one the baby received.

Jorge and Jeanine sat on the stoop in front of the building holding the infant, and then they didn't because it was taken away by the City. Jeanine explained that they had to go to the agency to see it. The agency controlled chunks of Jeanine's and Jorge's lives, because they'd had a child and they themselves were legally children and on drugs. Jeanine said she was trying to stay straight.

Jeanine became pregnant again. Then this child was taken away from her, and Jorge and she started getting high again. Then Jorge got deeper into shit, and into more trouble, and they both went down, down the well together, and the third baby was taken away. All the kids were placed in foster care. Then Jeanine went to prison. The Lopezes said Jorge was in Puerto Rico. Jorge was in jail. He and Jeanine were over.

If Jeanine wasn't on the street, dealing, if she wasn't in jail upstate, she lived at her mother's.

Looking out the window, Elizabeth remembered the afternoon Jeanine came over and slept on her bed. She remembered it as if it were yesterday. Roy was at work. Jeanine'd been up all night. Her mother wouldn't let her into their apartment.

> — Until I was about five, we all lived together. It was, like, happy. My mother had four
> girls and four boys. My mother separated from my father, she became a drunk, started
> using drugs, heroin, and when they got back together, he molested me, and he ended up

molesting my little brother and sister. I think he molested my other brother too, but I'm not sure. They don't speak on it. It caused problems between my mother and me. She blamed me for it. She was in denial for a long time. It happened to my little brother and sister when I went to jail the first time. My father was a really messed-up guy. He used to be a numbers man. He took money and disappeared. Then she had another boyfriend, but she's always insecure about me and her men, like maybe they want me, or I want them. I'm like, please, these old men, get out of my face.

Elizabeth was thinking about how she'd do in jail.

— It's all how the mind handles it, if they break your spirit. I guess it's tough because people tell you when to eat, when to sleep, when to shit. And they do any little thing to provoke you to get into trouble to lock you in solitary, make it hard for you to get out. 'Cause if you're in the city, you can do up to a year, and you have a day to go home; but if you're upstate, they can keep you from going home, they can hold you there. You're dead. You hear from the outside world, but their life goes on without you, so it's like you don't exist. I didn't have a hard time. That's probably why I don't fear going back. But I don't want to go back. Some people go in with this attitude, they try to be too tough, and people beat them up. A lot of people from this neighbourhood go. A lot of people have been in jail before — the more times you go, the more people you know. It's like you're a fixture. It would be very hard for middle-class people, people like you. My mother'd been incarcerated before I was ever born.

Jeanine slept for a while. Then she woke up and they had coffee at the rectangular table in the kitchen.

— Do you hate your mother?
— No, I love the old goat. She's a pain in the ass. I want to hurt her sometimes. We've had fights.
— If you don't buy her drugs.
— She has a fit. You pay to stay home, you pay to stay somewhere else. I gotta give her drugs, because I know she has a fit. She's had a hard time. My mother's father raised them. Her mother abused them from when she was little. My mother was in the hospital for three years because she was getting beaten very badly. Then they grew up in homes, because they took them away from her father because back then it was a man with little girls. Then my mother came back home, and she was with my father since she was thirteen years old. My father was older, twenty-six, she was like thirteen, or something. Hello. She should have realized then the man had a problem.

Elizabeth nodded sympathetically.

—Jorge used to beat me. First of all, he had an inferiority complex. I had to teach him how to read. The home setting was not happy. Very disturbed. He had the heroin habit. His sister died from AIDS, from shooting up.

Emilia's funeral. Jeanine couldn't handle it, too heavy.

—Jorge killed somebody during a robbery. They're not too kind with you taking somebody's life to deprive them of their property. If you kill somebody in a crime of passion or self-defense, it's one thing; but if you kill someone to take their property from them, it's worse. Jorge's crazy. The heroin, man. When he was so sick he didn't want to hear nothing, and he had attitude, and he wanted to beat everybody up, and blamed the world cause he was sick. When he was straight he didn't want to be bothered; he wanted to enjoy his high. There was no in-between. He became crazy shooting up towards the end. He didn't cry for anything. He cried when my kids were taken. But this guy didn't cry for nothing, except one day his fucking set of works got clogged, and he cried like a baby. That's when I really started staying away from the house. It gets to the point where I'm like numb, I really am.

Elizabeth wondered how Jeanine protected herself on the corner.

—The customers are more dangerous, because you don't know them. Though I got my leg broken out there, when the boss guy came out with a bat because somebody said someone was selling something besides his merchandise. We don't harm customers, in fact, people in the neighbourhood say they feel safer coming home because they know we're standing there. I'll walk down a drug block before I'll walk down a deserted block. People are not likely to try and drop someone on a block where there's drug dealers, because they're afraid. I'm not afraid of my colleagues, I'm more afraid of my customers, because I've been raped by customers. One girl was chopped up in pieces, we don't know who did it. You get some weird customers, they come out and like they're mixing. These are people who don't get high on a daily basis. Some do — they're real cool. Some people that don't, they're mixing alcohol or coke, heroin and pills and everything all at one time. They're not stable. Plus whatever problems drove them to get high. They want to take you somewhere. It's bad to get in a car, I used to, but I had an incident. Sometimes I have customers, when I see them really messed up I don't want to sell to them. They're more dangerous to us than anyone. Most of the regular cops don't bother you. Sometimes they have nights when they want you off the corner, they come by, slow down and say, take a walk. There's this older black guy we call Batman. He beats up the guys. He just gets out of the car and beats them up. He won't even take them to jail. Just beats the shit out of them.

Batman the cartoon or because he uses a bat?

> — He's a black man. I'm black myself, but this guy's blacker than my shit. He's even got
> this gold ring that has this Batman picture. His partner is six foot seven — they call
> him Robin. He's terrible. They're terrible. But they won't beat up the girls. There aren't
> that many girls out there, but they won't really beat us up. Which makes them angry,
> they get more angry at us because they can't really search us. But there are more female
> cops now, before you never saw them. This younger guy, he used to always want to talk
> to you, offer you help. If he arrested you, it would be because he felt like you needed a
> break. There used to be two sisters down the block. They were saving their money to go
> to school, so the cops wouldn't arrest them.

Jeanine ate a sandwich. Elizabeth told her about wanting to murder someone, anyone, when she
couldn't sleep. Jeanine laughed at her.

> — Some nights are really messed up. It gets bad out there. A lot of people are high.
> A lot of people learn to get it for themselves. We're middlemen, we're going to purchase
> it from a certain place. They don't want to commit a felony themselves. They might get
> beaten or they might get hurt, so they're willing to pay us double the price to get it for
> them. But a lot of customers are getting bold and they're going themselves. Some people
> got cleaned up. Once you could make a thousand dollars just out there a night; these
> days if it's a hundred bucks you're lucky. Coke's played out.

Jeanine drank some more coffee. She had a shower. She came out wrapped in a towel.

> — All the guys I have used to be cops. Isn't that weird? All the cops come over to me. It's
> weird. They like me, they're trying to get me off the block, but they end up giving me
> money to buy drugs. Cops come and buy drugs, not from here, from elsewhere. From
> other precincts, whatever. The guy I've been seeing for a while, he's married, and he
> wanted me to stay stuck in the house, and it was just not a healthy situation. If she's
> here, I wouldn't see him for three or four days in a row, then I won't see him for two
> weeks. A really uncomfortable situation, and I become very obsessed with him, and I
> didn't think that was cool. Somebody else's man. He's alright, he used to be a cop. He's
> a very nice guy. Some no-good man — that's my worst addiction. I'm addicted to no-
> good men. Or being addicted to anything, you know what I'm saying? Your body has to
> keep up with your mind. I'll run to avoid sitting and thinking and facing reality. A lot of
> people in the neighbourhood speak to me, want to help me, say I'm nice. I don't belong
> out there. I tell them, I don't know. It's my lifestyle now.

Elizabeth said it was a job, she saw her working on the corner almost every day.

— My job? Yeah, it's my job. True. And before, there used to be a lot of money. The flow was nonstop. A lot of people got clean. A lot of customers went bankrupt. Lost their jobs. A lot of customers had to stop to maintain their lives. A lot of men, their wives don't know what they're doing, and they screw up and their wives find out. There's women too, but it's usually couples if there's a woman involved, or like a lot of teenagers. I won't serve to teenagers, but there's college kids buying weed and stuff, then you see a lot of girls. A lot of people are smart enough to give it up instead of giving up their lives. Or it's too expensive. Sign of the times.

Jeanine looked at the clock on the kitchen wall. She had to make her group therapy session. She dressed, brushed her hair and put on orange lipstick.

— The last two months with my leg broken I couldn't report, and I couldn't get any outpatient therapy. It wasn't my fault. You go there, a group meeting, which is so stupid. I can't understand why parole and probation want to send you somewhere where you sit around and hear stories about drugs. Even in jail. I go to jail and sit in these little encounter groups, and every time I come out the drug I try is different from the one I used before. Because I heard about it in some meeting. They make you go and by the time you're finished with these meetings you want to get high. It's like really ridiculous. I don't want to go back. I won't sell to someone unless I know them. So many under-covers, you can't even tell who they are. I'm still on parole. They can lie on you, just 'cause you have a record, you can go to jail forever, you know? You gotta be real careful out there.

It was Jeanine in the doorway. She was gobbling some guy's dick for the price of a rock.

— You gotta be real careful out there.

Elizabeth wondered if Ernest was awake, lying in bed, or at the window above hers. Maybe he was naked, at his window. Maybe he was watching Jeanine. Maybe he was summer hot or excited. Jeanine in the doorway. Elizabeth liked sex, she liked watching sex. Maybe Ernest could sleep through noise. Sleep through anything. Like Roy.

Lights on in two more apartments. Babies crying. Dogs barking. One horrific scream. Then silence.

Endsville

Roland Brener

Photographs by Cornelius Heesters

Endsville, is a miniature city constructed of brown cardboard, a transitory material most often used

for packing and shipping containers. It is an expendable, banal city—a place made to be

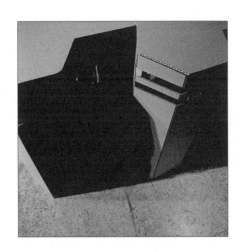

moved. Brener's projects often include subtle elements of motion, a swaying girder in an earlier installation

called *Capital Z;* or *Endsville*'s voice-triggered computer programs which randomly activate lights and a

soundtrack. Brener's non-place satisfies our desires for proprietorship but denies it at the very moment we

recognize we are strangers here, always a threat to the homogenizing mirror urbanity holds before itself. — C. H.

The places and moments of significance have been avoided. —Roland Brener

Perambulations of the Polis Desk

Edward Mitchell

Polis Desk was a collaborative response to the city of New Haven's request for an analysis of one of its troubled neighborhoods. *The Green*, originally Quinnipiac Indian territory, was based on the ideal nine square grid plan with a central green and is often cited as North America's first city plan. *The Green* was cut off from the city when the interstate highways were built in the 1960s — today it is rarely recognized as a part of New Haven proper.

The specific program and form of *Polis Desk*, as well as other related projects, were developed from a series of tours, short story lines of the city, documenting its histories and noting crossings that could constitute a new greening or mapping of the city. The Polis Desk tour, entitled *Perambulator*, begins with a newspaper account of a local Boy Scout Troop's discovery of stones — *xoanans* — that were inscribed with dates going back to the early nineteenth century, and were originally used to mark the boundaries of the city.

The Desk's design is based on the detritus found at the liminal boundaries of the polis as well as civic consciousness, and whose meanings are now lost. They are: The pericycle, a large wheel of files making up the record which comprises a new dictionary of emerging meanings — an archive of found souvenirs and abandoned objects as evidence of the various pressures which come to bear on the city limits. The detritus plowed up by the toe of the plow — doubling also as a tool for inscribing the town line — is then dusted by the brushes of the sweeper.

The desk operates as both a nomadic piece of furniture and a recording machine, policing the various points of entry, collecting improper acts into the record and redefining those acts as legal transgressions. By collecting and cataloguing the banal evidence left in the wake of transgressive activities, *Polis Desk* functions as an archive with which to refound the city.

—C. H.

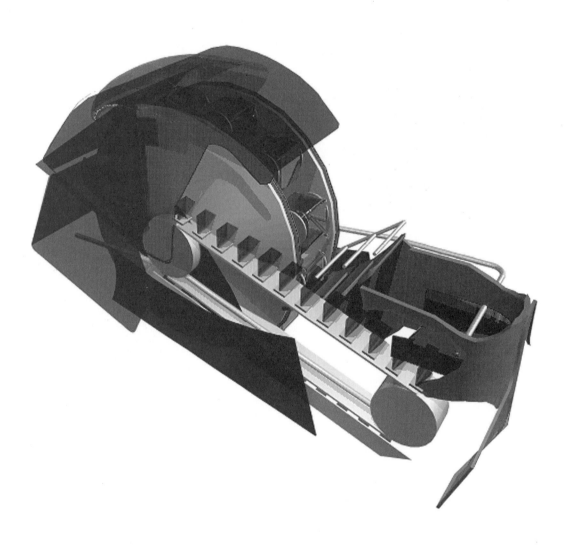

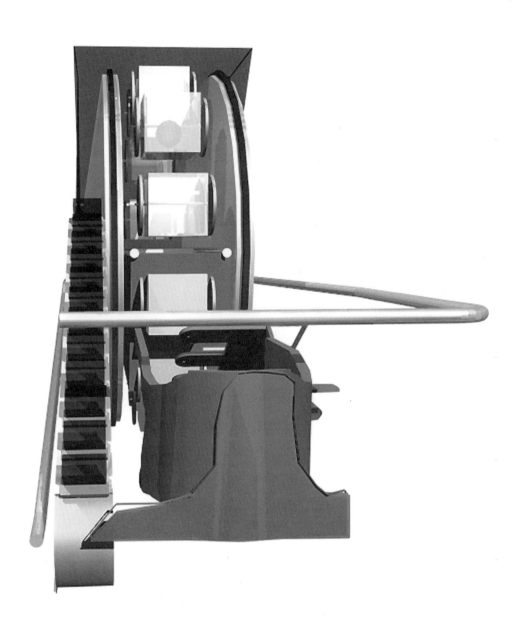

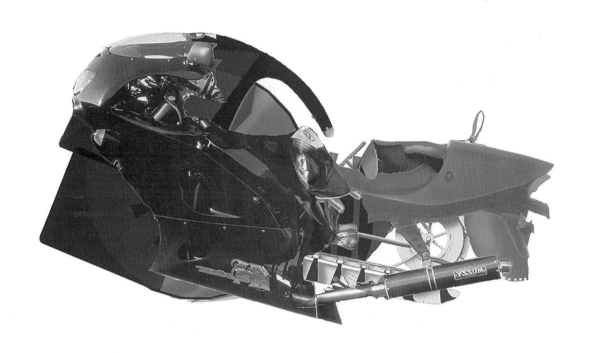

The Science of Strangers
Krzysztof Wodiczko interviewed by Bruce Robbins

Bruce Robbins: A passerby in the street sees someone holding a walking stick with a TV monitor on top like a hooded cobra. There is a moving image, there is the sound of a voice, perhaps an accented voice. The person holding the staff seems to want to make eye contact. What goes through the passerby's head? Another crazy foreigner? Someone who needs help walking? Moses in front of Pharaoh?

Some of the brilliance of this seems to me the play on what Debord calls "the society of spectacle," on the fact that people will not stop for human beings telling their story but will stop for a televised image of the same human being telling the same story. When the image replaces the person, when there's an obstacle between you and the person, there's a better chance of making contact. Is this what you had in mind? What sort of public encounter are you striving at or hoping to produce?

Krzysztof Wodiczko: It's very hard for me to present a theoretical model for what I hoped would happen, or even what I noticed did happen during these performative presentations. But it was clear that without this object, none of this would happen. Any kind of object held and operated by a stranger can be useful. But if the object performs and is attractive by virtue of being strange, it relates to the tradition of strangers, magicians, performers using instruments that come from somewhere else, to make magic, or just to sell something. In the environment of the contemporary city, too, a new object is always desirable. The first thing people wanted to know about the Homeless Vehicle that I designed earlier was whether it was something they could buy. Strange objects that are brought by foreigners are usually available for purchase.

The Alien Staff proved to be very effective because it was recognized as something familiar at the same time as something strange. It's like a cliché. A Biblical staff. It's clear people don't understand at first why it resembles something. Later they draw conclusions. Then there was the Wandering Jew myth. Some would see it as an icon of the Wandering Jew. At first people concentrate on the object, as a cliché. Then they get closer to see what's happening on the little monitor. It's very small. To get close is to cross a certain boundary. There's a face on the screen. A face, the face: the face of the Other. (Laughter)

Does Levinas laugh when he talks about the face of the other?

The face here is the face of a character and the face of an actor at the same time. The face of a media performer and an actual person. And there is the operator, an actual immigrant who is performing in relation to the pre-recorded image. The presence of the actual immigrant takes several forms. One of the forms is to embody disagreement with what was pre-recorded. Nothing here is very stable. It's quite open for exploration. When others ask questions about what's in the containers, for example, it brings up things that weren't said in the pre-recorded material. But very often the immigrant will also refuse to explain. They'll say, "It's none of your business. It's there because it's important to me." Other things are explained even if nobody wants to hear. Horrifying descriptions of the immigration department and so on. You ask for it, you get it.

Then there is yet another person, a person from the crowd — the beginning is the gathering of a crowd, and things are already leaking out of this two-person encounter into the crowd — which is listening to all of this and is voicing an opinion: "Well, excuse me, I'm also an immigrant," or

Alien Staff, 1993. Brooklyn, NY.

"I'm not an immigrant, but...." Levinas' "third" is the person who says, "I am not an immigrant, but...." This is the person who sees the whole situation from the point of view of a symmetrical democratic project. In France, which lives the classic democratic Enlightenment, the third is the person who says, "But wait, aren't we all members of one large community?"

This triple relation—me, the other, the third—can be reversed. Anyone of these can be the one who sees the triple relation. But the object helps in this process. It makes a multiple. This artifice, the Alien Staff, doesn't really exist for Levinas.

A Talmud for Migrants

Levinas implies the possibility that the other can be found within the other. In his Talmudic readings, there is that multiplicity.

He's describing the pact. The oral tradition, as he points out, is not only a commentary on written texts like the Torah; it's equally important to Torah. Some scholars demanded that God should read the Talmud.

Levinas' emphasis on Talmud as the most Jewish thing that exists is an emphasis on unending argument, disagreement, discourse. Maybe there's something Talmudic about what happens around the stick. (Laughter)

In a minor, microcosmic way, it's a history of the present. People live through being an Arab, or a Jew, or a Polish immigrant in Greenpoint.

It opens up for rereading, recollection, remembrance—all those things Benjamin speaks about—without a particular place, without the Temple.

If this equipment seems to be prophetic, it's because it puts every immigrant, every operator in the role of a prophet, interrupting history to open up a vision of community.

Each one brings their own experience, and in this experience is the seed of a new community. Of a world that would not ask the immigrant to integrate, but a world that would disintegrate, made of people who have disintegrated.

This connects with Socrates because Socrates did not tell people what to do. Socrates used an amazing discursive technique: he created situations in which people had to start thinking.

What is Socratic about the staff is the position of the performer in what used to be called public space.

Maybe a public place is being created in the very moment, the very act of performance, or in the act of dwelling in the polis.

Or, in Bataille's terms, a sacred place. Where people face each other's passions.

Not inside the church. Outside the Temple. Once the Jews concluded that they were not going to rebuild the Temple, Judaism became a much more popular religion, connecting the religious and secular community life.

I'm really fascinated by one aspect of your work that seems to me unique.

It seems to be designed so as to require a kind of narrative completion.

To stop and provoke kinds of conversation about it and between people who are involved in it is a kind of building block of some new community.

It's artistic work that provokes and invites intellectual and communicative activity in a very special way.

When you say a special way, I can only imagine what you mean.

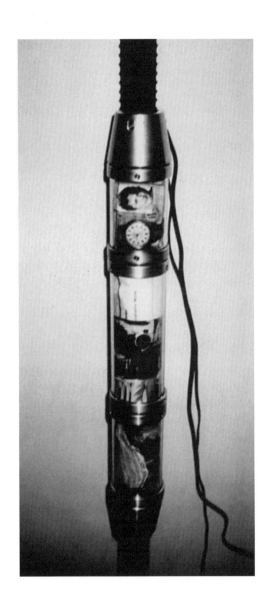

Alien Staff, 1993. Detail of reliquary section.

What I've tried to do, that I don't see being done enough, is perhaps the creation of some object or some intermediate form which inspires, and becomes a starting point for, the openings, exchange, and sharing.

And that is something that continues a tradition of the need of object or instrument, like a storyteller's instrument. A kind of magic staff that will make miracles. As in the Bible.

It is clearly stated in the Catholic version of the Bible that the staff is to make miracles.

In the Protestant version, it says to make a sign. But in both cases there is a magic to it.

Without the stick, people would not believe the person who was using it. But in this case the object can also become a center, a sacred place. Bataille defines the sacred place as the place where passions are unleashed, where something can be shared that has not yet been shared or is not supposed to be shared. It is a place of birth of some kind.

Communicating Objects & Subjects

This object is a performative object. I think we need more objects of this sort to come between an incredible explosion of unprecedented telecommunication technologies and a dangerous return to the tragic precedents of complete communication breakdown. How would you connect the Media Lab, the most advanced technological media experiments, with the situation of the ex-Yugoslavia? They are almost irreconcilable events.... In the space between these two points of reference, in normal everyday life, there is a need for people to recognize each other and take responsibility for each other, which is a highly difficult mission. There is a need to definitely recognize each other, face to face. How do we do this and at the same time create and take advantage of the global communication networks? It's a very personal, very fragile thing. And very direct contact, with all the resources, the historical documents or past cases, we can bring to it — how to bring forward the whole heritage of accumulated layers of the past and wrestle with it when we are actually facing each other?

To bring together communication technologies and interaction, direct contact, aesthetic work needs instruments, equipment, but it also needs to create events, acts, so that in facing those events people will start communicating directly.

In a way, the antique public space, this arena or stage, still exists. In fact it is a bloody scene, the stage of massacres, ethnic cleansing. You cannot simply say that the city is passé or that the human body is. Torture and killing remain the most important medium for the human body. What I am saying is that this is a necessary agenda for design.

There are a growing number of projects, which I really admire, by other artists on the Internet which are provoking or inspiring interaction and growing a kind of discourse. But what they don't propose is this bodily element; they don't connect electronic communication with the body and its experience, with direct contact. I'm not criticizing these projects. Actually I'm saying that the discursive aspect of my work is not so original because of this electronic work already done....

But you were just saying that the body must continue to have a place in what we've been calling the public sphere, that bodiliness is something that can't be forgotten. And one thing people appreciate about your work is the way it refuses the idea that the true public sphere in our time is cyberspace.

But I disagree with those who appreciate my work. Because their conservative reaction against cyberspace or the electronic public unnerves me. I think it is important to connect these different communicative situations and techniques in one work. We know the incredible growth of the

Alien Staff operated by Dgenevou Samou. Barcelona, Spain, June 1992.

Internet and World Wide Web also mimics dangerously the growing division between the poor and the rich, especially in the United States. This means a separation between the way populations communicate, producing a new form of alienation.

Estrangers

I have to ask a larger question about the politics of your work and its trajectory, about what the word "stranger" means to you.

If one were unsympathetic, as I'm not, one could say that to focus on immigration is to forget all the people who have not immigrated — to privilege, as we say in our jargon, the metropolis as the center of the story, and to drop out all the people who have not left the countries that immigrants have come from.

Is it to deal with an unhappy but somewhat privileged group?

That brings us back to Benjamin and Levinas.

To put emphasis on the stranger is to see ourselves, and to see ourselves as a democracy. It's the only way to know whether this democracy is human or ethical. We badly need strangers.

We call ourselves a community, we claim openness, rights, and so on, but we have no way to see that community. So it must be interrupted by strangers (Benjamin), who are more important than we are. (I don't consider myself a stranger, though I am of strange origins and have three passports.)

For Levinas, the symmetry of democratic process can only be sustained by an asymmetry of ethics. If the stranger to the city and someone born in the city are equal, and democratic equality is guaranteed by human rights and by the constitution, our obligation is to challenge that symmetry, to open ourselves to those who are less capable of taking advantage of their rights.

But it is we who are less capable of recognizing the needs of others, who do not fight for the rights of foreigners to vote. We impose taxation on everybody, but we don't demand that strangers have representation.

They are living here, they have children, they have nothing to say about how their children will be educated, and so on. There is a myth of equality, a myth of symmetry between us and them, that needs to be challenged. To make that symmetry possible, one has to act asymmetrically. You have to overexpose people who are underexposed.

This is also an aesthetic effort. There's a need for a bandage to cover the wound. But something at the same time that helps people articulate, recognize the origins of the wound.

Most of the designs I've made belong to this category of the bandage. The bandage also shows the location of the pain. It's in between, a communicative device. These instruments prove to be necessary, as the operators tell me.

After they go through all the trouble of gathering information and opening it up to everybody, they report that they can manage better. They can cope.

Apropos of the bandage, one of the things I like so much about the Mouthpiece, which is your other instrument for immigrants, is the suggestion that it's a monstrous gag. While it's a prosthesis helping people express themselves, it's also expressing the impossibility of speech. It's a sort of bandage over the mouth, blown up to monstrous proportions.

What I'm hoping to do with the new variant of the Mouthpiece, which is a truly monstrous prosthesis, a cyborgian bandage that overemphasizes the need for equipment, for aid. It allows the mouth of the speaker to be both covered and uncovered. The monitor section of the equipment, showing the lips of the speaker, can now be shifted, so that the operator can speak directly as well as with pre-recorded speech. Or it can be switched off.

Instrumental Design

The artifact is a kind of intermediate object that articulates, interrogates aesthetically, connects certain archetypes or certain ancient forms or myths, as the Alien Staff does. By an artifact I mean an extended gesture, modulated, refined, edited, or aesthetically conceived to the point of a kind of intuitive clarity or metaphoric quality or narrative, a confession or act of speech or exteriorization of something that is difficult to explain in normal language.

It connects those familiar icons with something new, iconographically and technologically, as a kind of design object, an inspiring instrument which proposes the possibility of new functions.

In this very moment when I say "art" I have to make it even more difficult because I have to say it is "design" at the same time. Let me speak of vehicles and instruments.

That is where you come from, right?

Yes. Industrial design. And for many artists design is a difficult area. What is expected from "art" objects or "artistic" acts or actions? An artistic event is a translation of some set of internal or external issues into form. In design, the situation is much more complex. It is a juxtaposition of connotation and denotation, the pragmatic and the symbolic, which demands acting, doing, operating, or experiencing. It has both practical and metaphoric aspects, it is feasible not only in objects but in the way one lives. It brings meaning to the idea of everyday life.

What kinds of changes in the Alien Staff do you have in mind?

I'm interested to see to what degree instruments of this sort can be more playful. Inspire more of an artistic or baroque use. In other words, if they can respond better to the gestural and narrative virtuosity of strangers. Of course instruments of this kind are not for every stranger. They are for special agents — or angels.

In ancient Greek, angels meant messengers.

Yes. Messengers who like to speak, who are angry enough, who are motivated. Sometimes even desperate. Or, say, initially reluctant, yet having an internal need to construct, reveal, or open up their experience and share it.

I am designing a tool or instrument which will create a new situation. That level of the unknown is connected with a kind of intuition of the present, a revolutionary intuition of the present. There's an intuition that those people will be able, for example, to come to terms with their impossible set of experiences, the impossible reconfiguration of their identity or the new forms, new connections, inside of them. Not to be completely alienated and frustrated. As they start recording and re-enacting their stories and reinterpreting, rhetorically articulating them in front of others, in interaction with the others, one hopes they will learn more about what they would like to say and also that they will learn to play with this somehow painful, difficult, and maybe tragicomical device, enjoy it in some humorous and baroque or maybe even rococo way.

I emphasize the possibility of modulating the audio-visual recordings with gestures or even allowing the other people around to participate in this re-play or re-enactment. The Media Lab at MIT is continuing the project that was developed by Theremin, a Russian inventor, and recently rediscovered: an instrument operated by gestures.

I would like to test this gestural instrument. I have to build it to see how one could become a virtuoso of his or her own story, also maybe adding new components to the story, discovering more and more aspects of the experience and making it into a more playful act of speech and also, psychologically, an act of self-construction.

The playfulness is definitely a psychological need here, for the operator and also for everybody else. In the space between strangers, and between strangers and non-strangers (if one can call them this way), this artifice which is already there as a kind of object could become more interactive and more interpretive or performative than it is now. I hope that it may be the birth of some other kind of instrument.

Tell me a little bit about the science of xenology.

By xenology I mean a field of knowledge which also connects with the field of experience. The field of historical intuition or present intuition. I want to propose an existential knowledge combined with life practice. A struggle of displacement. This has something to do with displacement.

Not especially transnational displacement? It could as easily be an internal or domestic displacement?

As inside of yourself.

Oh, I see. Strangers to ourselves, as Kristeva says.

Yes. This external and internal displacement is about crossing the boundaries inside of yourself. Because there are all those different borders one is discovering. Maybe they were there before. But one recognizes this whole incredible world which is normally not recognized by people who stay in one place for too long. One can definitely learn a lot from strangers. Those who move less should listen very carefully to those who move more. And maybe the opposite.

But the fact is that xenology would be experiential, theoretical, and artistic. In the further development of my project, xenology could be its aesthetic, not just its cultural or theoretical frame. The xenologist would be someone who is more aware of the field, a kind of prominent scholar or practitioner in the field. Like a doctor. A Talmudic doctor exists as long as Talmud exists. Here we are dealing with an oral history, not written texts. There are cases. Xenology is not centered around sacred literature, but it could assign to certain fragments of this historical material something like the meaning of a sacred text. Maybe it should be more displaced, not fixed in one body like the Torah.

In your experiences of displacement, your wanderings, can you think of any discovery that might serve as an example of the sort of knowledge xenology would produce?

I learned about xenology from a person whom I know well, Jadwiga Przybylak. She runs a network of domestic labour for Polish immigrants. She cannot stop lending her experience, exchanging addresses, finding rooms for people, mediating. She is still working in the field of undocumented labour, or half-documented labour, or labour in the process of being documented. This is a rescue mission, part of the Polish culture of resistance and survival. She is an ethical advisor to Polish people. They call her. And sometimes they leave messages on her answering machine. Recently she started to connect those messages. Now she has a bank of cases, messages left about miserable experiences or comical stories. She is working, so she's not home, but her answering machine is on. And people call, and they cannot stop. There is so much traffic of telephone calls that it is almost impossible to reach her.

Jadwiga needed the Alien Staff when she began, simply because she had never acknowledged to herself that her experience is something very valuable and something to be proud of. She told me at first that she didn't want to be a part of the project. But she eventually started to search for relics. That was the first thing. She was interested to find a photograph of her nighttime cleaning colleagues at IBM. And she found it but she had to travel across the whole city to find one of these friends. She of course took a camera, because she's a photographer. She discovered what had happened to this woman. Something incredible developed around this person. She realized that there was so much to recover. She started to write down her memories about a time when she was enslaved, taking care of an elderly German woman who herself had been an immigrant to America fifty years before.

So Jadwiga started to write it down. This started to connect in her and finally led to videotaping and editing. And then more objects were found, usually so well hidden that she thought she could never find them. Because they were the most important objects that she had brought from Poland. And photographs and correspondence she received from someone in the immigration department.

Finally she put all this together and she started to speak, with an incredible ability to say things, and she grew to like it. She is always a consultant in the development of my projects. I cannot take any new steps, without talking to her.

Speaking for Others

Could you say something about the political uses you just mentioned — people who want to use instruments like this to represent others? Are there any examples that come to mind of people who want to use this technology less to speak about themselves than to speak on behalf of other people?

Everyone starts with his own misery.

But there's one person in a refugee camp in Poland, for example, who came from a very miserable situation in Morocco.

He had lost contact with his family and he claimed, probably rightly, that if he returned to Morocco he would be prosecuted because of his anti-fundamentalist stance. So he contacted his family by phone. This is what he actually started with. But then he brought a seriously prepared speech to be recorded that was about fear, a problem he thought should be addressed. Such a large part of the population of this planet lives in fear. He had a theory of fear, which came out of his own experience, and he proposed the theory to Polish people.

He speaks French. He got it translated from French into Polish. He asked Poland to recognize the need to help Morocco in this impossible situation where people live in fear. But he also asked the Poles to rethink the way they think about their own country and their own politics because of the danger of Catholic fundamentalism, which threatens to take over politics and eventually all human rights. Suddenly he was talking on behalf of Polish populations with which he had limited contact.

Actually, when I think about it, everyone mixes politics in, connecting the personal and the political. But only on occasion does it get dangerously close to using this equipment to address political issues more than their own experience. As Benjamin said, when you transpose the personal into the historical, that is what is revolutionary. They think this is the moment in which history has to be addressed. Because if one doesn't speak about it right now, things can irreversibly turn into catastrophe. Both in their lost land and in their promised land. This is how they are messengers.

Could you say something about any of the reactions to the use of these instruments either that you've seen or that you've heard about from people who were using them?

It has become clear that much more is happening with this stick than I anticipated. The reactions were usually good when there were both immigrant and non-immigrants around this stick. First of all, there was an attempt to exchange and share experience between the operator and other immigrants, maybe from other countries. There is usually very little connection between immigrants. And then there are the non-immigrants who, of course, might have imaginary relations to their memories of their own "first place." They might feel that in that sense everyone is an immigrant.

Everyone feels strange, everyone is alienated. But when they start getting into the details of the exchange of experience among immigrants, they realize that they are actually not part of the same conversation. They cannot be. They want to listen. Or, they want to speak more in order to dominate the discourse, to reinterpret the situation of immigrants for them. This was very apparent in France.

There were some types who immediately translated fragments of what they heard into a kind of rough theory, making it an act of their own speech, political speech. "Let me tell you what you mean," and "what does it mean from the point of view of democracy in general?" All of those concepts like egalitarianism that they carry from the 18th century — they truly believe in them in France. But usually it is so ridiculous that they are overwhelmed by the reaction. Or there is silence. A very thorough kind of silence. They are trying to learn based on some sense of ideals or recognized ignorance.

There was one moment that I found quite amusing. Conversation developed so well between the immigrants around the stick that they forgot about it. They ended up in a restaurant and the stick was just leaning against the wall. One of the immigrants from Morocco was laid off. And as a result of this she got a job from the operator, who needed a baby-sitter. Later, I took this as an important possibility for new equipment. There's something very pragmatic on occasion that comes out of all of the political and cultural debate, about national policy or legal problems they share, an exchange maybe of some addresses of lawyers, or god knows, some services. There is also the job market which appeared here.

So I realized that in some next generation or network of instruments I should design-in the legal and economic issues. The immigrant can become a "case." One could say, "Okay, actually this reminds me that I need to speak with someone because I don't know exactly what the situation is in terms of my legal status, which is changing all the time. And there are rumours. Is there any way I could find a job in this immediate situation? Is there anybody could help me? Maybe you could help me." At that moment, the walking stick could become a transmitter of this question, and the operator could also receive additional training as a messenger, a more informed messenger. In fact there could be a legal station on-line. It could be transmitted very easily to a satellite and it could go to a computer run in the base of the staff which could very quickly identify all of the options for the stranger. Because they have established trust, they have opened up a concrete case which is in itself public.

So there's a possibility of a very concrete service. The equipment would have to be transformed in relation to the growth of an organization or network. I'm in touch right now with legal services in Cambridge who help with immigrants. This group of lawyers (who are fascinated, they told me, by this project) think it will be very helpful to have some agents or angels to encourage these displaced people to help — free help. With the possibility of a larger group and a number of instruments and an electronic network, we'd have to really rethink the whole design part.

Inoperative Community

When you were talking about the new computer technology that you'd like to experiment with, I wondered whether you had recording equipment as part of the Staff, as a way of making it more interactive, producing something that would include the people around. And then I thought that, practically, this seems like the worst idea in the world because of the fears people have that it would be used as an instrument of surveillance.

Yes, even the idea that I presented is doubtful. How do you convince people that the possibility of digital transmission is really there and is not really a trick? How to open this up without scaring people to death? Another possibility would be to eliminate this transmission altogether and rely on live transmission, rely on the possibility of meeting the same person at the same time.... The operator could reappear the same time the following week. That is what happened in Greenpoint, on a Sunday in front of a church. It is a very important place in Greenpoint because it's a church attended both by Poles and Puerto Ricans as well as some other groups, not as many Polish as maybe one would hope, but some. And it is a sacred place because they share the same religion. And a sacred place could be used as a site for this performance. And as I said, someone asked "Will you be here next weekend?" In this question there is the possibility of a community, a newly born community.

Certain fragments of what Jean-Luc Nancy said about community seem strangely familiar when I observe what's happening around the stick. He proposed a different kind of community, and this helps me to understand my own work. He says that there is a kind of un-doing of community, an undoing of ties or pre-conceived notions of the commonality or communistic or communal. And this immigrant is refusing to accept any imposed notions, or ties, or connections with others. She's saying... "Please do not think that we all have the same situation or that I speak here on behalf of others. No, this is a unique experience I am opening up. I don't know what others go through. Telling you all the complexity, all of the problems I have with myself, with the way I was and I am no longer, with the things that change in me, it is difficult to actually accept what I am doing. All of the questions, all of the disagreements inside of me, this is something that you have to listen to. Because this is something that I cannot even say without a certain hesitation and pain."

I'd like to connect the Staff with this kind of community of un-working and un-doing, a community of refusing, of refusal to be fused — I think that is what Jean-Luc Nancy says, more or less — and yet also a possibility of community disseminated, contagiously spread by the immigrant, a community of all of those disagreements and problems inside of one person. The person will say, "Join me in this exploration and we will have in common all of our doubts about what is supposed to be our collective or community, what is supposed to be the legitimate bond between us." In this way, I could see this stick as, maybe for a moment or fifteen minutes, the point of a birth of a new community. A community that comes from inside the containers, from all those things that are contained in the video and the relics, but also from the play with them.

If I could make it more playful and interactive…laughter—all the jokes, the disruptions, the changes of topics, all the absurdity and impossibility of talking about identity. This is the new community.

But it will also be connected with a kind of Brechtian interruption, with what Benjamin calls the "interruption of history." As I've mentioned on many other occasions, the interruptions of the linear continuity of the history of the victors by this secret tradition of the oppressed which is non-linear and always negative and always disruptive, and always trying to recover its own history. This concept of un-community or this community of refusal of being fused could be connected with this concept of interruption.

Listening to you talk about Nancy and the notion of community, I thought that in a sense this is something you had already been thinking about from the moment you began playing on words with the Polis Car. On the one hand, noting the danger of surveillance, that is "police car," and on the other, trying to revitalize the notion of the polis, the community. It also seems that you are not just now beginning to play with fear. Your consciousness of fear has always been part of the aesthetic element for you, maybe even part of the Brechtian Verfremdung you mention—your work shouldn't be too warm and cuddly, it shouldn't be too user-friendly. There should always be an element of fear as part of the experience. Or perhaps you feel that there is an element of fear, hostility, negative feeling, which is inextricably connected with the hope for the building of community?

Yes. Because of the legitimacy of community. The community can only be legitimate when it questions its own legitimacy. This is certainly true in a so-called community of city inhabitants. New York as a community has to question itself immediately. "We New Yorkers." The homeless people can define what they mean by being New Yorkers, and this does not correspond to the others.

Time, Rhythm, Memory

Of course this corresponds to a myth of Constructivist and Productivist art: a design of new rhythms of art, not a design of objects. Rhythm of life process—there's a lot of mystification there, and a lot of utopia, clearly. But it is important. The issue is not to be utopian. The issue is not to create better or new art but to create new life. That was the assumption behind productivism—it is not about production but about moving closer to life, impatiently. Not just waiting for an aesthetic practice to transform life later on, not injecting some essence, through art, which will then re-emerge in the next generation as new perception or new imagination. No, let's do it now! In that sense I think design is as much a natural extension of art as politics is a natural extension of ethics.

I hope you know that you've been very important to theorists of space, people like Rosalyn Deutsche and Neil Smith, and they find that your work helps them think about space. Maybe it would also be interesting to think about you as working with time. You were talking about constructivism as a kind of experimentation with rhythms of life. The way that you use the ephemeral, the knowledge that such and such a projection will not last, won't be there, or the way you were just talking about the "same time next week" theory as a possible way of mobilizing the Alien Staff—all of these things make me think that in some way you are doing a kind of art in time. That time is the material you are working with.

Yes. It has something to do with the life of the city, inserting itself into the existing rhythms of life or ways of perception or interaction between different x inhabitants, their relation to changing circumstances. What was good yesterday might be wrong today, and might be idiotic tomorrow. That's probably what Brecht believed. If one disrupts the routine perception of everyday life, one has to be tactical and temporary by principle. And that was definitely endorsed by the Situationists. This is not only the beautiful theory of everyday life presented by Lefebvre, but also an extremely humorous kind of Surrealist touch. Life is also a kind of popular art, living your patterns and enduring. The disruption of this everyday life makes perfect sense as an aesthetic project because the everyday is already an aesthetic project.

Well, one of the reasons I asked you about time, and the work it seemed to me that you are doing in the medium of time, on the materiality of time, is because I'm very curious about the extent to which the question of the public is a question of time as much as it is a question of space. We ask, "what's a public space?" but of course in this speeded-up, speed-it-up rhythm we all know, the public is also very much a question of time.

In France, when I started to discuss what benefits the Alien Staff could bring to in immigrant populations, many of the activists and social workers told me it might be a necessary bridge between the new younger immigrants, people born of immigrant parents, who are still treated as immigrants in France, and their parents, from whom they are often alienated, and their parents' experience of crossing. Their parents are socially segregated, a population which it is hopeless to try to integrate — so the French say — so let's integrate the youth. The Alien Staff was understood as a possibility of a parent-children link that was something new. But this might require different equipment, or even a different cultural project than mine.

When Jadwiga took the Alien Staff to the New York Institute of Technology, she decided bravely to present herself as an immigrant and not as a professor. And most of her students are Long Island children of immigrants. Somehow, electrified or hypnotized by her presence with this Alien Staff, they suddenly felt a desire to see their parents. They recognized something similar between her and their parents, something that they never really understood.

The students completely changed their normal seating position in relation to her. They created a different space in the classroom. And she thinks that they respected her afterwards much more. Oral history, memory, the transmission of experience: these have something to do with time.

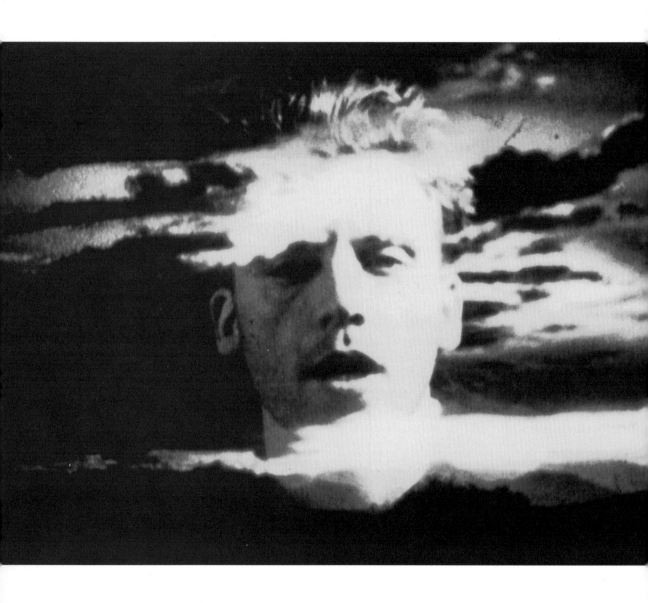

Positiv

Mike Hoolboom

Last night I had this dream that I'm living in a world where there's just two kinds of people, bodies and minds. Somewhere a bell rings and the whole world stops for recess so we all run out of school heading for the wall on the other side of the yard. I can feel my legs growing as I run and with one giant step I'm there, I'm at the wall watching everyone race towards me. And then I realize omigod, I'm a body.

Which is funny because ever since becoming HIV positive I've felt like a virus that's come to rest in this body for a while, that it really doesn't belong to me anymore, like I'm trying on a new suit that won't fit. I couldn't be the one who starts sweating at night for no reason at all until the sheets are so wet I have to ring them out in the morning, or the yeast in my mouth is so bad it turns all my favourite foods, even chocolate chocolate chip ice cream, into a dull metallic taste like licking a crowbar. I know then that my body, my real body, is somewhere else, bungee jumping into mine shafts stuffed with chocolate wafers and whipped cream and blueberry pie and just having a good time, you know?

There are days I wander through the streets like Michael Jackson, deciding to have that one's nose, those lips and your waiter's perfect clam-shaped ears. When I look around my apartment I think that everything has a warranty except my body, everything here can be replaced or traded in except for the cellulite army that has conquered your thighs, or the small hands that were always too clumsy to play Satie. When I was six and learning the scales I watered my hands everyday without result, until I realized that despite all the chaos and upsets and frustrations my life possessed a shape after all, a unity of design, and that shape was my body.

Some days when I go out I fall in love with everyone I meet. Do you get that? You wake up and everyone is impossibly beautiful and you know that while you've been dozing off they've been up all night on the stairmaster, the tummy-tucker, the waist-watcher. You walk down the street with these gods all around you and think that you don't have to die to go to heaven after all. Sometimes just a membership at the Y will do.

All day long you feel that you've undertaken a perilous descent because you're falling, falling in love, so it's a big relief when you finally get home and shut the door behind you and as you're taking off the day's uniform you happen to catch a glimpse of yourself in the mirror and there you are all at once, you're one body, one person again. Your skin is like a forcefield, it's the place your personality returns to when it's tired of wanting to be a guitar hero or a fireman or the sex slave of the Minnesota Vikings.

And then the doctor tells you there's something wrong with your blood, that you're HIV positive, and all of a sudden the body that melted at the sight of your first chocolate factory isn't yours anymore. There's something else inside and slowly this stranger, this uninvited guest, becomes more important than you. At first it's hard to notice because you don't walk through walls or shatter the Olympic record for embarrassing statements made at a party. A new word has taken the place of your body, so when you head off to the Madonna lookalike contest the little sticker on your chest doesn't say, "Hi I'm Mike" it only says "AIDS" because it's not you they're talking to anymore, it's the sickness.

In the old days, in the past, you were always excited to take up a new sport — synchro swimming, water polo, electric horseshoes — you tried them all, wondering if some slumbering chromosome might awaken and unleash a ferocious talent, but now even your lifelong dream of appearing on *The Price Is Right* seems a distant fantasy, and as you watch Bob Barker take the stage you worry he'll slip and fall. He seems so old and frail now and you wonder at the terrible toll it must have taken on him, to watch Middle America grow rich night after night, while he tried to hold the answers back, tried not to blurt them out before their time. Somehow his easy charm and quick smile was all you ever hoped for, and as he takes the stage again, a little stooped and wrinkled with a thinning head of grey hair, you realize he has decided to share his decline, that these many years before the camera have followed his aging and descent into infirmity, that he is a university of death where we will learn the secrets of our own ending.

You've grown apart from your family. You remember the day you decided to hitchhike to Vancouver with a large cardboard sign and a backpack filled with books and candles. Your mother drove you to the end of town saying, "That's it, you can't come back now. Good luck." That was the day you left home, crouched in the cab of a Molson's Brewery truck headed for Kapuskasing. Since becoming positive the war of silence has been called to a halt, the arguments dissolved beneath the sense that there's no longer time for that. You are haunted by the image of your own illness, bedridden and helpless, that you would once again become a child. This nightmare of dependency, of having to give yourself over to them once again, has kept you from them all these years, and now, strangely, through the agency of this disease, you've managed to return there, to the place where memory comes from, to the history of your failures, in the body of the family.

When I was six or seven my brother David got it into his head that if we could grow a third arm we'd be set for life, and for weeks we'd argue about where to put it — Dave figured it should come straight out of his chest for the surprise knock-out punch while I thought it should run out of my butt because I figured that furniture was going to be extinct. I thought it would just die out as we got older and that I'd want something to sit on. We made a little lotion out of eggs and arm hair and a little blood and every day we'd rub it into the spot where we wanted our new limb to grow. We never did grow that extra arm — but Dave did have three nipples — just like Gold-finger in James Bond. I guess it's not that unusual. But Dave always said that was the beginning of his double. He always kept a bandage on it so no one would know; one day it would take his place so he could get on with his real business. Or maybe — he'd wink at me — maybe he was already gone.

I think I always looked up to Dave a little bit — even during that year when he was painting everyone's car green, it just seemed like the most obvious thing in the world. Dave said that next to the brain, the smartest part of a guy's body was the balls because they were all wrinkled and veiny like the brain was, only there were two of them. For Dave everything came in pairs like Noah, and after jerking off into a petri dish he would study his cum for omens; if it came from his left ball then it was about the past, and if it was from his right ball it was about the future. He wanted me to try it, figuring the more samples he had the more he'd understand. But I was worried he'd mess up the changes going on in my body, that I'd never grow up, or that some-how, through his experiments, I'd become more like him as I got older. And I guess that scared me some.

He was the first one who was told you were sick, and you'd never seen him cry before, not since he was six or seven and that was just because he caught his hand in the door, and as you held each other and whispered I love you, you knew why it had taken so long to tell him. Your sickness was real now. From now on it would live in your brother as a reminder that we would never be young again, never young enough to change what had already happened. Before you spoke, your illness was a professional concern discussed with the doctor, drawn up in charts and tables, but as the illness spread so would the number of those who knew. If your body had become a danger in your sexual relations, with Dave it had become again a house, a place where blood was thicker than the years we'd grown apart, a place where the certainty of death was no longer disguised by our youth.

Every month you head off to the doctor's to get your blood tested. At first you couldn't believe that your whole body had so much blood in it. When they were through filling the tray you expected to float across the city, or bound over streets like the men on the moon, granted admittance to a new world where everything that lacked weight was familiar, every snowflake and pigeon feather and supermodel was a friend, all endowed with a grace one writer deemed the unbearable lightness of being. As the blood flows you think of Keith Richards, the Rolling Stones guitarist who tried to rid himself of his addictions by having all his blood replaced. What he hadn't counted on, after a lifetime of guitar heroes and record deals and trainers, was that heroin was a state of mind, a place he could return to after the last chord had faded, that to leave his addiction behind would require saying no to himself.

There's not much the doctors can do for you, except draw this blood out for tests. In fact the more your condition worsens the more tests are demanded, as they seek ever finer ways to monitor your decline. Your identity is clinging to these numbers, your viral loads, the ratios of enzymes and tissues that continue to betray you. At night, when you're alone, you try to visualize them, you try to imagine them as part of you, belonging somehow, but find that you can't. The disease seems always separate, and you wonder whether this lack of imagination will finally prove fatal. Because you're unable to embrace this intruder, it has no choice but to destroy you. You imagine your body like those maps of the second world war, with arrows marking troop movements and tanks, with trenches dug and landmines buried, the whole imposing a geometry of death over the earth. Each border remembers some lost battle, some revolution fought at terrible cost. As you continue to turn the globe between your fingers it comes to you: the division of geography into nations is also a map of the dead world, each line marking the place of catastrophe. Because the number of the dead far outweighs the number of the living, we've divided the world into nationalities in order to mourn it more perfectly. And our mourning together, this must be the thing we call a country.

You think: it's hardest for your friends, when they met you for the first time there was no way to know that they would have to bury you one day. You all seemed so young, and while they've continued to age at the usual rate, all of a sudden you've grown old. You would like to apologize for asking so much of them. Because your slide into sickness is slow, monitored by the machines at the hospital, you don't notice at first that you're any different than you ever were, until they come to visit. And while they are gracious and kind and you love them so much, you read the whole cruel truth on their face. You watch yourself dying there. This look hurts you more than all the fevers and sweats and blind panics, because where once there was love, now there is only fear, and this vague terrible sense that all this could have been avoided if only you'd been a little more careful. Somehow you did this to hurt them because they weren't enough so you had to go out and get more, and after you crossed that line you were never the same.

Now that I have AIDS I keep tripping over myself, and sometimes when I'm talking with a friend I'll just nod right out and when I come to they have this terrible expression on their face like, "Are you alright?" And of course I am, I'm fine, I've always been fine, only they can't see that. My body keeps getting in the way.

Last week Donna came to visit, my best friend. She told me that 6,000 cells die in the body every day and that every seven years we're completely new people. Donna's always coming up with crazy shit like that. So I guess I just have to wait it out. I think I'm gonna remake myself as a fat ice cream queen with perfect skin. Donna says that sounds just perfect and then she kisses me because it's time to go. Visiting hours are over.

Islands in a Coded Urban Space — Berlin's *Wagenburgen*

Renate Berg

1. Self-portrait

Literally translated, *Wagenburgen* are the wagon barricades the pioneers used to erect to defend themselves from attacks in the Wild West, but it could as easily be translated as wagon park, carriage stronghold or portacabin site.

In Berlin, *Wagenburgen* are communities. As of June, 1997 there were eleven *Wagenburgen* sites there where groups of people live in converted portacabins, circus wagons, caravans or trucks. The total population is about 500, and the two legalized larger sites — outside the city centre — have about 100 people each. The remaining nine sites are in the inner city, mostly around the area of the former Berlin Wall.

The *Wagenburgen* first developed in the 1980s, when the squatter movement expanded. In those days, Berlin showed a certain tolerance towards squatters, alternative projects, and sub-cultures, which were allowed to develop in niches in the divided city. The second phase started after the Wall came down, when the former 'no man's land' suddenly offered undeveloped open space. In those years there was an acute housing shortage, and *Wagenburgen* emerged all over Germany. We see ourselves as an alternative housing project promoting a different style of city life. We choose to live in wagons; they are not a self-help project to combat homelessness. The Berlin sites all have different spatial and social structures; they include people on social welfare as well as full-time professionals. The largest group amongst the wagon dwellers is part-time workers, free-lancers and people in further education such as apprenticeships or university. Most of the wagon dwellers are between 20 and 35 years old, although they include many younger and older people.

Beyond these groups, broader relations connect the wagon dwellers. In Berlin we have run for the past year and a half a weekly, citywide 'wagon plenum'. Since December 1990 there have been nation-wide meetings called *Wagentage* which are also attended — if only sporadically — by Swiss, Dutch and Danish wagon dwellers. These meetings take place more or less quarterly, each time on a *Wagenburg* in a different city. The programme includes workshops, parties, film screenings, concerts, theatre performances and so on. Within these networks we exchange ideas and develop close contacts with wagon dwellers from different cities. A growing number of people travel around and visit *Wagenburgen* throughout the country. Within the framework of these *Wagentage* we also publish our magazine *Vogelfrai* ('outlawed'), which contains news from the different *Wagenburgen*, such as eviction threats or site changes, reports on workshops, events listings, fairy tales or stories and small ads. We also publish more comprehensive discourses, and the magazine always contains the latest address list.

The seasons reveal much about the limits and the attractions of our wagon-lives. While the wagons are well-insulated and furnished with ovens against the winter cold, winter is nonetheless, an exhausting season, due to the long dark hours, cramped space, permanent dampness outside and a general lack of communication. Summer compensates immensely for these shortcomings, since we spend most of our time outdoors; the free space around the wagons becomes a kind of common living room. A lot of activities take place there which could not possibly take place in houses, such as cabarets and acrobatics or working with metal or wood. In this way, we combine living, working and spare time. Despite all these pleasant aspects, living in a wagon is a time-consuming affair. Organizing our every day life is complicated and the constant fight against eviction demands a lot of time.

The main attractions for us lie in the opportunity to live in a freely constituted community, to live ecologically, and the mobility inherent in a wagon.

Life in a wagon offers the opportunity to live within a loose and dispersed structure; the members can be individually very different. Any conflicts can be alleviated by adjusting the spatial divisions on the site and the community can autonomously shape the inner and outer space of our personal living environment. This loose form of community counters the anonymity of the metropolis. For this reason, and also in order to remain politically active, a well-functioning group structure is important; we carefully choose who we want to live with, and make these decisions through the agreement of the whole group. This kind of freedom — living without institutional controls, property managers, janitors, landlords or extortionate rents — is an essential attraction of life in a wagon.

A lot of people also move into wagons in order to live closer to nature and not feel locked away from the weather and seasonal changes. At the same time, we control to some degree our ecological situation. We strive to use our resources consciously: in our wagons we can choose our building materials, energy sources and furnishings, and we often use and recycle old materials which would otherwise be thrown away. The problem of supply and waste management is met with cost-effective and environmentally-friendly solutions. We fetch water in cans, and as rubbish collection is often difficult, we rely on economical consumption and avoid waste wherever possible. We also use solar cells, recycled rain water, reed sewage treatment, compost cesspits, and we plant vegetation to improve the soil. We mix our wish to live more ecologically with the dictates of necessity and the desire to achieve a positive impression in the eye of the public.

Many people are attracted to the mobility of life in a wagon. It is possible to change your spot on the site, or to change sites completely, or to travel around. This flexibility has become more and more popular; there is a trend towards self-propelled vehicles, which is partly due to our uncertain situation, partly influenced by the demands of the education and job market, and partly due to a basic need for independence and freedom. However, this mobility only works if there are enough sites where wagons can find a temporary home.

2. Our changing situation

In legal terms, *Wagenburgen* occupy, at best, a grey area. In German federal law there is more than one fundamental principle by which we can be made illegal, including building laws, camping and caravan guidelines, and environmental regulations.

Our original situation — which was bad enough — has seen massive changes in the past few years. In the course of neo-liberal city development, Berlin finds itself in the middle of a far-reaching re-structuring process. The fall of the Berlin Wall gave the initial boost to the development of "Enterprise Berlin" (so called by the reigning mayor of Berlin, Eberhard Diepgen), which is strongly supported by the city's conversion into the federal capital. The city is keen to create an investor-friendly ambience and the inner city of Berlin is under enormous pressure to be utilized and exploited. As Senator of the Interior, Joerg Schoehnbohm stated on the occasion of the eviction of the wagons on the East-Side-Gallery on July 17th 1996: "Berlin no longer exists just for its own sake but is the display window and representative of our state." The results of the city development thus far do indeed point towards the end of the history of tolerance in Berlin. Where the city used to brag about its subculture it now wants to get rid of it.

Already in the past few years there have been several evictions and relocations of *Wagenburgen*. By the end of the last parliamentary term, in October 1995, all wagon sites were to have been cleared — but officials were still talking about providing replacement areas. This plan was not executed as they were unable to find new space. We tried to initiate talks with the administrative authorities, one example being the round table talks we organized between August and

November 1995. But the administrative authorities did not take part, which prevented us from discussing concrete solutions. We had to realize that neither the local authorities nor the senate were interested in talking with us or in offering alternative spaces. Therefore we decided to discontinue the round table after several attempts.

A key moment in our history was the clearance of the East Side in July 1996, which was covered in the media throughout Europe. With about 200 inhabitants, it was the largest *Wagenburg* in Berlin, and was named after the nearby East Side Gallery, a remaining section of the Wall. The East Side had made headlines on several occasions, with stories about drugs (dealers and users), petty criminal activities as well as muggings resulting in grievous bodily harm and even manslaughter. The tabloid press commented on these incidents in their usual shock horror style, while politicians and the rest of the media polemicized against the wagon dwellers. There has always been a strong tendency to depict us as antisocials breeding criminality. In the course of the clearance, this process found its climax. Headlines such as "Tuberculosis, car wrecks and drugs next door to the railway station" determined public opinion.

The image '*Wagenburg* equals Slum' was confirmed, and if five months later a tiny newspaper article eventually stated that there was never even a single case of tuberculosis, nobody noticed. Other wagon dwellers saw the East Side as a melting pot which threatened to become a slum. But we have always insisted that the problems of the East Side have to be solved on both an individual and a social basis, that not all *Wagenburgen* are the same, and that evictions do not solve problems but simply move them to a new area.

After the clearance, the senate followed up with a decision to evict all inner city *Wagenburgen* by the end of 1997, and even the sites which had been legalized were only to be kept for a short time. The senate pointed out that "*Wagenburgen* are no qualified solution for re-integration into society and permanent avoidance of homelessness for their inhabitants." They searched for a so-called alternative site for all *Wagenburgen* on the outskirts of the city, which we called an internment camp. But this concept is no longer an option. The senate decision was amended in April 1997: the sites are still to be cleared by the end of this year (1997), but no alternative sites will be provided, since they are not considered financially viable.

In the autumn of 1996 we started another attempt to negotiate with the senate. It failed after about six months, since the conservative party (CDU) stuck to the line of action described above. The extent of the threat is interpreted quite differently amongst the wagon dwellers, but we have all recognized a turn for the worse, especially in connection with the so-called 'Capital Madness' ("Hauptstadtwahn"). We have always been of the opinion that we were never particularly desired, since we could not be utilized. Now we are an even greater obstacle in the face of 'utilization pressure'. On top of that we are now seen as a disturbance to interior safety. Growing privatization, the retreat of the state from social tasks, and increasing control and repression are now indeed part of the threat we face.

3. Resistance

There are many activities with which we might counter the threat of eviction, including: negotiation attempts with the communal legislative body and authority; public relations work, which is divided into press coverage and other activities such as stalls at street fairs, open days, action weeks, etc.; co-operation with universities; networking attempts with alliance partners such as the inner city action group, churches, social initiatives; and contacting investors.

Our intention is to preserve the possibility of life in a wagon and to give it a secure legal basis.

First and foremost, we try to remain on our current sites. We are not opposed to alternative sites, but they would have to fulfill certain criteria: not on the outskirts, not too noisy, the soil not totally sealed, appropriate infra-structure and a little bit of vegetation.

In our struggle against the eviction threats we have so far reached our limits rather quickly. We were skeptical about the negotiation attempts with the senate; it seemed obvious that it was impossible to obtain legal assurance for all *Wagenburgen*. We worried that we would be split, an event which has fortunately not materialized thus far.

Our main approach, which we have been advertising to the public and to communal authorities, is to promote the project character of the *Wagenburgen*, i.e. the fact that we pursue alternative, cultural, social, ecological or artistic ideas. We sell this in order to justify the idea that we are entitled to live in the inner city, especially since we live on 'choice cut' (*Filetgrundstuecke*) plots . Since the state is increasingly retreating from its social and cultural tasks, we see this as a chance to slip into the resulting vacuum. This would mean an institutionalization of the *Wagenburgen*; we would have to agree with certain rules and regulations, and we have asked ourselves what price we are prepared to pay. Some of the *Wagenburgen* have managed to straddle these issues with minimal compromises.

It was obvious however that those *Wagenburgen* which were not prepared to get into local politics were going to be the first to be hit with displacement or eviction. The bitter reality so far, is that there has been little interest in our attempts: all our efforts have been in vain.

4. Models

Wagon dwellers manifest ideologies ranging from 'critical of the system' to 'in radical opposition'. At the same time we are not a fundamentally oppositional force nor a homogenous movement. The contradictions of life in a *Wagenburg* make this clear:

1 The search for clear community structures which at the same time value individuality and the need to retreat.

2 The move away from the ever-accelerating social rhythm of urban modernity into a more time-intensive, slow organization of every day life, which at the same time adapts to modern dynamics and flexibility through our own mobile home.

3 The need for protection within a group in the face of being exposed and open because of a lack of walls.

4 The escape from anonymity into a social context while still desiring to live in a big city.

5 Moving away from the ethos of exploitation but at the same time doing our share to build and maintain an infrastructure and organize our daily lives.

6 Creating a space where nature and environmental influences can be physically experienced while facing the challenge of doing so in a severely ecologically disturbed metropolis.

Our heterogeneity and contradictions make the 'model *Wagenburgen*' a concept that cannot be generalized. After all, our biggest conflict is the permanent need to justify ourselves in the face of the pressure to open ourselves to and provide services for the general public, although most of us just want to live the way we have chosen.

**

Just as they are most threatened, the *Wagenburgen* are growing. The increasing polarization of society makes more and more people want, or indeed need, to live in a wagon. This becomes a problem in larger *Wagenburgen* which are no longer self-administrated. While smaller communities are still capable of voicing their interests and organizing themselves as groups, the communication problem in larger *Wagenburgen* makes this basically impossible, and this very scale threatens our communitarian ideals.

Indeed, the fear that *Wagenburgen* are threatened by a partial but possibly growing slum problem is justified, as the example of the East Side illustrated. Therefore, the most important aspect of our resistance is public relations. Without public support our bids for legalization will always face resistance in the name of the public interest, which is itself under the influence of the ignorant tabloid press and the senate. The struggle against marginalization and ghettoization has to be considered in connection with social fragmentation, which is why we should pursue cooperation with other oppositional forces.

On the other hand, we have to ask our fellow-citizens why the multi-layered structure of a city should be brutally destroyed. The current development plans call for a total replanning and reduction of free areas and public spaces. The open areas of the inner city are increasingly coded; they are all being utilized to make capital productive. Even if we accept the transport and communication value of these spaces, we have to ask whether the planners might not be shooting themselves in the foot by re-building the cities in a manner that seals off other possibilities. The cities might turn out to be no longer viable or desirable, neither for the population itself nor for commercial developments. The multi-coloured and non-conforming sub-culture that includes the *Wagenburgen* may therefore in the end find another entitlement.

October Group

October 25–26, 1996 was a collective action in solidarity with the Metro Toronto Days of Action. To protest the Conservative provincial government's anti-urban policies, a ten-foot diameter transparent tube one hundred and fifty-feet long was installed on the air grate in front of Toronto's City Hall. It was made of .006 inch-thick polyethylene vapour barrier and inflated by exhaust from an underground parking garage. An inscription was stencilled in a single line down each side. The structure was prefabricated and accordion-folded to be moved; fixed along its edges were light wood 1x2's and these had been pre-drilled for butterfly nuts that dropped into the steel grate. Twenty people acting simultaneously installed it in ten minutes. This drew security's attention and the vent was quickly turned off, but environmental monitors automatically turned it on again at 6:00 a.m. It was then agreed that the construction would be removed at 8:30, but by that time striking parking attendants from nearby rallied to its defence with their pickets. The "banner" thus remained until the rally on the square ended at noon. In a short, glorious morning, hundreds of people traversed the noisy, wind-whipped tunnel in a spontaneous parade of cameras, strollers, bikes and placards. With a single slit along the top it was gone.

In addition to its directly political motives, the project reflects the need for new, more culturally effective forms of political protest. Compared to the technical perfection and ubiquity of advertising and official media, the forms of public speech for political art seem hopelessly uncoordinated, trivial, even quaint. What is needed to revitalize our forms of political occupation is not to compete on the spectacle's terms, but a new canniness and economy. The tube reclaimed the device of the tent city one of which occupied Queen's Park at the same time, but responded to the fact that tents are now primarily associated with family leisure and escape from the city, not emergency shelter. While being like a tent in that it was light and temporary, this new form was emphatically urban, suggesting a subway tube, linear city or sci-fi time-tunnel. It materialized, at a collective scale, the desperate situation of a person seeking refuge on an air grate. The inscription, the length of which alone forced its reader into motion, aspired to be both more affective (… HAVE MERCY I CRY…) and more specifically accusative (… THE GREED OF DEVELOPERS …) than typically reductive political slogans allow. By paraphrasing a poem from the student revolts in the early nineteen-seventies and joining this to a fragment of an essay by Velimir Khlebnikov, a Russian revolutionary poet, the text sought to raise historical consciousness of an unfinished project. On the transparent surface the letters were simultaneously visible from inside and out, frontwards and backwards. Their reader was immersed in a passage of discourse. Even in the employment of the hackneyed notion of the winds of change there is a difference: from this uncanny wind tunnel, air blew out both ends with equal force.

HAVE MERCY I CRY FOR THE CITY (Mike Herron); TO ENTRUST THE STREETS TO THE GREED OF DEVELOPERS AND TO GIVE THEM ALONE THE RIGHT TO BUILD IS TO REDUCE LIFE TO NO MORE THAN SOLITARY CONFINEMENT (Velimir Khlebnikov); HAVE MERCY I CRY...

Ground Plans For Paradise
Forced Entertainment & Hugo Glendinning

East

Mary's Place	The Chicken Ranch
Frankfurt Jail	Megaphone House
Baader Minehoff House	Border House
The Funny House	Home House
Hidden House	The Big Butch Building
High Life House	The Dallas Book Depository
The Ellis Home for Runaways	Sniper House
Whore House	The NUM HQ
Work House	The Big Texas Building
Hammer House of Harm	The Big Helen Keller Building
Notre Damme	The Big Overgrown Building
Spook House	Gareth Blonk's Electrical Wholesalers
The Big Fun Building	52 Cromwell Street
Ciccone House	Club of No Regrets
The Big Mexico Building	Graceland
Beaten House	The Tower of London
The Burning Building	The Sleep Labs
Mock Tudor House	Fax It to Me House
The Fake Country Pub	Shift House
Hotel Russell	The Dub Club
The Valium Rooms	The Kelly Home for Missing Persons
Siege House	The Anderson House
Dependence House	Victory Mansions
The Big Blacklist Building	The Institute for Continuity Research
Exhaustion Works	Rachel X's Love Lab
The Halliday Inn	The M.I.T. Lab for Darkness Research
The Ray Newe Bail Bond Agency	The Agony Building
Tripwire House	The Tower of Bethlehem
The Houses of New Parliament	The Big Cromwell Building
The People's Court of Street Justice	The Dust Halls
The King Mob Building	The Pearl Machine Works
The Union Jack Club	The Wire Workers Union Hall
Timex House	Thieves House
Stones Brewery	Scarcity House
The Mirror Building	The Big Rationing Building
The Ice Palace	The Church of Chance
The Navigation Pub	Pig House
Penal House	Dyson Steel Works
The Stardust Building	The Wapping Plant
Intruder House	Stevenson Street Works
Windy View House	The White House
Mandela House	Permutation House
OJ House	Pandemonium House
Unpredictable House	The Adidas Building
Dr Livingstone House	The "OK" Club
The Big Sinister Building	The Fila House
New Rose Hotel	"Say Yes / Say No" House
Free Trade House	Hello Harry House
The Big Sherlock Holmes Building	The Sewage Tower
The Palace of Versailles	Decision House
Stomach House	The Roy Castle Housing Project
Heat Works	Peter Pan House
Heat Treatment House	Walt Disneyland
The Kidney Building	Tired Tower
The Big Anachronism Building	The Libel Halls
The Blue Eyes Building	The New Bastille
Hospitality House	Liberace House
The White Meat Tower	Televisionland Tower
The Razor Wire Hotel	Toxico
The Prebaltistkia Hotel	Have-A-Go House
Harvest Festival House	The Burns Unit
Hanging House	Neo-Gothic House
	Substandard House

Lillington Towers
Semtex House
The Big Sharon Stone Building
Himalaya House
Fraction House
Numerator House
Ransom House
Human Race House
Football Tower
The Big Sid Vicious Building
Foreskin House
Rape House
The Big Complicated Building
The Big Simple Building
The Big Boarded Up Building
Devil House
The Cartoon Club
The Scum Club
Mikhail Gorbachev's Dacha
Intention Tower
The Big Shop Building
Piercing House
Ronnie Scott's Free Jazz Club
The Big Giraffe Building
The Big Black Pope Building
The Rodney King Tower
Panhandle Tower
The Bloody Awful Building
The Listed Building
Slow Death House
Lie Detector House
Cut Price House
The Discount Store
Cantonna House
Child Abuse House
Slapped Down House
Injection House
Entebbe House
Dominant House
Everybody House
Stripped Naked House
Falling House
The Big Nervous Building
The Dangerous Tower
Product House
Problems House
Scenario House
Librium Buildings
Infection House
The Small Contagious Building
Military House
The Noise Building
Fireworks House
Vertical House
Horizontal House
The Butterfly Club
The Dumb Club
The Spanner Club
Anorak House
Panopticon House
Difference Tower
The Smelly Building
The Big Badly Painted Building

The Big Emergency Building
False Report House
The Big Multiplier Building
Job Club
The Wicker Boys Club
The 400 Club
Scavengers House
The Barter Club
Sex Worker Tower
Crap House
Broken Glass House
Sambo House
Samba House
The White Trash Tower
Blind House
The Big Flooded Building
Shit House
Spunk House
Dirt House
Stink House
Mickey Mouse House
Kray Twins Tower
The Big 40w Building
Winter Buildings
Zip House
Crucifix Steel Works
The Kennedy Space Centre
Yvonne's Place
Kelly's Casino
Bitch Buildings
Race Baiting House
The White Lies Building
Improbable House
The Peoples Museum of Sex and Industry
Loss House
The Big LSD Building
Eurodollar House
The Ace Casino
Cupid Towers
Aphrodisiac House
The Cheap Building
Loss of Virginity House
The Big World War One Building
Dilapidated House
Manor Beer & Social Club
Wakefield Young Drinkers Club
Saatchi House
The Big Damascus Building
Carole's Petrol Pub
The Big Meteorite Building
Hi-Fi House
Motown House
The People's House
The Big Council Building
The Jules Verne Building
Esperanto House central
Heartbreak House east
The Big Interrogation Building
The Big Tranquillity Building
The Big MI5 Building
The Institute of Theoretical Warfare
Dave's Spanish Bar
Blackmail House

Bleak House
The Fire Station
The Institute of Theoretical Physics
The Winter Palace
Heartbreak Hotel
The Kodacolour Building
BUPA Hospital
The Big Poland Building
The Big New Communist Man Building
The Big Tarkovsky Building
The Big Chemistry Building
The Suicide Building
The Museum of Love & Drunkenness
The Museum of Religion & Atheism
Simeon's Tower
The Last Chance Saloon
The Big Cholera Building
The Palace of Science and Culture
Freebase House
Hotel Amnesia
Hotel Eden
The Roman Hotel
Money U Like
Drugs R Us
Macdonald's
The Big Neon Building
Zoo Station
The Big Zodiac Building
The Royal Institute for Blind
Hoffman Centre for Blood Transfusion
Dave's Glue Club
The National Centre for Tropical Diseases
Poltergeist House
Trump Tower
The World Slave Trade Centre
The Green River Building
The Kum Bak Club
The Paradise Building
The Tony Hotel
Clown Alley
The Institute for Invisibility Research
The Big Mechanical Building
The Tall Club
The Women's Refuge
The Haunted Building
The Radar Station
Radio London
The Big Dancing Building
The Electrical Building
The Passion Building
The Loveless Hotel
Dark House
Revolution House
The Big Joe Klieg Building
The Big Gary Glitter Building
The Palace of History
The Big New Moon Building
The Blood Building
The Weeping Building
The Big Chocolate Building
The All Union Workers Hostel
The Dorman Home for Fallen Women
The Dorman Home for Fallen Men

Geomancy House
The Big South Africa Building
Deserters House
The Big Nocturnal Building
Assassination House
The Palace of Narcolepsy
Strongbow Cider House
The Dead Building
The Money Building
Precarious House
Nothing House
The First Fireproof Hotel
The Big Deng Xiaoping Building
Helen's House
The Towering Inferno
The Rand Think Tank on Sex
The Institute of Possible Futures
Crack House
Paul's Shooting Gallery
Wireless House
Void House
Number One Building
Number Two Building
Number Three Building
The Midland Bank
The Big Barclays Bank
The Pentecostal Church of Elvis Alive
Coventry Cathedral
The Free Church of England
The Friends Meeting House
The Chech Club
The Big Howard Hughes Building
Frank Dobson Builders Merchants
The Institute of Loss
Centurion Glass
The Big Binary Building
Retail World
Tempo House
The Everything a Man Could Want Bar
The Big David Mellor Building
The Big Antonia de Sanchez Building
The Air Products Building
Hotel Regent
Hotel Alsace Lorraine
The Kings Planetarium
The Department of Transport
The King Kong Building
Giant's House
The Oliver Machine Works
Redemption House
The Big Eclipse Building
The Department of Health
Thirsty Tower
The Private Building
The Big Sceptics Building
The Big Fujicolour Building
Black City Morgue
The Patents Library
The Library of Classified Texts
The Fish Market
The Big Pre-Fabricated Building
Harry's Bar
The Big Astrid Proll Building

Naylors Bomb-proof Hotel
The Englishe Building
Patriot House
The Big Steve Rogers Building
Wrong Number House
The Hate Library
X-Ray House
The Big Mud Building
The Big Karl Marx Hotel
The Regicides Building
The Big Botany Building
The Library of Stories and Chronicles
Kit Burn's Rat Pit
McGurk's Suicide Hall
The False Memory Building
The Big Fingerprint Building
The Big Telly Savalas Building
The Big New Spain Building
The Cold Building
The Deep Sleep Building
Liar's House
The Big Concrete Building
House of Chance
Backward House
Helen's Hot Hotel
The Sleep Inn
Fulsome Prison
Armley Jail
The Mile High Club
The Sands Hotel
Centre Point
The Chrysler Building
The Love Building
The Fear Building
Jay's House
The Meat Market
The Reichstag
The Big Empire Building
The New Bank of All England
The Whispering Tower
The Newey Plastics Building
Carpetland
The First Fainting Building
The Second Fainting Building
The Poor House
The Bull & Patriot Pub
The Fast Horse Pub
The Institute of Believing
The Joy Building
The Sex Tower
The Rover Car Plant
The Telephone Exchange
Videoworld
The Big Theory Building
Dante's Inferno
The Big Police Station
The Palace of Invention & Lies
The Big Damp Building
Crisis House
The Big Petro-Chemical Building
Nixon House
The Big Nature Building
Mathematical House

Dobson's Laundr
The Borges Diner

North
The Big Deception Building
Conveyor Belt House
Eternity House
Crooked Tower
Philosophy Tower
Comedy Club
King George V Buildings
Thought Buildings
Cardiac Tower
Cherry Blossom Chapel
Hotel 17
The School of Hard Knocks
Horror House
Early Madonna Buildings
Muggers Buildings
Truncheon House
The High Risk Hotel
Fahrenheit House
The Silent Hotel
Lion King House
The Cock and Bull Pub
Volitional Buildings
The Kingdom of Heaven Guest House
The Big Norway Building
The Big Preposterous Building
The Spit Club
Scargill Buildings
The Daydream Hospital
Yuri Gagarin Hostel for Cosmonauts on Earth
The Bar None
The Onion Club
The Carnival Club
The Big Shaking Hotel
Bad Maths House
Crooked Buildings
Last Chance House
Blast House
Blind House
Shape House
Star Trek House
The Fist City Gym
Drive-By House
The Big De-Magnetized Building
Green Fields Tower
Insomnia House
Erection Buildings
Plankton House
Thorazine Buildings
The Big Trick Building
The Swastika Hotel
Houston House
Cold Calling House
Straitjacket Buildings
Inflation House
Graffiti Mansions
Landslide Mansions
Blackpool Tower
The Big Inevitable Building
The Pleasure Rooms

Error Buildings
RAM House
Crooked House
Thoughtless Buildings
House of Incest
Deep Hidden House
Dave's Uncomfortable Clothes Shop
Tamezepan House
The Anonymous Hotel
The Gray House
Kasmir House
Lipstick Buildings
Malvinas House
The Second Fainting Building
Dead Man's House
Formula House
Rick's All Nude Revue
Thorax House
The British Embassy
Impotence Buildings
The Home Hotel
The Zodiac Building
Troublesome Towers
Hotel Green Eyes
Mourning Tower
Blue Screen House
The Big Padlocked Building
Narcotics House
The Crawl Club
The North Circular Club
The Prophecy Rooms
The Secret Hotel
Infatuation Buildings
Disarray Buildings
The Animal Morgue
The "Ear, Nose and Throat Hospital"
The Big Reaganomics Building
The Big Tolstoy Building
The Hard Drive Hotel
The Institute for Human Nature
Former Lover Buildings
Satan House
Zulu Buildings
The Bible Belt Club
Occupation House
Abolishon Mansions
The Chelsea Hotel
The Danger House
House of Nowhere
New World House
Trap House
Breeze Buildings
Sincerity Towers
The Big Explosions Building
Cacophany House
The Big Pointed Building
The Big Reversible Building
The Warm Water Hotel
Jumping House
The Second Wives Club
Hotel Irrelevant
Precarious House
Armistice House

Enemy Buildings
The Bad Dream Building
The Big Biology Building
Nietzsche House
The Power Tower
The Incorporate Hotel
Hacker House
Late 50's Buildings
Charles Mansions
Half-Moon Hotel
Secret House
Speak Bitterness House
Tesco House
The H-Block
Twat Motel
Pete's Chop Bar
The Cursed House
House of Silence
Ego House
House of Toss
Personality Buildings
Radio House
Tottenham Hotspur Supporters Club
The Broken Heart Club
The Snow Factory
Blank House
The Big Regular Building
Heroin House
Kryptonite Mansions
Light Bulb Buildings
Forest Buildings
The Big Persia Building
The Leaning Tower of Destiny
Arabia House
The Big Alphabet Building
Illogical Mansions
Donald's Drive In
The Bad Daughter Motel
Paschendale House
The Dead Drunk Club
Voodoo Tower
Unheimlich House
Contradiction Buildings
Smart Arse Hotel
Gaunt Buildings
Scrotum House
The Mercy Chapel
The Big Sideways Building
The Stud Club
The Soviet Belgian Embassy
Factory Mansions
Precision Hotel
Man on Moon Buildings
Paparazzi Mansions
Banal Buildings
The Big Hundred Years Building
The Open Wound Motel
The Monkey Club
Heather's Laundromat
Lethargy Mansions
Kerb Crawler Buildings
Profumo House
Coward House

Suffragette House
The Free Church of Philadelphia
Aligator House
The European Court of Human Rights
IFOR House
U-Turn Mansions
Tiannemen House
Flammable House
Rent House
The Big Unconscious Building
The Heidegger Hotel

South

The Big Super-Ego Building
X-Certificate Mansions
The South African Embassy
Bank of Nowhere
Hotel Adventure
Longevity House
The Big Instructions Building
Autumn House
The Big Incomprehensible Building
The Swab Rooms
The Milky Way Club
Counterfeit House
Incision House
Target Practice Hotel
Half-Way House
Suspicion Buildings
The Ping-Pong Club
Shakespeare Mansions
The Dirty Dealing Club
Gasoline House
Romance House
Strange Man Buildings
Firing Squad House
Retro House
The Gravity Hostel for Girls
The Hard Man Hotel
The Big Singing Building
Hotel Anatomy
Movietime Motel
Year Zero House
Heroine House
Motherfucker House
The Big Word Building
Andy's House
The Big Id Building
Infinity Buildings
Block Building
Index House
The Big Magic Building
Dave's Children's Prison
SuperFly House
Downfall Buildings
The American Dream Disco
Fart Buildings
Repetition House
Geopolitics House
Safe House
Hand Job House
Marcie's End of The Pier Amusements
Weight House

House of Money
Myth House
Inconsiderate House
The Summer Club
Innuendo Buildings
The Penn/Davies Amateur Strip Club
Sleepwalkers Tower
The Futures Market
Corpse House
The Big Unstable Buildings
Big Number House
The Big Logical Building
Dave's Reality Parlour
Telepathy Buildings
Improper House
Rupture Buildings
Hotel Emotion
Mystery Buildings
Inflatable House
Dick House
The Tower of Salt
Speaking Stones Guest House
Right Wing Buildings
Push & Shove Buildings
Perfectionsit Buildings
The Big Argentina Building
Brave House
Club Med
Law & Order Tower
No Surrender Mansions
Dave's Amateur Hospital
Negative House
Office Wonderworld
Disaster Mansions
The Heartbeat Club
Hotel Impossible
The Goal Hanger Hotel
Hotel Hypothermia
Biro House
The Cuddles Club
Helpline House
The Institute of Realness
Injection Buildings
Lusten/Lasten Buildings
The Ghetto Tower
Parasite House
The Loaded Dice Hotel
Piss House
National Insurance House
Procedures House
Rat Fuck House
Epiphany Tower
Inebriated Buildings
The King of Spain Club
Olde Macdonalds
Post Coital Buildings
Loss of Faith Buildings
The Big Ratings War Buildings
Womb House
The Skin Graft Hotel
The Big Transparent Building
Trouble Towers
The Big Smoking Gun Building

Vomit House
The Sweat Shop
Wire Tap Buildings
The Spirit Club
United House of Terror
Unspeakable Buildings
The Big Tabloid Building
Telesales House
The Big Ruthless Building
Play Ball Buildings
The Rat Race Place
Spice House
The Scrum Club
The Stepford Wives Club
Ultimatum House
Wank House
Retribution House
Slight Fever House
Rope Buildings
Rent-A-Mob Buildings
Hot Dog House
The Big Infested Building
The Big Pessimisitic Building
Cryptography Buildings
Endorphin House
Mock-History House
The Big Constipated Building
The Tall Dissapearing Building
The Big Radiator Building
Bravado Buildings
Hal House
Hotel Irrational
Ontology House
Air Gun House
The Big Parole Building
Psychedilic House
Blonde House
The Big Carbohydrate Club
Clit House
Entropy Buildings
Hysterectomy House
Rift Tower
Sodium Buildings
Top Dollar Buildings
The Walt Disney Wedding Chapel
Erasure Mansions
The Big Grammar Building
Hotel Optimism
Lino Mansions
Pre-Pubescent Buildings
Dave's Rave Club
The Fluids Club
Homeboy House
The Big New Ocean Building
Chewing Gum Hotel
Dave's Impossible Nightclub
The Che Guevara Wedding Chapel

West
Carpet Wonderland west
The Bank of Toytown
The Bank of Russia
The Second City Zoo

Deng's House
Psychic Dancehall
The High Five Bar
Papa Legba's Place
Iron City House
The Stock Exchange
Derivatives House
Dead Dreams House
The Basic Building
The Board of Unsafe Structures
The Capital Tower
The Capitol Tower
Cunt House
The Shelter for Hopeless Men
The Grand Hotel
Universal Studios
The Big Language Building
The Big Politics Building
The Big Venezuela Building
Blast Theory House
Bimbo House
The Post-Darwin Zoo
Pharmaceuticals House
Shit Tower
Son of Sam Residential Home
The Church of Cash
The Kelly Residential Block
The Drug Club
Knife Tower
The Tower of Babel
Post-Babel Tower
Free Market House
Bull Market House
The National Centre for Hope
HIV House
Profit Tower
The Institute of Correction
Vandal Tower
The Big Jane Building
The Pain Saloon
The Horse Club
Gorby's Tower
Madeliene House
Boredom House
Thatcher Tower
X House
The No Shit Trading Co.
The Slit Club
The Post Office Tower
The Leaning Tower of Derby
The Last Building
Fiasco Tower
Purgatory Point
The Slip Street Building
Boys Tower
The Small Genes Building
Slow Time House
The Walt Disney Holocaust Museum
Microphone House
Reuters House
Terrible Tower
Percentage House
The Big Intravenous Building

Lottery House
The Chance Street Building
Hand-Grenade House
The Library of Love
Duracell Tower
Iran / Iraq House
The Blood Club
Smack House
The Big Bruise Building
The Big Asbestos Building
Diagram House
The Gold Building
The Zinc Building
The Big Stone Building
The Small Stone Building
The Bob Marley Building
Contentious House
Race Tower
Millennium House
Avanti House
Bev's Bunker
Beginners House
The Big Spinning Building
Stillness House
Black City Dog's Home
The Big Ground Zero Building
Fallout House
The Big Business Building
Sunset House
Subway House
Desire House
The Fools Paradise
Mike Kahill's Hospice
House of Games
Ill-Repute House
India House
Africa House
Hotel Margaret
The Sheffield Novotel
Chianti House
UK Plc
The Museum of Things Lost & Found
Peyton House
Burnside Buildings
Hardcore House
The Debtors Prison
New Dollar House
The Palace of Rest
Hoogstraten House
Bitter Buildings
Sunny Gyms
The Fattening Rooms
Mistake House
The Sperm Bank
The Blood Bank
Hurricane House
Lymph House
The Tower of Reason
The Library of Congress
Out House
The Big Bunuel Building
Hotel New Hampshire
The First Electric Hotel

The Hotel California
The Hotel Hiroshima
Bullet House
Wigan Casino
Gold Rush Amusement Halls
The Millionaires Bar
The Red House
The Blue House
The Yellow House
Korea House
Magnetic House
The False Translation Building
The False Hope Building
Crazy Tower
Comintern Tower
Venture House
Guttenburg House
Hawkins House
Koblenz Federal Archive Building
Wonder Weapons House
The Big Italy Building
Photocopy House
Submarine House
Berlin Technical University
The Jigsaw Building
The Stork Club
Kafka Towers
Prehistory House
The Big Feudal Building
The Big Republic of Ireland Building
IRA House
UDA House
Punch & Judy House
Zion House
The Free Rasta Hotel
The Diamond Hotel
Eighth Day House
Deep Throat Hotel
The Clean Sheets Motel
The Premature Baby Unit
Kim Philby House
Tyson Tower
The Poverty Zoo
Coronation House
Charles & Camilla Tower
Lesbian House
Kev's Tattoo Parlour
Rascals Sauna & Video Lounge
T-Cell House
The Adult Building
The Big Historical Truth Building
Aerosol House
The Big Polaroid Building
The Pig Pen
House of Spirits
Class War House
Bargain House
Mr Buyrite
Trademark Tower
Pee Wee's Playhouse
The Big Blue Blood Building
Kota Kinablu Hotel

Ground Plans For Paradise is an installation/collaborative project designed to conjure a vast imaginary city using model buildings, street indexes, photography and occasional performance. Created by the UK-based performance ensemble Forced Entertainment and their long-term collaborator Hugo Glendinning the project draws on the reality of city life and on the utopian dreams which urban spaces can inspire. Using 1,000 balsa wood tower blocks, each of them named and lit from inside, it creates an abandoned metropolis which viewers are asked to fill; imagining the lives, people, and stories that might belong there. This deserted space — inhabited, or dreamed perhaps, by the sleeping figures in Hugo Glendinning's photographs — feature the names of places and of streets from both real and fantastic cities. © Tim Etchells (Artistic Director, Forced Entertainment) 1997

Ground Plans For Paradise was originally commissioned by Leeds Metropolitan University Gallery & Studio Theatre with funds from the Arts Council Of Englands Live Art Commissions scheme. Subsequent presentations of the piece have been at Quarterlight (Sheffield) and at Cubitt Gallery (London) with the support of the Paul Hamlyn

Cities in the Global Economy

Saskia Sassen

The specific forms assumed by globalization over the last decade have created particular organizational requirements. The emergence of global markets for finance and specialized services, the growth of investment as a major type of international transaction, all have contributed to the expansion in command functions and in the demand for specialized services for firms.[1]

Why and how do cities matter in today's global economy? Is there something different about their role today from twenty or thirty years ago? This is, inevitably, one particular angle into the question of the importance of cities today, since most cities have probably had few interactions with the global economy and have felt only minor repercussions from its growth. But it is an important issue to pursue because many experts and policy makers appear to be convinced that globalization and the new information technologies mark the end of the economic importance of cities.[2]

1. Geographic dispersal and central control.

The dispersal capacities emerging with globalization and telematics — the off-shoring of factories, the expansion of global networks of affiliates and subsidiaries, the move of back offices to suburbs and out of central cities — led many observers to assert that cities would become obsolete in an economic context of globalization and information technologies. Indeed, many of the once great industrial centers in highly developed countries did suffer severe decline. But, against all predictions, a significant number of major cities also saw their concentration of economic power rise. Why?

There are three features of the global economy today that explain why cities, and particularly the network of thirty to fourty global cities matter. First, the global economy is not simply a market; it is a system that needs to be implemented, coordinated, managed, and serviced. Much of this specialized work is concentrated in cities. Secondly, the privatization of public-sector firms and the deregulation of a growing number of activities have brought with them a privatizing of governance funtions. We see a shift of such functions from the world of government to the corporate world. This entails, to a good extent, that the work of governing the private economic system gets done in cities — in the form of various legal, accounting, managerial tasks, business associations, etc. Indeed, one of the key, though rarely recognized, features of the global economy today is the formation of an intermediary, institutionalized world of high-level financial, legal, and accounting firms that have emerged as strategic agents, often replacing some of the functions fulfilled by national governments before privatization and deregulation. Third, the digitalization of a growing sector of the economy has underlined the importance of access to that infrastructure, and for leading sectors it will have to be state-of-the-art infrastructure. Leading economic sectors will find what they need in the major international business centers which have enormous concentrations of such infrastructure.

Let me elaborate briefly. The combination of geographic dispersal of economic activities and system integration which lies at the heart of the current economic era has contributed to new or expanded central functions and the complexity of transactions has raised the demand by firms for highly specialized services. Rather than becoming obsolete due to the dispersal made possible by information technologies, a critical number of cities: a) concentrate command functions; b) are post-industrial production sites for the leading industries of our period, such as finance and specialized services; and c) are national or transnational marketplaces where firms and governments can buy financial instruments and specialized services.

The number of such cities, their shifting hierarchy, how novel a development they represent, are all subjects for debate. But there is growing agreement about the fact of a network of major cities both in the North and in the South that function as centers for the coordination, control, and servicing of global capital.

Introducing cities in an analysis of economic globalization allows us to reconceptualize processes of economic globalization as concrete economic complexes situated in specific places. A focus on cities decomposes the nation-state into a variety of sub-national components, some profoundly articulated with the global economy and others not. It also signals the declining significance of the national economy as a unitary category in the global economy.

2. The new urban economy.

This new or sharply expanded role of a particular kind of city in the world economy since the early 1980s basically results from the intersection of two major processes. The first is the sharp growth in the globalization of economic activity. This has raised the scale and the complexity of economic transactions, thereby feeding the growth of top-level multinational headquarter functions and the growth of services for firms, particularly the growth of advanced corporate services. The second is the growing service intensity in the organization of the economy, a process evident in firms in all industrial sectors, from mining to finance. This has fed the growth of services for firms in all sectors, and for both nationally and internationally oriented firms.

The key process from the perspective of the urban economy is the growing demand for services by firms in all industries and the fact that cities are the preferred production sites for such services, whether at the global, national or regional level. The growing service intensity in economic organization generally — and the specific conditions of production for advanced corporate services, including the conditions under which information technologies are available — combine to make some cities once again a key "production" site, a role they had lost when mass manufacturing became the dominant economic sector.

A central proposition here is that we cannot take the existence of a global economic system as a given; rather, we need to examine the particular ways in which the conditions for economic globalization are produced. This requires examining not only communication capacities and the power of multinationals, but also the infrastructure of facilities and work processes necessary for the implementation of global economic systems, including the production of those inputs that constitute the capability for global control and the infrastructure of jobs involved in this production. The emphasis shifts to the practice of global control: the work of producing and reproducing the organization and management of a global production system and a global marketplace for finance, both under conditions of economic concentration. The recovery of place and production also implies that global processes can be studied in great empirical detail [See Sassen 1991; 1994].

Two observations can be made at this point. The first is that to a large extent the global economy materializes in concrete processes situated in specific places, and that this holds for the most advanced information industries as well. We need to distinguish between the capacity for global transmission/communication and the material conditions that make this possible, between the globalization of the financial industry and the array of resources — from buildings to labor inputs — that makes this possible; and so on for other sectors as well.

The second is that the spatial dispersal of economic activity made possible by telematics contributes to an expansion of central functions insofar as this dispersal takes place under the continuing concentration in control, ownership and profit appropriation that characterizes the current economic system. More conceptually, we can ask whether an economic system with strong tendencies towards such concentration can have a space economy that lacks points of physical agglomeration.

3. Global cities and global value chains.

The vast new economic topography that is being implemented through electronic space is one moment, one fragment, of an even vaster economic chain that is in good part embedded in non-electronic spaces. There is no fully virtualized firm and no fully digitalized industry. Even the most advanced information industries, such as finance, are installed only partly in electronic space. The same is true of industries that produce digital products, such as software designers. The growing digitalization of economic activities has not eliminated the need for major international business and financial centers and all the material resources they concentrate, from state-of-the-art telematics infrastructure to brain talent.

Nonetheless, telematics and globalization have emerged as fundamental forces reshaping the organization of economic space. This reshaping ranges from the spatial virtualization of a growing number of economic activities to the reconfiguration of the geography of the built environment for economic activity. Whether in electronic space or in the geography of the built environment, this reshaping involves organizational and structural changes. Telematics maximizes the potential for geographic dispersal and globalization entails an economic logic that maximizes the attractions and profitability of such dispersal.

The transformation in the spatial correlates of centrality through new technologies and globalization engenders a whole new problematic around the definition of what constitutes centrality today in an economic system where a) a share of transactions occurs through technologies that neutralize distance and place, and do so on a global scale; b) centrality has historically been embodied in certain types of built environment and urban form, i.e. the central business district. Further, the fact of a new geography of centrality, even if transnational, contains possibilities for regulatory enforcement that are absent in an economic geography lacking strategic points of agglomeration.

4. New forms of marginality and polarization.

The sharpening inequalities in the distribution of the infrastructure for electronic space, whether private computer networks or the Net, in the conditions for access to electronic space, and, within electronic space, in the conditions for access to high-powered segments and features, are all contributing to new geographies of centrality both on the ground and in electronic space. What does this mean for cities?

One issue I would like to emphasize is the importance of conventional infrastructure in the operation of economic sectors that are heavy users of telematics. This is a subject that has received little attention. The dominant notion seems to be that telematics obliterates the need for conventional infrastructure. But it is precisely the nature of the production process in advanced industries, whether they operate globally or nationally, which contributes to explain the immense rise in business travel we have seen in all advanced economies over the last decade. The virtual office is a far more limited option than a purely technological analysis would suggest. Certain types of economic activities can be run from a virtual office located anywhere. But for work processes requiring multiple specialized inputs, considerable innovation, and risk taking, the need for direct interaction with other firms and specialists remains a key locational factor. Hence the metropolitanization and regionalization of an economic sector have boundaries that are set by the time it takes for a reasonable commute to the major city or cities in the region.

The irony of today's electronic era is that the older notion of the region and older forms of infrastructure re-emerge as critical for key economic sectors. This type of region in many ways diverges from older forms of region. It corresponds rather to a type of centrality — a metropolitan grid of nodes connected via telematics. But for this digital grid to work conventional infrastructure — ideally of the most advanced kind — is also a necessity.

The new growth sectors, the new organizational capacities of firms, and the new technologies — all three interrelated — are contributing to produce not only a new geography of centrality but also a new geography of marginality. The evidence for the U.S., Western Europe, and Japan suggests that it will take government policy and action to reduce the new forms of spatial and social inequality.

There are misunderstandings that seem to prevail in much general commentary about what matters in an advanced economic system, the information economy, and economic globalization. Many types of firms, workers, and places, such as industrial services, which look as if they do not belong in an advanced, information-based, globally oriented economic system, are actually integral parts of such a system. They need policy recognition and support: they can't compete in the new environments where leading sectors have bid up prices and standards, even though their products and labor are in demand. For instance, the financial industry in Manhattan, one of the most sophisticated and complex industries, needs truckers to deliver not only software, but also tables and light bulbs; and it needs blue collar maintenance workers and cleaners. These activities and workers need to be able to make a decent living if they are to stay in the region. (See *Social Justice* 1993; *Competition and Change* 1995).

Yet another dimension not sufficiently recognized is the fact of a new valuation dynamic: the combination of globalization and the new technologies has altered the criteria and mechanisms through which factors, inputs, goods, services are valued/priced. This has had devastating effects on some localities, industries, firms and workers.

Notes

1 Services for firms are usually referred to as producer services. The producer services, and most especially finance and advanced corporate services, can be seen as industries producing the organizational commodities necessary for the implementation and management of global economic systems. Producer services are intermediate ouputs, that is, services bought by firms. They cover financial, legal, and general management matters, innovation, development, design, administration, personnel, production technology, maintenance, transport, communications, wholesale distribution, advertising, cleaning services for firms, security, and storage. Central components of the producer services category are a range of industries with mixed business and consumer markets; they are insurance, banking, financial services, real estate, legal services, accounting, and professional associations.

2 There have been several firsts by major organizations when it comes to including cities in analyses of general international issues. Let me just mention two: the recent OECD meeting at the ministerial level, on "Cities and the Global Economy," held in Melbourne in 1995 and the 1996 project by the Council on Foreign Relations on "Cities, the world economy and foreign policy." Also of interest here is that in 1994–5 the World Economic Forum — an international forum for business executives of multinational corporations — launched a Club of Megacity Mayors, a first in its 15-year history. In a somewhat different vein, the World Bank now asserts that to understand macroeconomic performance we need to assess urban productivity.

Bibliography

Abu-Lughod, Janet Lippman (1995), "Comparing Chicago, New York and Los Angeles: testing some world cities hypotheses," *World Cities in a World-System*, Edited by Paul L. Knox and Peter J. Taylor, Cambridge, UK: Cambridge University Press

Cohen, Michael A., Blair A. Ruble, Joseph S. Tulchin, Allison M. Garland, eds. (1996), *Preparing for the Urban Future. Global Pressures and Local Forces.*, Washington D.C.: Woodrow Wilson Center Press

Competition and Change, The Journal of Global Business and Political Economy (1995), Vol. 1, No. 1

Le Debat (Summer 1994), *Le Nouveau Paris* (Special Issue), Paris: Gallimard

Drennan, Mathew P. (1992), "Gateway Cities: The Metropolitan Sources of US Producer Service Exports," *Urban Studies*, Vol. 29, No. 2, 217–235

Dunn, Seamus, ed. (1994), *Managing Divided Cities*, Staffs, UK: Keele University Press

John Friedmann (1995), "Where we stand: A decade of world city research," in Knox and Taylor, 21–47

Frost, Martin and Nigel Spence (1992), "Global City Characteristics and Central London's Employment," *Urban Studies*, Vol. 30, No. 3, 547–558

Futur Anterieur (1995), *La Ville-Monde Aujourd'hui: Entre Virtualite et Ancrage* (Special Issue), edited by Thierry Pillon and Anne Querrien, Vols 30–32, Paris: L'Harmattan

Holston, James, ed. (1996), *Public Culture, Cities and Citizenship* (Special Issue), Vol.8, No. 2

The Journal of Urban Technology (1995), *Information Technologies and Inner-City Communities* (Special Issue), Vol. 3, No. 19 Fall, King, A.D., ed. (1996) *Representing the City. Ethnicity, Capital and Culture in the 21st Century*, London: Macmillan

Paul L. Knox and Peter J. Taylor, eds (1995), *World Cities in a World-System*, Cambridge, UK: Cambridge University Press

Richard T. LeGates and Frederic Stout, eds. (1996), *The City Reader*, London and New York: Routledge

Mittelman, James, ed. (1996), *Globalization:Critical Reflections, International Political Economy Yearbook*, Vol. 9, Boulder, Co.: Lynne Rienner Publishers

Saskia Sassen (1991), *The Global City: New York, London, Tokyo*, Princeton: Princeton University Press

———— (1994), *Cities in a World Economy*, Thousand Oaks, California: Pine Forge/Sage Press

Simon, David (1995), "The world city hypothesis: reflections from the periphery," in Knox and Taylor, 132–155

Social Justice (1993), *Global Crisis, Local Struggles* (Special Issue), Vol. 20, Nos. 3–4, Fall–Winter

Stren, Richard (1996), "The Studies of Cities: Popular Perceptions, Academic Disciplines, and Emerging Agendas," in Cohen et al., 392–420

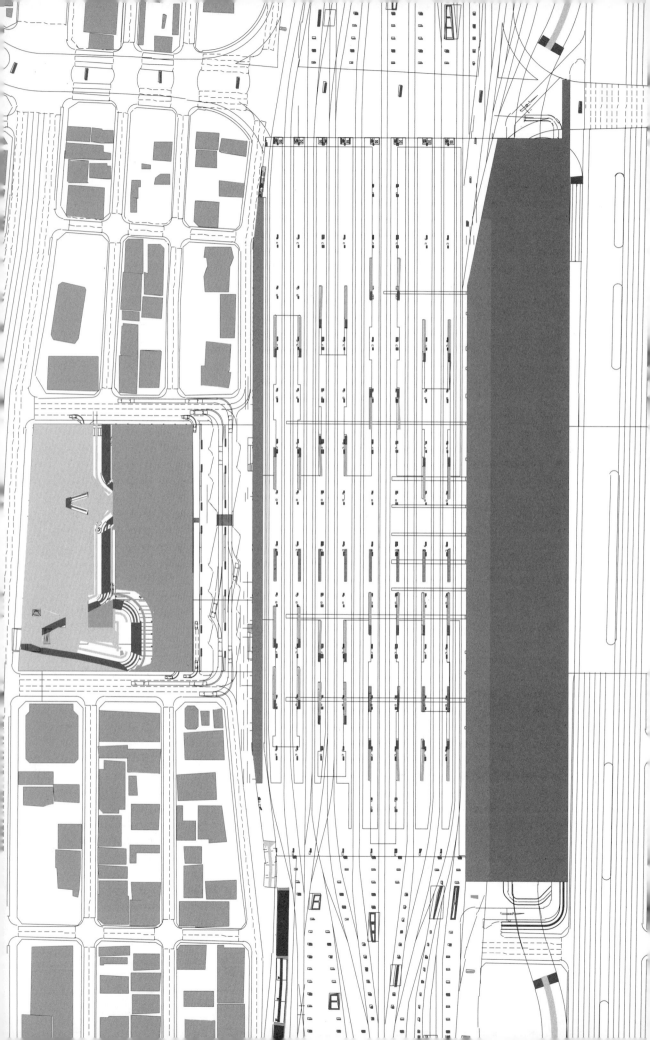

High Speed Railway Complex: Pusan, South Korea

Foreign Office Architects

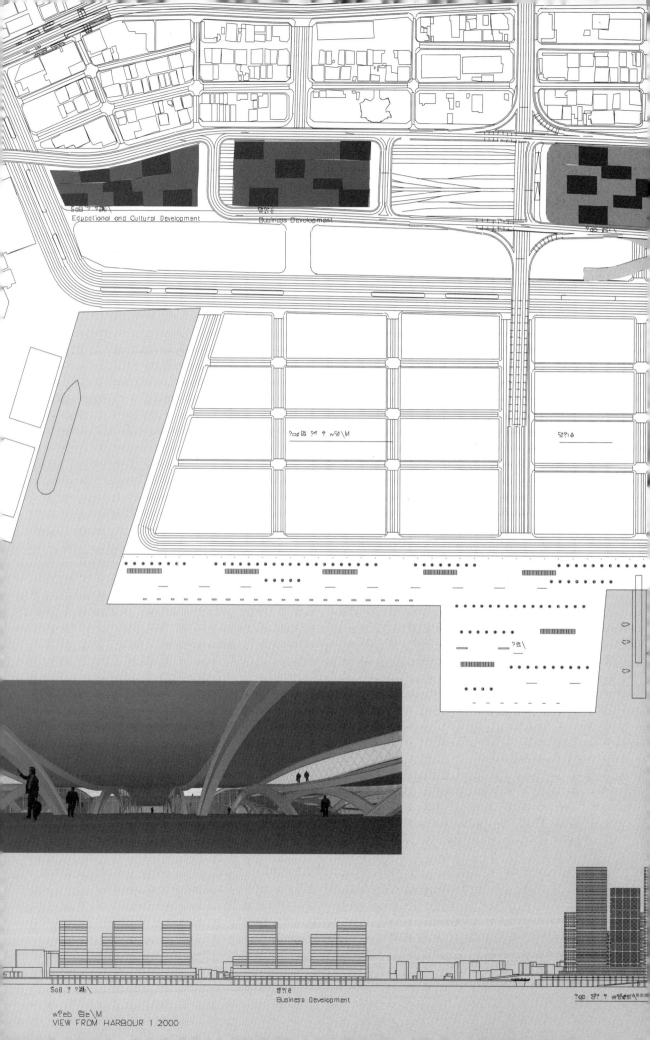

Educational and Cultural Development

Business Development

Business Development

VIEW FROM HARBOUR 1 2000

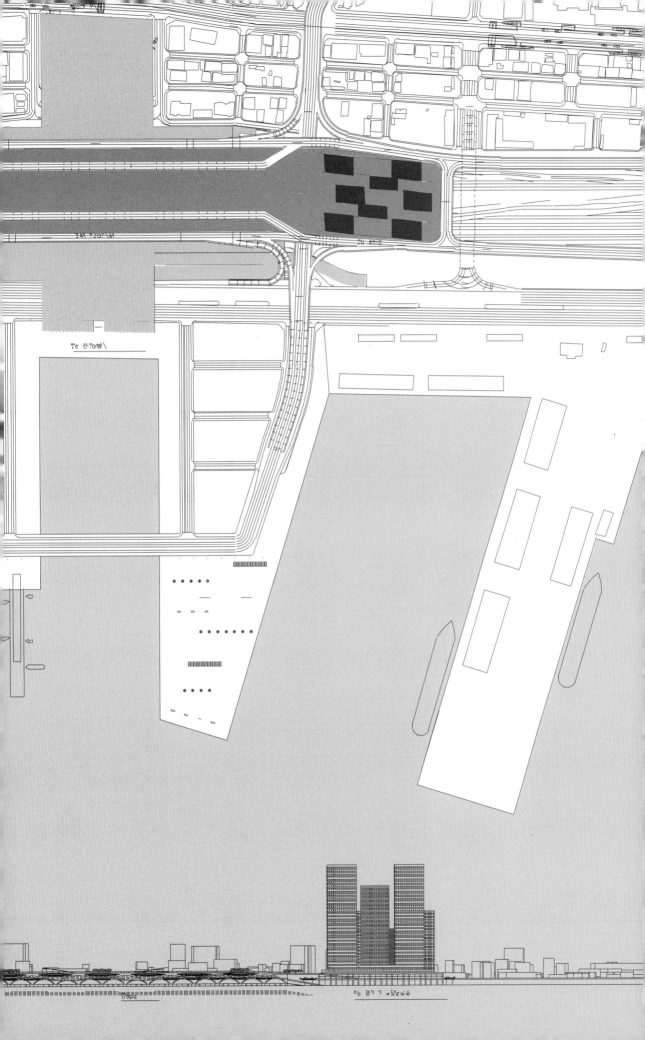

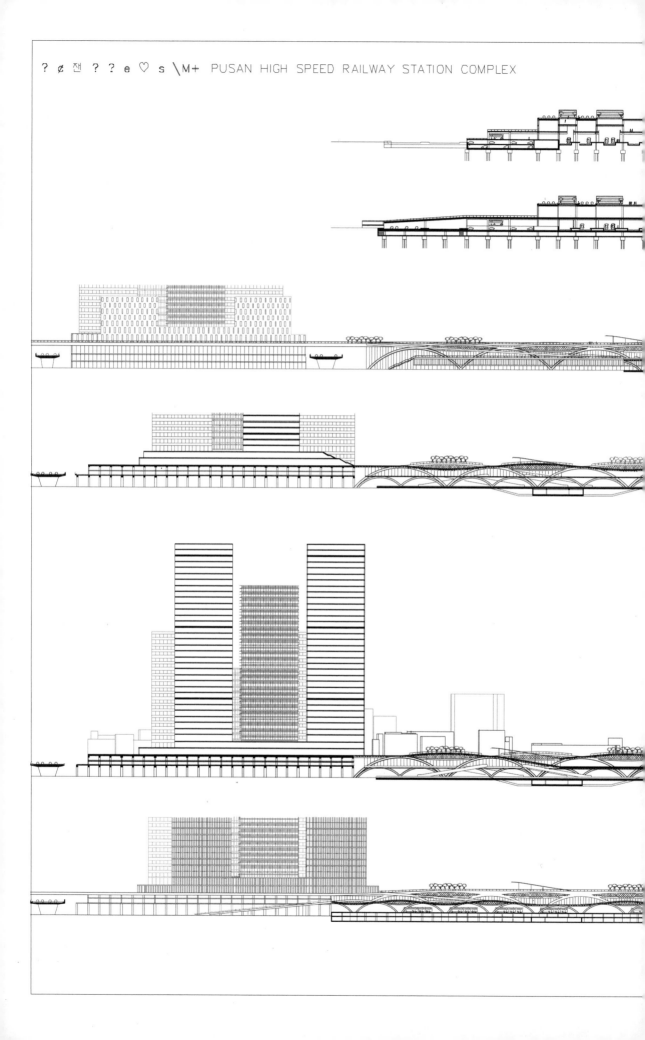

PUSAN HIGH SPEED RAILWAY STATION COMPLEX

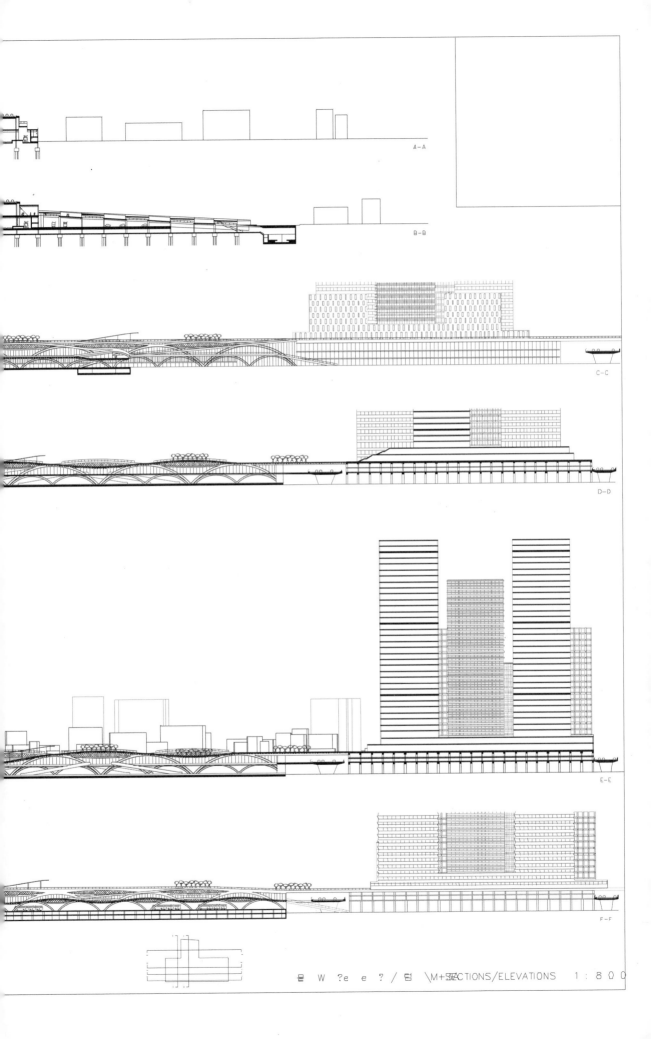

A-A

B-B

C-C

D-D

E-E

F-F

W ?e e ? / \M+SECTIONS/ELEVATIONS 1:800

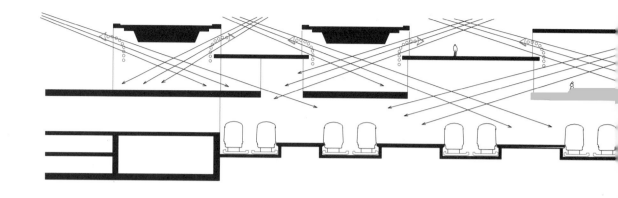

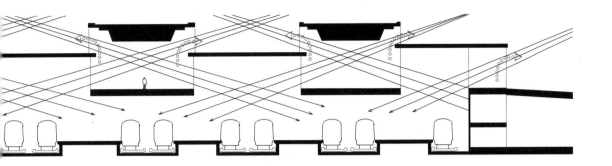

←	?繪í SUN PENETRATION
◁₀₀₀₀₀₀₀₀	贈碇 VENTILATION

?ae\U+253C碇 \U+2563 ?ae?繪í
NATURAL AIR AND SUN PENETRATION

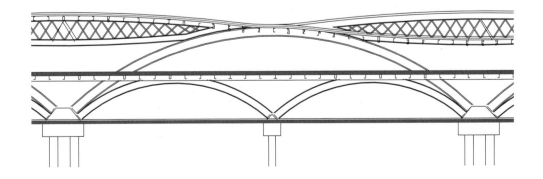

This project extends the architects' on-going research into new spatial models that would provide more open infrastructures for urban life than those of the past. Where the tradition of railway stations would monumentalize travel with great halls and conspicuous objects set into the city, FOA's proposal treats the terminal as an extension of the urban ground — a shredded surface of woven undulating bands striated in the direction of the tracks. This structure serves to connect different transportation modes smoothly to each other (regular and high speed trains, subways, buses, taxis, and parking) as well as to the city and waterfront. An artificial park on the terminal's roof lifts the ground over the tracks to link the city with the water and regain visual propriety over the bay. Rather than fixing the image of the station in a symbolic object, this project extends the public landscape of the city into a dense yet fluid labyrinth of mobilities, connectivities, and frameworks for urban experience. By dissolving the station into the city, this tapestry of opportunities is seamlessly and invisibly integrated into the flows of life for hundreds of thousands of people for whom travel has become everyday, no longer an event but still harbouring latent potential. Future urban development is strategically concentrated in two micro-cities at either end of the platforms. Extruding the organizational structure of the station into an irregular striated matrix, these clusters of towers would intensify the urban life of the area and would provide the station with an indirect visibility, its monumentality figured as the void between them. — D. M.

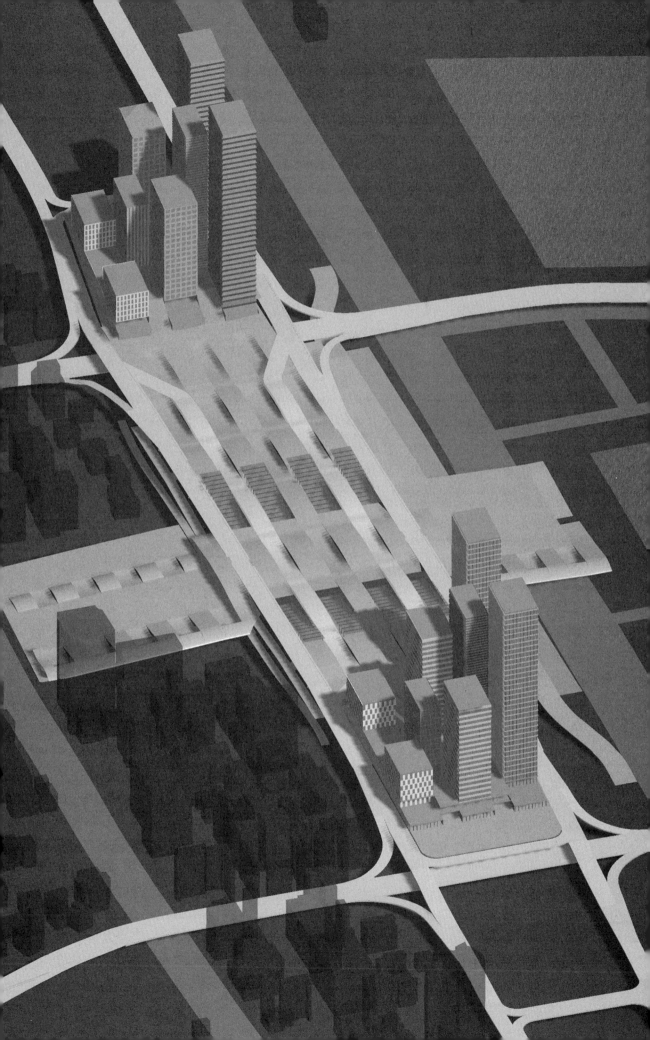

A Natural Extension

Vivian Flynn

In 1979 Vivian Flynn embarked on a project titled *A Natural Extension* — planting hundreds of Canary Island Pine seedlings in an area measuring eighty-five feet by two hundred four feet, following the contours of the shadow cast by the SST Concord. Vivian Flynn contends that the airplane shadow is "not out of place anywhere" — it has become a *natural extension* of the modern experience.

There is a certain poetics of displacement in Flynn's work. The airplane's shadow indexes the exponential speed that is the mark of our century, and yet it also represents the jet-lag that is the ponderous growth of a natural world. The reach for the heavens of these flying Canary Island pines evoke our Platonic dreams — a song of flight and release, liberating us from our terrestrially-bound condition. The technological and the natural conflate — a world (as constructed) and earth (as presented) — *A Natural Extension* tests the viability of the open space between these conflicted terms as well as our relationship to the ethical space between the two.

— C. H.

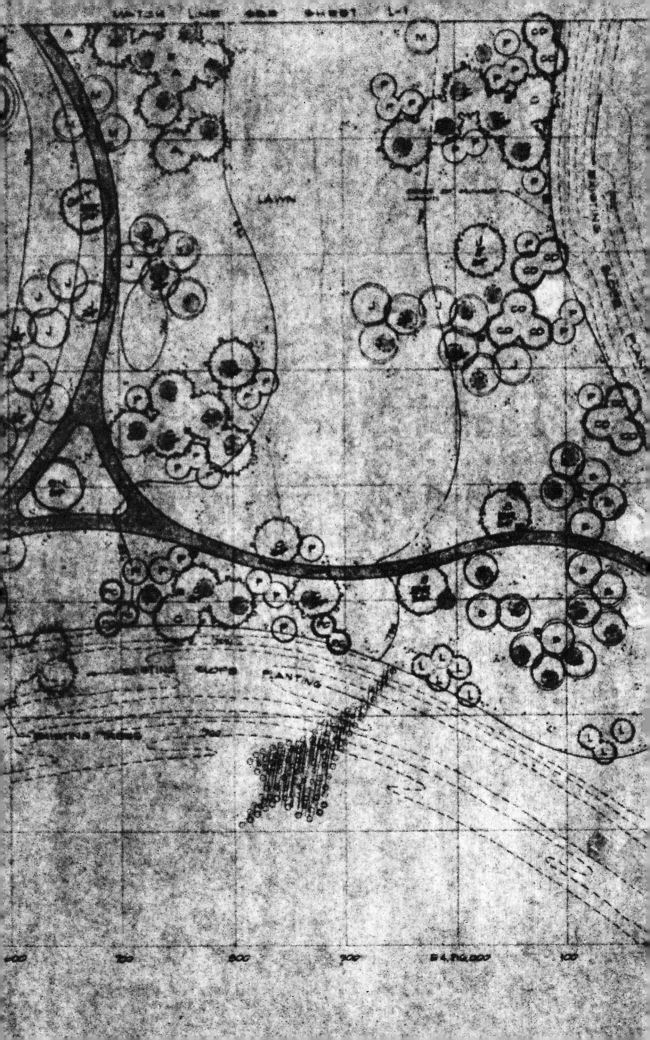

Cybermonde: The Politics of Degradation
Paul Virilio interviewed by Philippe Petit

Excerpted and translated by Julija Sukys

This text was originally published as *Cybermonde : la politique du pire* (Paris: Les éditions Textuel, 1996). The full text is forthcoming in an English translation by Michael Cavalieri (Semiotext(e), 1998. PO Box 568 Brooklyn N.Y. 11211).

The loss of the world or how to retrieve the body proper

Phillipe Petit: How does your understanding of time fundamentally differ from that of philosophers like Paul Ricoeur and Gilles Deleuze?

Paul Virilio: Ricoeur and Deleuze are philosophers, whereas I'm an urbanist. I don't say this out of modesty, because philosophy is born of the city. It isn't born in marshes, in the middle of the ocean or in the mountains, it's born in the city. I'm a man of the city and the question of time and the inscription of this time in a given place occurs in the city. St. Augustine's *The City of God* is, in a sense, a book about urbanism. Not a book about holy urbanism, but one simply about urbanism. There are no politics without cities, without the history of cities. The city is the major political form of history. My work is a work on narrative, but also on journey. Perhaps this is the difference between myself and Ricoeur, but not Deleuze. I do not work on object and subject — that is philosopher's work — but rather on the journey. I have even proposed to inscribe the journey [*trajet*] between object and subject and to invent the neologism "trajective" to go with "subjective" and "objective." So, I am a man of the trajective and the city is a place of journeys [*des trajets*] and trajectivity. It is the place of close proximity between people, of the organization of contact. Citizenship is the organization of journeys between groups, between people, sects, etc. When we say that citizenship is tied to land and to blood, once again we forget the journey, meaning the nature of the proximity which links human beings to one another within a city.

The immediate proximity that comes with the agora, the forum and the parvis; metabolic proximity with the horse; mechanical proximity with the train and the transportation revolution; and finally, electromagnetic proximity with globalization and the real time which carries it to real space. All of history has been an urbanization of the borough, the city, capital, metropolis, and today, the megalopolis. We've seen the tragedy that this brings about in the suburbs.... Catastrophic urbanization takes form once the city spreads out too far.

Yet, despite the Internet and electronic highways, we do not ask ourselves whether or not we can urbanize real time, whether or not the virtual city is possible. If the answer is no, then we are setting ourselves up for a general accident, the accident of history, the accident of accidents that Epicurus spoke of in relation to history. If, through the globalization of telecommunications, we cannot urbanize the real time of exchanges — that is, the live city-world — the real-time city-world, history and politics will be at stake. This is a great tragedy. I am not saying that it is a foregone conclusion, I'm simply asking the question.

You quote St. Augustine; does this mean that for you the refiguration of human time begins only with the existence of the city in its major political form?

Exactly. I'm a man of the city-form, a formalist because above all I'm an urbanist. Urbanism has been much criticized for being formalist because it gave form to societies — on the whole, we have seen what this produced — but we forget to say that this also gave rise to Venice, Naples, Bologna and the wonderful cities of the Middle Ages. Two questions come to mind: first of all, will there be a cyber-*città* after the cine-*città* and the tele-*città*? If the answer is no, is it over? *Finita la comedia*, as the Italians would say. Next, is form still possible if we lose place? Can *hic et nunc* endure when one loses *dasein*? When one loses it for oneself, one loses it for the other. There is a danger surfacing — in fact, it's the fulfilment of Nietzsche's hope, which goes against Christ's statement by turning it on its head — *love your foreigner as you love yourself.*

The question of neighbour and foreigner is the question of the city. My neighbour is the person next to me and the person with whom I create and defend the rights of the city. Those outside the city are effectively strangers, enemies, and today the question of loss comes up once again. Yes, we must love the foreigner, that is, the stranger, but not to the detriment of our neighbour!

You're not very cosmopolitan…

I'm a "citizen of the world," I don't want a return to nationalism, but if tomorrow we begin to love only our stranger without realizing that we hate our neighbour because he's there, because he stinks, because he's noisy, because he drives me crazy and because he calls to me, as opposed to the stranger that I can click off… so if tomorrow we begin to prefer the stranger to the detriment of our neighbour, we will destroy the city, or rather, the rights of the city….

For you, the question of the rights of the city and that of the loss of the Earth are inseparable from the question of the body proper, meaning the body situated in space and time. Could you elaborate on this point?

The question of corporeality touches all of us — and I use the word "touch" specifically. There are three bodies which are prominently linked: the territorial body, which is that of the planet and of ecology; the social body; and finally the animal or human body. This makes it necessary to resituate oneself in relation to the body, to resituate one's body in relation to the other — the question of proximity [*prochain*] and alterity — but also in relation to the earth, to the world proper. There is no body proper without world proper, without situation. The body proper is situated in relation to the other, to woman, friend, enemy… but it is also situated in relation to the world proper. It is "here and now," *hic et nunc*, it is *in situ*. To be is to be present here and now.

The question of telepresence delocalizes the position, the situation of the body. The whole point of virtual reality is essentially to negate the *hic et nunc*, to negate the "here" in favour of the "now." I've said it before: here is no more, everything is now! The reappropriation of the body, which uses dance as the major form of resistance, is not simply a question of choreography, but a question of sociography, of relation to the other, of relation to the world. If not, the result is madness, namely the loss of the world and the loss of the body. Technological time-limits that provoke telepresence seek to have us definitively lose the body proper in favour of excessive love for the virtual body, for this spectre which appears in the "strange dormer window" and in the "space of virtual reality." Here looms the considerable danger of losing the other and of the decline of physical presence in favour of an immaterial and ghostly presence.

Godard used to say that the Houphouët-Boigny Cathedral was already an image of synthesis. Could one not say of Patrick d'Arvor, that he is already an image of synthesis? I mean that even before falling into the virtual, he's preparing himself for it!

What's more, beyond the television and its decor, the entire city is teetering on the brink of the virtual, and with it, the individuals who are preparing to live there. The city has always been a theatrical apparatus with the agora, parvis, forum, drill ground [*place d'armes*], etc. It was simply a place where we could be in community, a public place. Today, television replaces the public space with the public image, and the public image is expelled from the city. The public image is not in the city, or for that matter, in the "tele-*città*," the already virtual city where we pretend to cohabit because we watch "*20 heures*" [the news] together. I believe that what is at stake behind the question of virtual space is the loss of the real city. I am an urbanist and for me the real city is the site of the social body, the site of population. Today, 80 percent of the French population is assembled on 20 percent of the territory, and tomorrow that figure will reach 90 percent. And it's on a world-wide scale that the city is attracting population. Therefore, a kind of city of cities is constituted: the city of telecommunications, the city of the Internet. Aside from the virtual bubble of the market economy which is generated by program trading, by automatic quotations, stock exchanges, a virtual urban bubble develops where public space has definitively yielded to the public image. And the propaganda surrounding the Internet and electronic highways seeks to urbanize real time just as we de-urbanize real space. Our cities, not only Saõ Paolo or Calcutta, but equally Washington and the Paris suburbs, are in an absolutely catastrophic situation. Today, they are on the brink of implosion. There is a tendency toward the disintegration of the community of those at hand in favour of the absent — the absent who have abandoned themselves to the Internet or multimedia. It is an event without comparison. It is one of the aspects of the general accident. The fact that we are closer to those who are physically so far away than those right next to us is a phenomenon of the political dissolution of mankind. We now see that the loss of the body proper brings with it the loss of the body of the other in favour of a kind of spectrality of the physically removed person, of him who is in the virtual space of the Internet or in the window of television.

Are you not being slightly alarmist? Are we really so obliged to surrender to the technological apparatus that surrounds us? Are we condemned to perish?

I have no ready-made solution, because these situations are beyond us. What I can say is that we cannot indefinitely lose the relation to the body, that is, to physical corporeality, as opposed to physiological, and we cannot allow ourselves to lose the relation of the body to the world because of teletransmission. I believe we've reached a limit. I think that the realization of absolute speed infinitely imprisons us in the world. The world is shrinking and already there is an emerging sentiment of incarceration that young people may not yet sense. Foucault's master concept of the eighteenth century — that of imprisonment — dates not from the eighteenth century, but from the twenty-first. Once we have all the interactivities we want, once we can go to Tokyo in two hours thanks to supersonic air planes, it's obvious that the feeling of the narrowness of the world will quickly become unbearable. We will have lost the grandeur of nature. This is an *unbearable* occurrence. To lose one's body to autism or schizophrenia is also unbearable. Now, I believe that because of technology, we are in the process of losing both the body proper and the world proper in favour of the ghostly body and the virtual world respectively. The question which arises is that of re-establishing contact. Earlier I said that there is no gain without loss. The world being a limited space, the day will come when the losses become unbearable, and the gains non-existent. The twenty-first century will probably be the century of this discovery: that the losses will overpower the gains. The loss of the world proper and the loss of the body proper will have to be compensated for, because it will have become unbearable for all. Not only for the poor, who already find themselves in an impossible situation, regressing incredibly, in underdeveloped countries as well as our own, but even for the rich: going to seaside resorts as if that meant a discovery of the sea; jet-setting — an exhaustion of the world! To rediscover the tactile, the sensation of walking, the feel of rock-climbing, of navigation (Gérard d'Aboville, the rower, is a kind of prophet) these are signs of a different kind of divergence, of a return to the physical, to the material, signs of a rematerialization of the world.

Seeing as we've been robbed of terrestrial space, could we not imagine a glorious escape to the sky?

This was one of the hopes behind deterrence. After the conquest of the air, which permitted World War II, the conquest of space permitted deterrence. It is because of the fact that the Americans ended up dominating in space that the Berlin Wall fell and that we found a kind of peace through deterrence. In a way, escape into space was also a loss of Mother Earth, of the world proper, and an attempt at going to colonize other planets, other satellites. "A great colony means a great navy." ["*Qui dit grande colonie dit grande marine.*"] An extraterrestrial colony means great astronautics! I believe that today this illusion has already disappeared. *Apollo 13* is no fluke. We are heroizing an accident. I find that very positive. I've read the astronaut Jim Lowell's memoirs. The crew is about to overshoot the Earth because they don't have enough power to propel themselves back into the orbit that will allow them to return. The astronaut asks his colleagues the following question: we only have one last shot with the rocket, it's possible that it won't be enough to get into the orbit that will allow us to re-enter — what do you want to do? They all answer: we prefer to burn in the highest strata of the atmosphere, to return carbonized to the Earth, than depart into the great cosmic void. It seems to me that this choice translates quite well the necessity not to return to the Earth, but to return to a real space and to the world proper, meaning the body proper, as the body and world proper are inseparable.

Isn't this return to the world proper something of an illusion?

My work is that of a limited man who must treat a situation without limits. A man who became interested in speed at the moment we achieved maximum speed, three hundred thousand kilometres per second. I'm incapable of imagining this situation in terms of propositions. I can only say "no." The problem is this: isn't the question of pain following anxiety a question of reality? No longer physical pain, in the sense of "that hurts," but in the sense of a history banging up against an impossibility. The history of my generation just hit the impassable wall of real time. We cleared the last two, the sound wall and the heat wall. The sound wall with the supersonic airplane, the heat wall with stratospheric combustion which allows us to reach the speed of liberation (28 000 km/h) and thus, to send an individual into orbit. Now history, our history, has just crashed into the wall of real time. Everything I've said in my books on the relationship between politics and speed is reaching its limit. Unfortunately, we won't accelerate anymore. Unfortunately, history will have reached its maximum speed. This is a question that I have no answer for. What I do know is that this general accident, this smashing into the time wall, is an event that will make us slow down, make us regress, go backward. This regression is an after-effect of the attainment of maximum speed. It's still too soon to say what form it will take. I have no solution to give. What I can say is that the solution will be arrived at via the urban question.

In losing the city, we've lost everything. In retrieving the city we will have won everything. Today, if there is a solution, it is in the reorganization of common living space. We must not allow ourselves to be betrayed, fooled by the tele-*città* after the cine-*città*. We must stand up to the drama and tragedy of the city-world, this virtual city which delocalizes work and the relationship to the other.

My solution is that of the urbanist that I am. Let's work in the city, and we will work at politics. In a way, this is a regression, as the word "politics" comes from *polis*, "city." We've crashed into the wall and we're returning to the city.

This desire to return to the city is honourable, but do you not have a tendency to sensationalize in your description of our technological environment?

One could find my approach negativist. It absolutely is not. Quite simply, I am obliged to work alone on negativity, while most intellectuals have already become collaborators, even promoters of technological developments. Some even speak of attaining "civilization" through information technology. So, through my work, I am trying to reset the clock. I'm not afraid of being a prophet of evil, because there is no one else who will do it.

I myself am passionate about technology, and I know that no territory exists independent of transport or information, and this has always been the case, even when we travelled by donkey. My work therefore tries to illustrate Aesop's phrase "What is the best and the worst thing? Information." Actually, he says "language," but I prefer to say that it's information.

The Internet, electronic highways, and the multinational corporations that are preparing to orchestrate the globalization of information use millions of dollars to plug their products. Faced with this, I can't help but put on the mask of Cassandra to show the hidden face of technology, its negativity.

You use the word "drama" to talk about the fusion of biology and technology. In what way do you think that computer-assisted medical intervention can be a drama?

The word "drama" is not the word "tragedy." It refers to the living. The third revolution is that of transplants. It's the colonization of the living body by biotechnology, and we have no choice but to use the word drama, because it affects the living. Cloning is a drama of the living. The receipt of a pacemaker or additional memory by the body or mind is a drama. Before elaborating on the question of biotechnology, I'd like to stress the fact that I use the word "dramaturgy" as opposed to "thaumaturgy." The thaumaturge is one who performs miracles or pretends to perform them. Today, all the thaumaturges proclaim any technological object to be a miracle, be it Bibop, the Internet, or a computer with voice recognition. The thaumaturge kings are numerous and nobody denounces them. The only one who opposes the thaumaturges is the dramaturge, who is not against the event itself, but who wants to show its drama, who wants to show that something is being lost.

There are no gains without losses. There are no technological gains without losses on the level of the vital and the living. What is real at the level of space that is minimized and reduced to nothing is real at the level of memory. We are developing additional memory, dead memories to complete, but also to replace the living memory, the memory of man. Biotechnology is the next aspect of the technological revolution. After the communications revolution, the attainment of absolute speed, and the reduction of the world to nothing, we are going toward the ultimate danger, the knowledge of the living reduced to less than nothing. By this I mean the artificial introduction of micro-objects into the body, of which the pacemaker is a precursor. You will tell me that this keeps people from dying. Of course. I have friends who have undergone heart grafts and some have pacemakers. I have nothing to say against a graft which makes it possible for a sick person to survive. On the other hand, some of these technologies sometimes become life-support technologies, which then find themselves in competition. When Marvin Minsky asserts that tomorrow miniature computers will be able to help an individual's memory, we are no longer in the domain of therapy, but in that of the man-prosthesis. Technology is colonizing man's body just as it has colonized the Earth's body. Highways, railroads and airlines have colonized the territorial body by organizing it. Today, it is the animal body that is in danger of colonization by micromachines.

You are horrified by the smart house, by la domotique *and telework, you disparage the use of a computer at home, which, according to you, reduces discovery and learning time. Can these tools not be used to positive ends in schools?*

Of course. Last year I pledged an investment to my own institution, *L'école special d'architecture* in Paris, to be paid over several years for its computerization. But the question of *la domotique* is related to that of living space, of the domicile — *domus* means house — and to the question of the relationship to the body of the inhabitant. We have had a relationship to the body through Le Corbusier and all the ancients, which was that of the *modulor*.[1] Man's body is the reference of his habitat. The ergonomic dimension of the body must be considered in its habitat. So, new technologies avoid movement in everyday life. In *la domotique*, instead of television channels, we click on the lights, the heat and the opening of the shutters. We don't go to the window to open it anymore, it's enough to click it. Therefore, there is a kind of reference to a handicapped body, no longer to a locomotive body. The overequipped able-bodied person of *la domotique*, the one who lives as the *home automation*, is the equivalent of the equipped invalid. I took part at an exhibition for the handicapped at La Villette that was called "*L'homme réparé*" ["The repaired man"]. I was surprised to see that these men in scooters were scandalized at the sight of teletechnology. I saw reactions of amazement at the fact that these able-bodied people were using the technology meant for invalids who, for example, are unable to move to open a window.

Today the screen of video surveillance is tending to replace the window. A video surveillance screen can replace a window without piercing a wall. In supersonic air planes the windows will be replaced by videos. Pilots will see the landscape through video, and unfortunately, this is what's happening to our relationship to the outside world. It used to be that when one wanted to know what the weather was like, one would look out the window to see if it was a nice day or not. Today, we turn on the television for the news or the weather forecast. But, to go even further, in 1995, thanks to teletechnology, we invented the virtual doorway. Next to the virtual window — the video surveillance screen — we invented the unthinkable, the virtual vestibule, the virtual entrance.

What is it?

It's a sitting room where you invite the ghost, the clone for a visit.

Could you give an example of it?

A vestibule is a semi-private, semi-public room. Someone knocks and you either let them in or not. It is therefore a quasi-virtual room of transition that is beside the kitchen — a warm room where we receive guests. With the data suit and the head-mounted display, we put the finishing touches on a kind of virtual vestibule that we call a virtual doorway. If two individuals are suitably equipped, they can meet each other over a distance through electromagnetic transmission. To be precise, the doorbell rings, someone is tele-arriving, so you have to put on your data suit and enter the calling room to see, hear and touch your guest, all through an intermediary clone. You will feel the sensations of the other body, knowing that it's in New York, for example, in another vestibule. The other body, of course, will experience the same sensations. It's a kind of in-home teleport. *La domotique, l'immotique* — the "domotized building" — lead not only to the disappearance of the city, but to the disappearance of architecture as an element which structures the relationship to the other. The visit of this clone has nothing to do with the visit of a man or woman. What's more, you can click it on and off. For an urbanist like me, these images are catastrophic from a political point of view and for the relationship with the other.

A few good reasons to join the resistance

We read the following in the November 4, 1995 edition of Le Monde: *"The image that many French have of their country on the eve of the twenty-first century continues to be steeped in a nineteenth century reality. They think that France is still a rural country, while the majority of its inhabitants live in cities." Do you agree with the idea that we still live in a largely rural imagination?*

Sadly, the bourgeoisie agrees with that. But I don't think that the majority of the French population — and certainly not the youth — live in that world. The city/countryside opposition made the nineteenth century, and the downtown/suburb opposition has made the twentieth. Thus, we are in this very last opposition. For the most part, except for the bourgeoisie, we are in a culture of the city in relation to the suburbs. We cannot conceive of the city without an opposition. It is either in opposition with its hinterland — this would be the nineteenth century — or in symbiosis with its hinterland, as in the preceding centuries. Today, our city culture opposes the centre to the periphery, the downtown to the suburbs. This opposition poses a threat to democracy and the culture of this *fin de siècle*.

In La vitesse de libération, *you make a comment that could complement the editorial that I just quoted: "After the no-man's land of the deserted countryside, how should one tomorrow imagine the 'no-man's time' of a planet where the interval of the local space of the continents will have abandoned its primacy to the interfacing of global time of the information highways?"*

The opposition that is on its way for the twenty-first century is not that of city/countryside anymore, nor is it even that of city/suburbs. It's the opposition of sedentary/nomadic — not in the sense of a Jacques Attali or Félix Guattari. There are those who are made sedentary by a job, who have homes, and there are the nomads, who are no longer localized, and who drift from one precarious job to another. The twenty-first century is preparing for the return of the opposition of the sedentary and the nomadic in the continent — Europe — that has been the most sedentary in history.

That which you call post-industrial upheaval is leading to the abandonment of the downtown core. How do you understand a city without a centre?

This means that a new centre is preparing itself. We are witnessing a phenomenon of migration from mid-sized cities to global cities, megalopolises. Mid-sized cities are forming partnerships with each other to resist the attraction of big cities like Paris or London. Thus, there is a creation of an archipelago of cities that benefits centre-cities which are no longer necessarily nation-capitals, but simply places of survival, where there is still work or where one can still subsist by panhandling. This phenomenon of metropolization has already existed in the Third World, where, following the countryside, small towns are deserted for the big cities. This is the globalization of urbanity. The centre is no longer the centre of the city, though certain cities become the centre of the world — Singapore is a good example of this. Suburb-cities are replacing the suburbs and the downtown core with relation to a global city. Parallel to this metropolization, a hypercentre, a metacity is claiming its place — a virtual city that exists only through the urbanization of telecommunications and which is in gestation on the electronic highways. This city is everywhere and nowhere, and each of these city-worlds is a neighbourhood, an *arrondissement* of this hypercity which resembles the virtual bubble of the economy. Therefore, there is a first movement of the metropolization of city-worlds, and a second movement of the creation of a global hypercentre from a virtual city which would make global cities of neighbourhoods, and from all other cities, it would abandon suburbs to dereliction, like the outskirts of Paris are today.

From the point of view of urban space, how would you criticize the position of Georges Frèche, mayor of Montpellier, who considers that the department is no longer a suitable unit of measurement for the codification of urban and regional politics?

Georges Frèche is an historian and he reacts as an historian. When he says: "The department was a measurement of land that a man could cover on horseback in a day. Today, its equivalent is the region, because one can go farther by car." It's an absolutely barbaric comparison. This is an error in the consideration of the journey [*le trajet*]. A journey is a unit of time and place, even an absence of a unity of space, like with telecommunications. And Georges Frèche is still back in the transportation revolution, not understanding that we're already dealing in units of telecommunication, teleshopping and telework time. Perhaps his vision is no longer departmentalist, but it's still regionalist. It is therefore not European, and even less so, global.

In your afterword to L'Insécurité du territoire, *one gets the impression that the opening of borders frightens you. To a certain extent, are you not confusing Schengen or la Grande Europe with information highways?*

I'm not unnerved by the opening of borders: I'm not a nationalist. On the other hand, I am unnerved by the suppression of borders and by the very notion of geographical limit. I see in this a denial of localization, which goes together with the immeasurable quality of the technologies of real time. When one removes a border, somewhere it is replaced. When we say "The border doesn't exist anymore," this means that we've masked the new border. And I believe that the new borders are related to the use of time, more so than to the use of space. A border, a limit, and the sectioning off of a field are related to a use of registered land or departmental space. Now, there is unfortunately a use of time that overshadows the use of space. We should be talking about this limit, rather than denying its existence. The frontier is somewhere. When we oppose Europe and Africa, in reality the frontier is now only aerial or maritime, which is a denial of geography, place, and relation. We don't plough the sea, but it has become the last frontier.

A man like Georges Frèche has forgotten that the city is the major political form of history, it has a limit. Is a city without limit still a city? My answer is no.

So Los Angeles isn't a city?

It's still a city because it has its opposition inside it. Its borders are in the interior. It is a city that spreads out over ninety kilometres. But it's not the size that creates the border, but the spot where the border is located. In Los Angeles, the borders are inside the city. They are between gangs, between social and ethnic categories...

To no longer take the exterior border of a city into account, whatever its size, is to force this frontier to establish itself inside the city.

Moreover, you quote the mayor of Philadelphia?

Yes. At the time of the first riots in the 60s, the mayor of Philadelphia said: "The borders of the country unfortunately go through the city."

Does this movement frighten you?

Totally. The moment we eliminate national frontiers, we create interior frontiers and frontiers of identity which inevitably lead to war. Thus, the city and its limit go hand in hand. The city is the law, and the law is the limit.

What does "preserving a national framework" mean once we want to gain access to a supranational state like Europe?

The nation-state is pulled in two directions, torn between two necessities. Upward, in the European, even global community, where the nation-state is surpassed by the possibility of a transnational state, and downward, through the will for regional emancipation and decentralization. This double movement is suicidal for democracy and politics. Once we uproot the nation-state both at the top and bottom, no transnational state will subsist and we will be on our way to civil war, as is the case with Eastern Europe.

   We should have gone from a national state without going through decentralization, which could only be realized in a transnational state. From the moment when the state gave the region power, and began losing its own power on a much greater scale, we've been heading for catastrophe. I am for the transnationalization of Europe, but I'm not for a simultaneous movement. If the European State had been established, perhaps we would have been able to decentralize. But to decentralize at the same time as we are creating the European community, seems irresponsible to me. This double movement was also followed in Eastern Europe at the end of the Soviet Empire. They dissolved themselves. We are dissolving ourselves in a different way. Less violently, for the moment, but it has not been proven that the feudalization of the regions will not result in conflicts similar to those of Eastern Europe — I'm thinking of Yugoslavia — tomorrow. It is, therefore, the simultaneity of the two movements that seems doubtful to me today.

   When de Gaulle held his referendum on regionalization, the French were against it. It was imposed upon them, exactly like in Czechoslovakia, where it was the politicians who provoked the division of the country. The Czechoslovaks didn't want it.

So you were in favour of conserving the centralization of the country?

Until we had moved beyond the nation-state. In making Europe, it would have been preferable to take advantage of French and English centralization, without following the example of the *Länder*[2] in Germany.

Won't the European choices in the domain of electronic highways complicate the situation?

Yes. Remember that there is always territory and property. The crisis of new technology is a crisis of property, no longer on a city-scale, but on a world-wide scale. On top of that, the electronic highways, the virtual city, and the megacity cause a final rupture, which is the ordering of real time. The constitution of an information city, of an *omnipolis*, of a "city of cities," is coming to make future geopolitics even more confusing.

   Geopolitics still reigns in the nineteenth and twentieth centuries. In the twenty-first century, we already enter chronopolitics, where real time is brought into real space. At the same time, the real space of the nation finds itself upset by the advent of the urbanization of real time and the creation of a virtual hyperville, which accentuates the chaotic quality of our era.

   The model of our world which lies behind the information delirium is Babel; the Internet is already a sign of this. The megacity is Babel ... and Babel is civil war!

You're quite a pessimist!

If I exaggerate a bit, it's because few others do. My work is interdependent with other works on the city. It only exists in relation to thought about the city, and this thought is largely guided by a belief in technological progress. The same idealism that provoked the catastrophes and devastation of the twentieth century is starting up again today. I am absolutely not against progress, but it is unforgivable, after the ecological and ethical catastrophes that we have known—Hiroshima as well as Auschwitz—to let ourselves become trapped by a kind of utopia that allows one to believe that technology will finally bring happiness and greater humanity. My generation cannot let that happen. Apart from Hanna Arendt, we haven't really returned to the debate. So, I do the work of a firewall, of a member of the resistance. Serge Daney said: "In wartime, no one talks about the resistance." Thus, new technology and the media, in a broad sense, are the Occupation. My work is one of the "resistance," because there are too many "collaborators," who, once again, are going on about salvation through progress, emancipation, man liberated from all constraint, etc.

Merleau-Ponty developed a philosophy of perception, Gilles Deleuze developed a logic of perception, and in your last book you speak of an ethics of perception which, according to you, should be taken into account. In the end, aren't you defending a politics of perception?

In any case, I'm opposed to a politics of perception which is already in place through television and through the reign of video surveillance. If I speak of an ethics, it's because the politics is already in place. A colonization of the gaze, induced and constrained by the staging of information and by the temporality and instantaneity of the editing and framing of events, seems an important event to me. But the politics of the gaze is television, and this politics will develop with new receivers.

A positive and accidental example of live television is the liberation of Nelson Mandela. He was supposed to be freed at three o'clock in the afternoon, and all the televisions of the world were poised to witness his exit from prison. The liberation was delayed. It was out of the question for the networks to throw back to the studio because nobody knew when he would be freed. Thus, television was caught in chronological time. It was no longer in the time of immediacy, because the time of liberation was unknown, and incertitude prevailed ... and during that half hour while we waited for Mandela to come out, we watched young girls play amongst themselves, we zoomed in on cars that arrived, but were empty, etc. Television had become, if not mute, at least involved in the wait once again. It was no longer situated in the event that had just taken place or that was just taking place, instead it was waiting for an event to happen. For once, it was outside of this ocular training, of this training of the gaze to immediacy, which is, in a sense, an asphyxia of the perception of the telespectator.

Of the probable war on the reconquered landscape

You are a disparager of electronic money, and the appearance of economic bubbles worries you. Also, you have often talked about the stock market crash. What does an urbanist like you have to say about money?

The return to a barter system in the suburbs and in the run-down cities of England is definitely not a good thing. It's an economy of survival, one does what one can with what one has, but I will not let myself be trapped by the side-stepping of money and the return to bartering. This is a sign of serious regression — the virtualization of economic power. Wealth and speed have always been related, one being the hidden face of the other. *Monétique* translates very well this movement that made circulation synonymous with money. Money is nothing, circulation is everything. Originally, money was not what it is today. One paid with grains of salt, shells, or small bronze coins, so with very concrete, material and, above all, countable things. Then, a first dematerialization occurred with the promissory note and the cheque. The countable loses its dimensions. Salt has three dimensions, the promissory note only has two. With electronic money, this dimension disappears in an electromagnetic implosion.

And equivalence disappears at the same time?

Yes. And the speed of circulation has taken the place of money. The production which resulted from this three-dimensional money is itself liquidated in favour of pure speculation, of a purely electronic game. The movement toward dematerialization that we've already analyzed on the level of the city and the neighbour, reproduces itself with regard to money. It's the same logic — the aesthetics of the disappearance of production and its monetary referent. With the trading programs of the stock exchanges that are now one, we have passed the speed limit of exchange. Wall Street, London, Frankfurt, and Tokyo are all a single stock exchange. All I can do is stand up against this passage to the absolute limit.

What kind of space does your relationship with the land inspire you to defend?

I am a traveller. Italian on my father's side, I don't feel that I'm a nationalist. By language, I am French, but I don't feel rooted in any one country. I'm an Italian *beur*,[3] and therefore, in exile. Nevertheless, I long to delve into the depth of space and time, the depth of relation to the other and into the thickness of meaning. Gilles Deleuze worked a lot on this level. My interest in him is undoubtedly related to that.

There's only one step between land and house...

For me it seems that architecture is the first measure of the earth. Its purpose is not to house or shelter man from bad weather, the cave did that very nicely. Thus, we live proportions that instil meaning on a neighbourhood scale, as well as a world-wide one. The proportions that we adopt in a house are the beginning of a relation with the world, and the quality of the landscape is related to the quality of architecture that we live. If I speak of grey ecology, it's because this question of proportions will be posed on a world-wide scale, but it has already been posed on a city scale. Living in a neighbourhood is not living in a house or apartment. The dwelling is the measure of proportions and, therefore, of my relation to the world. Architecture is a measure of the world.

We talk more and more about preserving the landscape. We build landscaped parks on old Citroën build-ings; in the Limousin region we are trying to save the Millevaches Plateau.... What does a politics of landscape mean for you?

Obviously, it's a job of recuperation from the effects of a great disaster: that of the European terri-tory being allowed to go fallow. Fernand Braudel said in *L'Identité de la France* that immigrants have never been a problem — all of Europe is a story of immigration — but, on the other hand, a Europe without peasants has never been seen. The European space used to be a veritable garden. Its great desertification and its lack of cultivation are a great tragedy, and like all tragedies, it must be corrected. Today, to correct means to mask. The attraction of the landscape is a nostalgia for the extraordinary gardening of *la douce France* of the peasants. Landscape is beyond the environment, but at the same time, it's a band-aid on a wooden leg. Three terms are very close: surroundings [*milieu*], soil [*terroir*], and territory [*territoire*]. Soil is the most fundamental [*foncier*][4] inscription in an urban or rural space. Territory is already an emancipation of soil through means of trans-portation or communication. The *milieu* is physical, yet abstract. Today, interest in landscape passes through the discovery of a landscape of events. We must reintroduce man and events into the landscape; if not, we will have been collaborators in the desertion of the countryside.

What is a "landscape of events"?

If you take the rural landscape, there are more landscapes than events. If you take the urban landscape, there are more events than landscapes. Many more things happen between people in the city than in the Beauce, even if there are events that cross cultures, seasons, etc. Thus, today it is essential to pose the question of the landscape of events — and not the question of land art that is hidden behind the museum studies debates of today. How do we regard what happens in that which moves little or not at all? How to conceive of space as a stage for people and not simply a more or less nostalgic object of contemplation? We must reinvent a dramaturgy of landscape. A staging of the landscape with actors, not only spectators, has to be recovered. The landscape that we lost to undercultivation used to be a landscape of events of cultivation by men harvesting the vine, wheat, etc. The history of the countryside is an eventful history much more important than that of the city, but we've forgotten it.

Could you give me a particularly liveable example of landscape?

Every man has an inner landscape. For some, it's the sea, for others it's the mountains, the countryside, or the desert. Each person has his own inner tableau. My inner landscapes are the coastline and the desert. I'm a shore man, not a sailor. I need a clear and changing horizon. My favourite landscape is the coast of Brittany with its cliffs and this conflict between solid and liquid. I also like its meteorological character as it changes with wind and light. It's a relative landscape, a landscape of interface between the land and sea. A place where relativity acts through dynamic and static forces.

And the desert?

It resembles the sea. It gives the feeling of our presence on a planet. I like landscape where one feels the planet, where the territorial body of the planet earth is perceptible on a reduced scale. I like a place that gives a glimpse of the global, and I like the global when one can perceive it starting from the local. We shouldn't lose one or the other, but keep both together.

Translator's notes

1 The ideal body whose proportions were used by Le Corbusier as the measure for all of his architecture.
2 *Länder*: term used for the member states of the Deutsches Reich in the constitution of 1919. The term came back into use in 1945 in the Federal Republic of Germany.
3 *beur*: a *verlan* (a form of slang whereby certain syllables of a word are inversed) version of the word *arabe*. It signifies a person born in France of immigrant parents from the Maghreb.
4 fundamental (*foncier*): a play on words. It means both 'fundamental' and 'land.'

Communication Park

Dennis Lago

Images by Public Thing International

> Outside facing the city, the arena displays a lifeless wall; inside is a wall of people.
> The spectators turn their backs to the city. They have been lifted out of its structure
> of walls and streets and, for the duration of their time in the arena, they do not care
> about anything that happens there; they have left behind all their associations, rules and
> habits. Their remaining together in large numbers for a stated period of time is secure
> and their excitement has been promised them.
> —Elias Canetti, *Crowds & Power*

Canetti's description will be familiar to anyone who has attended a large, staged event where a mass of people has assembled with a common interest. The "arena" experience would seem to be a cultural constant and, in fact, Cannetti's analysis claims this ahistorical relevance: all detail has been stripped away with the clear implication that what remains is essential, and thus timeless. But consider events at Toronto's major stadium in 1993. At the end of that year's television season forty thousand people gathered to watch the final episode of the sitcom "Cheers" at the city's largest public venue, the Skydome. The spectators here turned their backs not so much on the city as on each other. Their experience of gathering was mediated almost completely by the massive screen. At intervals the roving eye of a television camera fixed on a section of the audience and transmitted their image to the "Jumbotron." Only this enticed people to behave as a crowd: cheering, waving, shouting, until the spotlight illuminating them went out. Outside the camera's frame of light the crowd was stagnant, indifferent to its own presence and potential.

Of course, in the case of the arena the question is not whether this suspension of potential is to be welcomed or condemned. (In Canetti's description we can only view the crowd's promised "excitement" with apprehension.) What needs to be registered here is the power of communication and information technology to radically alter our experience of public space even to the point of

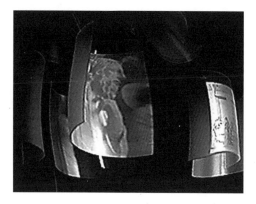
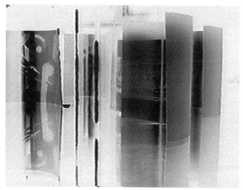

nullifying the visceral experience of gathering in one place with forty thousand others. And if this is true of the arena, what of the "structure of walls and streets," the "associations, rules, and habits," out of which Cannetti's citizens and these atomized spectators have been "lifted"? How has communication and information technology transformed our experience of public space in a more general sense, beyond the towering walls of the arena?

As the Skydome example suggests, communication and information technologies have led to an increasingly mediated social life, an eroded sense of place, and so an impoverished civil experience in both a moral and aesthetic sense. But to formulate an answer in terms of technology alone is akin to attributing the Coliseum with the power to incite bloodlust in Roman citizens. To make technology culpable is to accept the proposition that its power has been fully realized, that its potential is exhausted by its commercial applications. To propose the opposite — to uncover the salutary potential of the information and communication technologies that are transforming urban experience — is to situate these technologies within a society whose dominant interests are served when their potential to enrich experience is thwarted. Thus situated, technology is revealed not as ascendant over, but as subservient to long-standing and all-too-familiar imperatives.

In "Speech and the Silence of the City," Raymond Ledrut describes this society in the following terms:

> In opposition to a more concrete urban world where urban space is at the same time
> political and everyday, the city is submitted to the norms of an abstract space which cor-
> responds fairly precisely to the constitution of a political organization — the State —
> external to the daily activity of citizens and to their attachment to the places they live
> in. The dominant class of today is closely linked to the State and very feebly rooted:
> this is the neo-bourgeoisie which transforms all places into a space both commercial
> and planned, the space of organized quantity. There is no longer any land, there are
> only plots [Ledrut, 125].

What Ledrut describes as the state also encompasses corporate governance since both institutions operate and survive by quantifying public space. This "space of organized quantity" appropriates public space through the addictive ideas of necessity, functionality, and efficiency. Urban morphology is "submitted to the norms of an abstract space" not simply by being quantified. These abstract norms are codified in the monumental grid of the "plan" and the sub-systems of managerial infrastructure that take form within it: roads, sewers, zoning, etc. A building is given form because of the functional order of the parking garage below, or a community is planned around the carrying capacities of fibre-optic lines. How we create our urban environment is determined by the values attributed to these sub-systems. As a pervasive structure this immediately suppresses growth based on the intrinsic qualities of place and immediately precludes the city's creation as a collective oeuvre, as "unmanageable growth."

It might seem that these managerial sub-systems and the technical fields associated with them are of purely technical, and not political, significance. But even the most apparently practical technologies can allow political action of the most unmanageable sort to be effectively controlled. During the Toronto riot of May 1992 police utilized traffic to restore control. They first divided the crowd according to block structures by bottlenecking the traffic at main intersections, then quickly released the flow of automobiles into the pedestrian crowd. Traffic signals became powerful instruments of control, easily utilized because they have the power of social habit and not of direct authority. In this way the apparently objective utility of the "grid" in which we live applies a powerful mapping dictum upon public consciousness.

Under managerial infrastructure we essentially inhabit maps and—as the above suggests—maps always carry an agenda beyond the purportedly objective framing of information. Maps engineer control, which has more in common with predictability and profitability than with living. In fact, mapping is an early example of how public space becomes appropriated through an abstract representation of space that is monumental both in its scope and in its ability to eclipse all existing or possible alternatives:

> In European peasant societies, former commons were subdivided and allotted, with the help of maps, and in the wilderness of North America, boundary lines on the map were methods found impossible to challenge. Maps entered law [Hartley, 285].

Presented as an objective service, mapping claims an immediate centre and maintains and deploys principles of inclusion and exclusion: a perpetual marginalization machine. Maps became a peculiar hybridization of both law and currency that charted activities and placed value on the place of their materialization.

The same process was at work in the gradual development of maritime navigation and here the monumental nature of Ledrut's "abstract space" is only more apparent. The seas were originally travelled on nomadic principles based on the intrinsic qualities of wind, sky, and water. Environmental phenomena were read not for signs indicating relative position, but for the temporal events these phenomena augured: a storm, a landfall, the discovery of a fishing ground. In fact, the space revealed in such contingent knowledge allowed only for the sort of episodic movement we find in oral narrative. Programmatic, imperial movement required forms of navigation that monumentalized the ocean into an ever-present position and quantified it: the gradual development of magnetic bearings, latitude, and longitude. As with the mapping of the land, a grid of semantic order was laid over this "smooth space par excellence" and, with the grid, a way of living based on a deep relation to place perished [Deleuze & Guattari, 479].

In terms of contemporary urban experience, mapping principles have evolved into "location technologies" [Stone, 36]. Now clusters of data serve us as "magnetic bearings" in the urban landscape. When we use credit cards, security passes, health or bank cards in conjunction with service instruments such as automated teller machines, computer terminals, or direct debit devices we contribute to a burgeoning reference geography which locates bodies in relation to contexts, not in them. We create a sort of meta-urbanity, a paradoxical urban experience in which we find extreme individual isolation in the midst of extreme visibility, extreme accountability, and indistinguishable or "placeless" locations.

The interrelated networks of constantly renewed data created through this system—a system that is largely dependent on public space to provide it with physical interfaces—represent a powerful new form of mapping, a subtle and unforgiving new form of regulation. Like earlier mapping, it represents a "perpetual marginalization machine," but it is all the more powerful because

  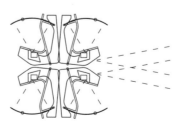

its striations are no longer limited to the three dimensions. Where participation in public life once required the ownership of land by both law and social norms, citizenship now entails the "ownership" of a trace of one's presence through overlapping and now "converging" fields of data. Ledrut's formulation — "There is no longer any land, there are only plots" — should be updated: There are no longer any plots, there are only paths.

Of course, Ledrut's concern lies with the "concreteness" of the citizen's actions, the degree of meaningful participation allowed him, and therefore his attachment to place. Under the guise of providing us with services location technologies establish the relative worth of citizens — and so the degree of participation allowed each of us — in a far more thoroughgoing and unforgiving way than hitherto experienced. As such, they represent a further entrenchment and refinement of social stratification. But it should be recognized that in Ledrut's formulation the "neo-bourgeoisie" lives in a world of "plots" along with the disenfranchised, however much it benefits. Both classes are equally resident in an abstract world, equally alienated from a "concrete urban world where urban space is at the same time political and everyday." Our main concern lies then, not with the emerging definition of citizenship as such, nor even with the unsettling prospects of surveillance and control that location technologies offer the corporation and the state. Our concern lies with the most apparently anodyne feature of location technologies: by creating an increasingly efficient feedback system by which our experience of and participation in urban life contributes to the refinement of a totalizing urban design, location technologies bring the realization of a completely managed environment into view.

Civic health requires public spaces that resist the fixed interpretations required by the imperatives of predictability and profitability — spaces that are directly lived and formed. And yet, it may be that technology itself offers us new forms of participation, new spaces not yet appropriated by our managerial elites, and new ways to circumvent corporate and bureaucratic control.

In the early phases of its development and growth virtual space seemed to offer just this. As is well-known, the Internet was originally conceived by the military as a decentralized communications network that could withstand heavy damage. Yet, the Internet quickly became an incubator of communities based not around shared physical space, but around shared interest or purpose. The academic and research users who had access to it constituted an elite. Nevertheless, the newly developed forums required active participation and a deep relation to the discourses carried on within them. Furthermore, the space that had opened up in virtual reality initially seemed difficult to quantify and commodify and so seemed resistant to managerial control.

The appearance of the World Wide Web represented the end of managerial tolerance of such a direct utilization of technology. With it came the establishment of private commercial networks, government censorship, advertising, statistical surveillance, demographic analysis, and risk management. The community that utilized the Net before it became the "information super-highway" bemoaned its commercialization, but its voice has been drowned out. The current preoccupation with security and bandwidth on the Web signals its incorporation into existing management

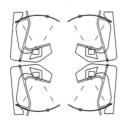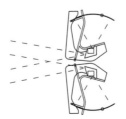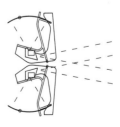

paradigms. It is seen primarily not as a public space, but as a means to more efficiently deliver conventional goods and services or pre-packaged information (such as complete programs in the proposed computer without memory.) Passive consumption is replacing participation and is being sold to us, along with the Web, as the fulfillment of interactivity.

This eclipse of a thriving unmanaged community by commercial interests is hardly unprecedented. The fact that this community was formed in and around new communication technologies should be enough, however, to indicate that technology does not itself dictate the uses to which it is put. And the eclipse of this community offers at least a momentary drama in which technology has appeared in the streets without its "courtiers" — the managers who would identify themselves with technology's power and present themselves as indispensable to its realization.

"Communication Park" was an attempt to heighten this momentary drama by proposing it be read as a political conflict over public space. In part this was to be achieved by literally bringing the technology out into the street. The site of the installation was propitious: an empty lot in Toronto's commercial core along Yonge Street; the city's north-south axis. Despite its prime location, the lot had remained undeveloped for a long time and so seemed ripe for reclamation. Coincidentally, the installation was also to occur during the 200th anniversary celebrations of the surveying and construction of the street itself. Yonge Street, the world's longest road, remains the most enduring legacy of the Imperial Grid Survey which quantified the immense lands of the undeveloped colony. A great tangent drawn with no relation to the lands it traversed and the peoples that inhabited them, the street represents a monument to the abstractions of colonial power. Thus, it seemed to be an ideal venue from which to question the conditions to which civic space must conform; to contest the legitimacy of the commercial interests manifest in the urban landscape surrounding it, and the abstractions that buttress these interests.

But if the site itself was charged with political relevance, this was not sufficient to initiate reflection on dramas of appropriation. After all, the grid laid down with the road itself literally created the colony which gave rise to the modern Canadian state — not in spite of, but because of its monumental illegitimacy. The site represented, at most, a suggestive gap in the fabric of an axiomatic and therefore all but invisible abstraction. If the archaeology of the site was to be uncovered, this could only be achieved by way of a less remote contest over effective ownership of public space.

The park was to challenge the image, text, and sound monopolies of the commercial space that surrounded it by providing an arena for public expression and debate, thus giving access to the participatory communities of the Internet. For this reason, the site was to have two addresses: a street and an electronic address. And by reclaiming a portion of the urban grid for this virtual community — newly threatened by commercial and managerial incursions — the park would attempt to situate the battle over the use of this technology within a long-established pattern of appropriation. By uniting two loci of public action — civic space and virtual space — it would illuminate both.

   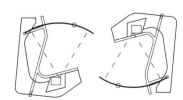

Physically, the park was to develop around a number of projection surfaces and around standards emitting audio messages. The former were envisaged as nine feet by fourteen feet sections of arced Lexan glass sandblasted to produce a surface capable of receiving a projected image from a conventional computer interface. The latter, housed in weather-proof casings, would cycle through curated content and would project contributions received at the park's Internet address and through on-site terminals. Content was to reflect a variety of contexts including the on-going debates of "newsgroups" and specifically a forum to be established on a local server. The audio standards would similarly cycle through aural contributions submitted by poets, musicians, community activists, or simply individual users of the park who wished to contribute. In all cases the contributions would represent a direct authoring of place and so demonstrate information technology's ability to determine space without creating the mass inertia of the Skydome event or the placeless fixity inherent in location technologies.

The objectives of such a project and its potential effect on our civic life must be weighed against the near complete dominance of commercial interests which characterizes our age. After eclipsing countless local, national, and indigenous cultures, capitalism and the abstract, monumental space it projects seems to be gaining the potential to cover its own traces, to eclipse even its own history. That the Luddites' cause is now commonly understood as a sort of intransigent backwardness indicates not merely the uncontested dominance of Ledrut's neo-bourgeoisie. It indicates that we cannot even articulate the question the Luddites found so pressing: "Who and what will technology serve?" Their struggle — one that is not against technological progress as such, but that is against a managerial elite which has chosen to interpret technology's usefulness according to its own narrow interest — has become incomprehensible in a post-industrial world. With the blurring of class divisions the impetus, and thus the ability to critique technology has waned and the abstract world of "plots" (and now of "paths") is becoming unassailable. In such a world resistance can find little purchase. However, if the citizen is not to become indistinguishable from the consumer, this critical project must continue.

Works cited

Elias Canetti (1960), *Crowds and Power*, London: The Penguin Group

Gilles Deleuze and Felix Guattari (1987), *A Thousand Plateaus: Capitalism and Schizophrenia*, Minneapolis: University of Minnesota Press

J. B. Hartley (1988), "Maps, Knowledge and Power," *The Iconography of the Landscape*, Denis Cosgrove and Stephen Daniels, eds., New York: Cambridge University Press

Raymond Ledrut (1986), "Speech and the Silence of the City," *The City and the Sign: An Introduction to Urban Semiotics*, M. Gottdiener and Alexandros Ph. Lagopoulos, eds., New York: Columbia University Press

Allucquére Roseanne Stone (1993), *Sex, Death, and Architecture*, Architecture New York, November

Delightful Horror!

A Visitor's Guide to carPARK at the Horseshoe Falls

Pina Petricone

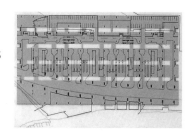

Niagara Falls have historically provoked meditations on the sublime. While varying in their expression, what has largely tied these meditations together is the association of the Falls with what has been called the "natural sublime." From within this frame, the Falls have been defined as an awesome force of nature that inspire existential contemplation and difficulty. In particular, Niagara Falls are ascribed with the power to precipitate a vertiginous fear in the observer. This is not only because of the magnitude of the Falls, but because, in their nature, they stand as a reminder of the limits of thought and existence.

It can be argued that the Falls of the late twentieth century have all but disappeared as a natural object for sublime contemplation. If only to re-affirm long familiar images and sentiments, 12,000,000 people still arrive each summer to experience the authentic tourist attraction, the Horseshoe Falls. These visitors continue to measure their experience against their expectation of sublime emotions, only to be disappointed, of course, by their lack of appropriate appreciation. The adventuresome traveler of the nineteenth century has been replaced, it seems, by the more passive, consumerist, pleasure seeking twentieth century tourist. Every moment at the

750,000 USA GALLONS OF WATER DROP

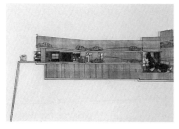

ticket booth Standing in the throng of people on the pavement, immediately above the white uproar of the cataract, one can't help wondering, in fact, if there isn't some therapeutic or self-defensive intention in all the rubbish with which the spectacle has been surrounded. What else could one do with it? In making such a stupendous gesture, nature embarrasses us... We are not explorers, we are not believers ... we are not nineteenth century romantics, we are just tourists.
— D. Jacobson

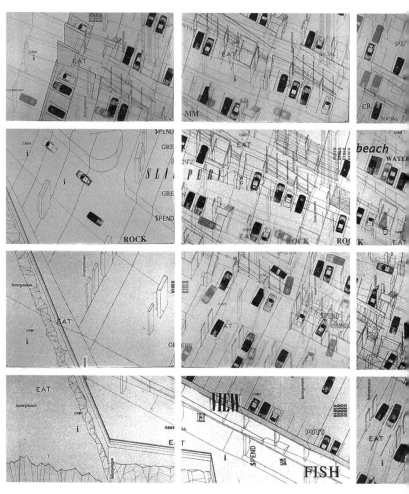

EAT "When danger or pain press too nearly, they are incapable of giving any delight, and are simply terrible; but at certain distances, and with certain modification, they may be, and they are delightful, as we every day experience."
— E. Burke

Level 1

o u t e r   l i m i t

OND, WHILE 12,000,000 PEOPLE VISIT THE FALLS EACH SUMMER

MM the resulting passion is Astonishment — "the state of the soul, in which all its motions are suspended, with some degree of horror." Described as a passion, astonishment is compared to the ultimate passion of fear. "No passion so effectively robs the mind of all its powers of acting and reasoning as fear. For fear being an apprehension of pain or death, it operates in a manner that resembles actual pain." Thus, sublime effect is gauged according to degrees of mental debilitation — often via terror.
— E. Burke

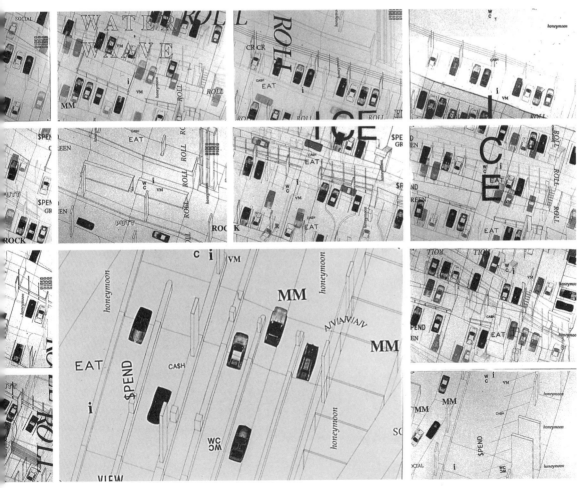

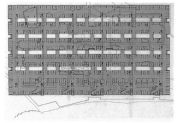

AVERAGE DAYTIME TEMPERATURES

ARE:

ROCK "The only difference between a cliff and a wall, a rock and a monument, was that of intention and self-conscious design."
— Anthony Vidler

beach "Niagara Falls is simply a vast unnecessary amount of water going the wrong way and then falling over unnecessary rocks. The wonder would be if the water did not fall."
— Oscar Wilde

now fetishized spectacle of Niagara is mediated by a grid of technologies, services, images, histories and desires that simultaneously trace and erase the Falls.

CarPARK is a hypothetical design that contemplates the possibilities of a "contemporary sublime" — one that via an artificial ecology harnesses the delightfully alienating crowd as the natural sublime substitute. It recognizes the loss and impossibility of recovering the sublimity of Nature, and in its place seeks to fashion a new source and experience of the sublime from the artifice of built form. Thus, carPARK works to evoke the sublime from within the crowded, carnivalesque and commodified spaces that define the modern Niagara Falls.

CarPARK is a three-level park-ing garage superimposed on the Table Rock overlooking Horseshoe Falls on the Canadian side of Niagara. A massive geological outcrop, Table Rock has been for centuries the principal site from which visitors have viewed the Falls. By occupying this site and pinching the existing viewing platform, carPARK directs attention away from the Falls and turns Table Rock's reference point inward, to the structurally ordered, yet simultaneously chaotic space of a parking lot. Adopting the logic of a matrix, the form itself is hyper-rational. It stretches two by three football fields in dimension. Its surface is bowed and striated into three levels, spaced by oblong columns that are aligned with

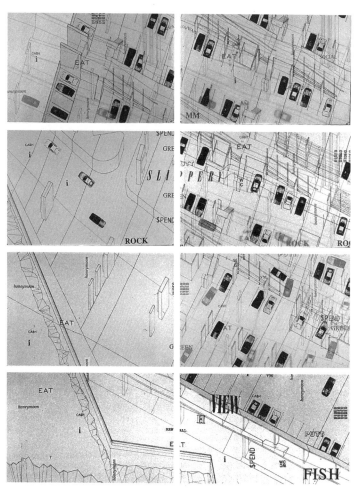

Level 2

inner limit

25°C; F–12°C; W–1°C; S–19°C; CARPARK–22°C TOTAL NIAGARA

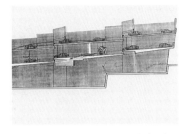

i "In reality a great clearness helps but little towards affecting the passions, as it is in some sort an enemy to all enthusiasms whatsoever. Essentially it is our ignorance of things that causes all our admiration."
— E. Burke

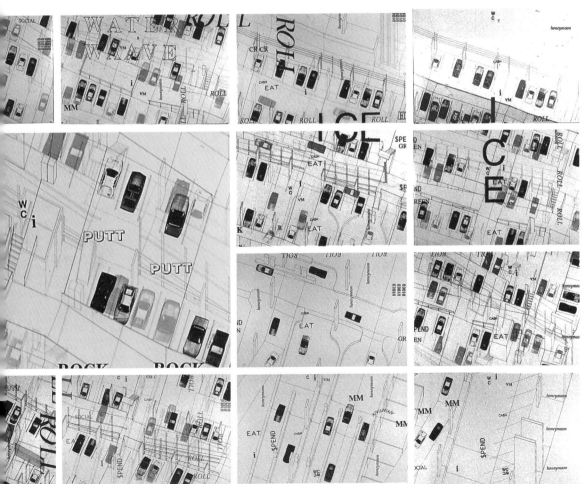

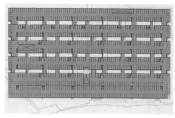
RIVER FLOW IS 1,590,000 USA GALLONS PER SECOND WHILE T

VIDEO "I wish'd an hundred times that somebody had been with us, who could have describ'd the Wonders of this prodigious frightful Fall so as to give the Reader a just and natural idea of it, such as might satisfy him, and create in him an admiration of this Prodigy of Nature as great as it deserves."
— L. Hennepin

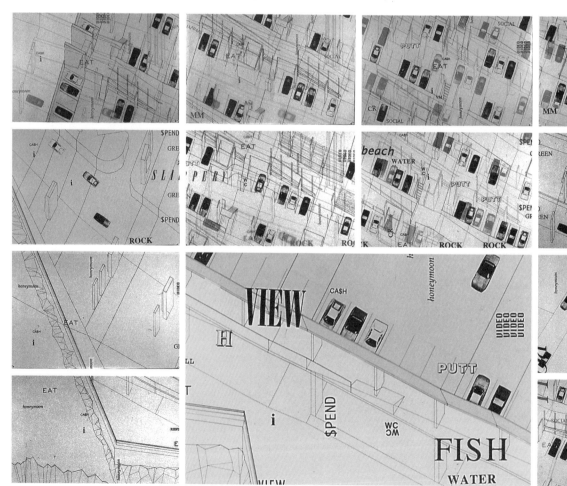

VIEW Travelers have always "carried their known familiar landscape with them and have had the trick of catching glimpses of it through the strongest lights."
— J. L. Lowes

honeymoon If, while resting on a summer afternoon, you follow with your eyes a mountain range on the horizon or a branch. This image makes it easy to comprehend the social bases of the contemporary decay of aura. It rests on two circumstances, both of which are related to the increasing significance of the masses in contemporary life. Namely, the desire of contemporary masses to bring things "closer" spacially and humanly, which is just as ardent as their bent toward overcoming the uniqueness of every reality by accepting its reproduction.
— Walter Benjamin

the parking grid. The levels of the parking garage are connected by a series of roads and ramps. Ascending from the Lower to the Upper level, regulated by gates, lights and parking icons, the visitors increasingly become distanced from everyday life. The first level functions as the entrance to the carPARK. The second level is the only point from which to view the Falls; it includes a small, squeezed viewing platform and the occasional window providing spliced images of Niagara. Finally, defined as the inner limit of the carPARK, the upper level is an optically sealed enclosure wherein the outside disappears.

CarPARK institutes a total experience by replacing the spectacle of the Falls: 4000 cars compete with the flow and noise of Niagara's thunderous cascade. CarPARK incorporates all possible service, leisure and recreational facilities into its fold to create an other-worldly environment. Its internal icon-ography and relentless repetition of parts guides tourists and choreographs the flow of traffic to create strategic moments of disorienting delightful horror.

In the end, carPARK is totally ageographic: as cars travel through its various levels not only does the world outside disappear, but the observer becomes subjected to an overwhelming form of alienation. Visitors are oriented exclusively by an infinite hyper-Cartesian order of colour, sound and coordinates. The park becomes the attraction and the Falls its backdrop.

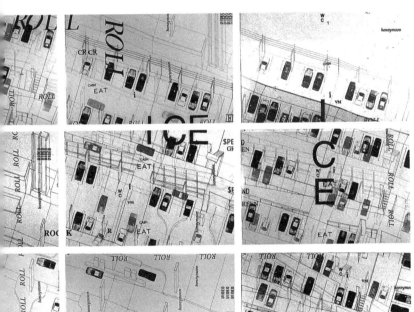

Gothic City

MVRDV, Rotterdam

Confronted with the regulatory matrix that tightly limits the production of architecture and urbanism in European cities, MVRDV point to new patterns and forms that have emerged in response to contemporary desires and modes of production, but distorted by the armature of normative conventions that would, in fact, deny their existence. For instance, the tax differences between Belgium and the Netherlands have given rise to a vast number of villas along the border, producing a linear town where no town has previously existed or been intended. Or consider that in the reconstruction of Berlin, a nineteenth-century urban model has been imposed forcing contemporary developments — much larger than in the past — to expand into vast interiors and underground concourses, which, ironically, turn the streets into minor incidents in the landscape of urban experience. Similarly, in the case of Amsterdam, heritage legislation mandates the strict preservation of the medieval facades as well as sightlines to them from across the canals, while leaving open the possibility of radically different interiors. Supermarkets, Chinese restaurants, megahotels, department stores and parking garages have begun to encroach upon the inner court-yards of the old blocks, yet remain invisible from the street. MVRDV's project, Gothic City, pushes this strategy of legitimate transgression to its extreme by first extruding the volume of buildable space from the interior of the block, and then carving it to stay just within the restrictions of the sightlines that must be respected. In this way, the maximal form of new building is projected — mutated precisely to the contingencies of the site. From a distance or a height not governed by the sightline regulations, a new "gothic" cityscape becomes visible, manifesting the quantities, scale and hidden logics of contemporary urbanism in a monstrous growth that remains, nevertheless, strictly legal and becomes, paradoxically, normative. —D. M.

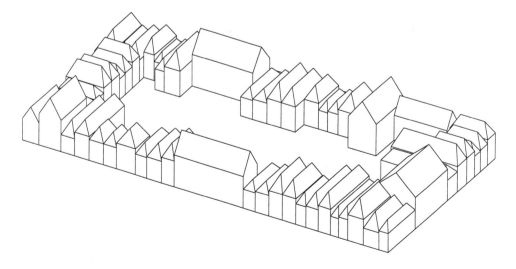

The Rules of Engagement

Catherine Bush

There was before. This is after.

She is on a plane, flying east across the North Atlantic. Curled in her window seat, she pulls a blanket around herself, face towards the oval window. Far below the moon laps at tiny waves. The lights in the plane are dimmed. Figures squabble on a row of movie screens, like reflecting mirrors, in cabin after cabin, accompanied by a whisper of voices, a chorus, from people's headsets. The engine and all the attendant machinery of air travel throb and whine, a constant sound that every so often changes, introduces a new pitch and drone, and the sound is like the vibration of fear that travels with her. She would have worn dark glasses except, on a night flight, it would only have looked suspicious. She has travelled under her own name because she had no idea how else to do it. It isn't likely that anyone will yet guess what she is up to or where she is going. Not yet. No reason that anyone will be waiting to stop her in London. And once there, well, she intends to disappear.

In the dimness, she rises from her seat, squeezes past the bodies next to her, pads down the aisle to the back where there is, mercifully, a toilet empty. The thrum of the airplane travels up through her feet. When she locks the door, the light flickers on and she peers towards the mirrored wall in front of her, touching her face lightly with her fingertips. A young woman in a flowered dress with long dark hair presses her square jaw, her wan cheeks, her high forehead, stares out of the mirror in shock and furious wonder.

There are invisible wings out there in the dark, wings that no one else can see, wings that trail from her shoulders and carry her in flight across the sea. Or, no — turbulence streams out behind her like a comet tail. She sees, through a scrim of leaves, two figures: one, tawny-haired, stands across a clearing back in Toronto. He holds a pistol. The other, dark-haired, lies sprawled on the ground. Blood soaks through his jeans. From his hand, too, springs a glint of metal.

As she slips back to her seat, her heart beats fast and shallow. She longs, now, to be prepared for anything. In the thick of a ravine — this is earlier, in the dozy afternoon of a freak Toronto heat wave in late September — the same tawny-haired young man stands before her and rips off his shirt with a look of such ferocity that she is astounded, ready to leap towards him or away. From his pocket, he pulls out a little blue-handled knife, tugs it free of its sheath. Without warning — before she could stop him, will he hurt her? — he turns the blade on the bare pink skin of his chest and carves into the flesh. Blood wells up — lines, a circle. Two letters, an A, an O. He dances in front of her, scarred, bloody-chested, arms thrown open wide, taut with pain and longing. "Alpha and Omega," he calls out. "From the beginning to the end. Because I'll love you forever, Arcadia."

The trick, she thinks, as she wraps the airplane blanket even more tightly around herself, is to believe you can begin again.

* * *

No one ever guesses what I do.

What I love is the expression on people's faces when I tell them, that instant of vulnerability and revelation, before they manage to recompose themselves. Sometimes the shift is as small as a quiver of the mouth, the flicker of an eyelid, a pulse of fear and dismay or fascination and surprise, but it's there nevertheless — a transformation.

"What do you do?" people ask. At dinner parties or pubs, the friends or friends of friends or strangers—an epidemiologist, a journalist, a psychiatrist, a botanical gardener, a man who mends musical instruments, a woman who choreographs the artificial stars at the planetarium.

I had been invited to a party by my friend Colin, an artist who, in order to support himself, runs his own video surveillance company. A drinks party, as they say in London, at the flat of a couple who both work as photographers' assistants. After handing me a glass of white wine, Colin disappeared in search of canapes into the next room.

There was almost no furniture in the flat, or, if there was more, its owners had hidden it, and what remained was draped in plain canvas broadcloth. A gilt-framed mirror hung above the mantelpiece. Black tulips—dark purple, actually—rose from window boxes outside the windows.

A man approached from across the room, a youngish man in a linen jacket of forest green and green-framed spectacles to match. His pale hair was slicked back. I had worn what seemed like suitable cocktail party wear, a long skirt that fell slim and silky over my hips and skittered about the ankles of my black lace-up boots. This is, in any case, the sort of clothes I like to wear. Dark red lipstick, of course—I hate to go out without it. My dark hair was pulled back in a loose knot. When I talk to people, I watch them closely, gauging their faces for a response, lightly touching the tortoise-shell combs tucked into my hair. Searching for the end of a thought, I'll pull out a comb distractedly and catch in the loose and wispy pieces. None of this is a disguise, although sometimes people act as if it is. There are no rings on my fingers. I sound English, though not completely. At moments my vowels waver, as if turning a North American street corner. American, people ask, or assume, but no.

The man in the green jacket greeted me demurely. "Have I met you?"

I said I didn't think so. "Arcadia Hearne."

"Arcadia," he said ruminatively, shaking my hand. "No, I don't think I have met you." His name, he said, was Peter Semple, and he was an economist specializing in the field of economic cannibalism, with a side interest in poison pills. He raised his eyebrows expectantly, as if in antici-pation of — what? — my shock or titillation. "Tell me what you do."

"Study war," I said, and took a sip of wine.

"Not really."

"I do. I'm a researcher, actually, a theorist. Associate director at The Centre for Contempo-rary War Studies. In Highbury Fields." This is not something I would ever have imagined myself doing at thirty-one. Not when I was sixteen, as a teenager in Toronto, not even when I left Toronto, ten years ago, at twenty-one.

He looked startled and as if he were trying to hide it. The muscles around his eyes quivered in a paroxysm of tiny movements as he leaned closer, intrigued nevertheless. "May I ask exactly what you do?"

"Write a lot about intervention. And the forms wars take in the post-Cold War era, which often involves talking about issues of intervention." I gestured with my fingers. "You know, should an outside force intervene in what may or may not be described as a civil war, and should one engage in something you could describe as war management, or is it even possible to think of inter-vening by taking sides. That sort of thing."

"Aha."

A drift of breeze blew through the partly open window behind me like a gust of longing. A woman in a white dress stopped in the interior doorway, glass in hand, then bore down upon Peter Semple.

I have a degree in War Studies, not Defense Studies, or Conflict Studies or Peace and Conflict Studies. I like the baldness of War Studies, the refusal to hide, the refusal to talk around what we are really talking about — and we are really talking about war.

This, if people ask, I will also tell them.

I left Colin at the Tufnell Park tube station and rode the Northern line south to Camden. When I resurfaced at street level once more, the light was beginning to fade, growing long and languid, though far from dark. The sun still hovered high above the horizon. It was late May, not mid-summer yet but nearly, the air billowy and warm, evening stretching out for hours as it does at this time of year in England. I made my way north along the High Street, plastic bag of pack-aged dinner in one hand, black soft-sided briefcase slung over one shoulder and banging against my thigh.

Stalls were being closed up for the night. A few limp t-shirts fluttered in a breeze. Racks of reflective sunglasses still blindly gleamed. On the stone bridge above the canal, a boy sat hunched over a guitar, blond dreadlocks quivering as his fingers jangled chords. A pale girl in a long skirt sat beside him, a German shepherd with a studded collar slumped on the pavement at their feet.

On the far side of the bridge, at the point where a path leads down to the canal side, a black man in a rasta hat knelt by a camp stool, weaving tiny corn-rows into another girl's hair. I made my way around them, down the ramp towards the green and gelid water. Ahead of me, long, brightly painted canal boats, a tourist company's fleet, were moored side by side for the night, abutting the old tow-path that ran along the bank.

I walked west, towards home, along the tow path. Blank-eyed warehouses loomed on either side of the water. After another moment, the banks widened, sprouting grass and tufts of nettles and little yellow flowers. A duck skittered across the water, hugging the far bank.

There was almost no one about, apart from a man in a grey business suit, back to me, strid-ing some yards ahead. What I love about walking by the canal is that it's like falling out of the city you know, like tumbling down a green vein, into a hidden artery that runs through the heart of

London. You're entering border country, city but not city. People disappear around corners on the canal path, never to be seen again. Or they appear as suddenly: a crowd of school children materializes without warning, yammering under a rainbow-painted bridge.

Some days I'll walk for miles by the canal, from Camden, through the Islington detour, to Limehouse, and back again. In some ways, it calms me, assuages me, haunts me. The canal reminds me, I suppose, of the ravines in the city where I grew up.

My phone began to ring as I unlocked the second of the two locks on my front door, top and bottom. As I pushed open the door, the ring, that two-note English purr, broke off and the answerphone clicked into action. I set down my bags. "Hey," said a voice, "it's me."

I lunged across the desk. At least in a small flat — a basement flat — it never takes very long to reach the telephone. "I'm here." Breathlessly. "Wait just a moment."

"Cay," sang out my younger sister Lux. "How are you?" A garble of other voices filled the air beyond her, as if she were in a train station or an airport. Or, for that matter, in the TV station where Lux works in Toronto, though I would not have been surprised to hear her say she was at the Camden tube stop, ten minutes away, or the offices of Euro Music TV, mere blocks from there, or anywhere else in the wide, wide world. You never knew with Lux. She had a habit of unexpected annunciation. Whenever her voice sprang without warning out of the telephone, I imagined her floating up above the earth, transformed into recombinant flecks of energy, ready to bounce down via satellite into any number of noisy cities at once.

"I'm fine," I said. "Where are you? Or do you want me to guess?"

"Want to guess?"

"Nairobi." She'd rung me once before from there to tell me she'd be arriving in London the next night.

"Nope," Lux said.

"Sydney." She'd rung me from there, too, heedless of time zones, at two o'clock in the morning.

"I don't know if you're getting warmer, Cay."

Pulling out my desk chair, I sat down and stared at the map of the world tacked to the wall above my desk. "Right." I could make out some of the voices behind her now: someone shouted, We're shooting, while someone else counted down, Five, four, three. "You're in Toronto. But you'll be in London tomorrow."

"Oh, almost bingo," Lux said delightedly. "Day after tomorrow."

"Do you need somewhere to stay?"

"No, it's business," Lux said. "We're staying at the same place we stayed in last time. That kind of grungey hotel near Picadilly. Well, it's OK. So do we need to make plans now or can I just call you when I get there?"

"How long will you be here?"

"Three days. Then we're flying to Johannesburg to shoot some stuff there."

"Are you? Ring me when you get in — only, Lux, please — don't leave it until absolutely the last minute."

"I won't," she said. "I'll call — I'll ring you as soon as I get in."

Arcadia. Lux. What sort of people would give their daughters names like these?

Our father was the one principally responsible. Benedict Hearne. When I was born, my parents were still living in Ottawa, before moving north, up the Ottawa River, to a little town upstream from the nuclear research station where my father had begun to work. Here all the families of the nuclear researchers lived in a town created for them, a tiny, perfect town, a suburb dropped down in the middle of the woods. Our streets were crescents of white bungalows. Our school was a spreading brick low-rise from whose flag pole hung the quivery red maple leaf of the Canadian flag and a green flag emblazoned with the grinning face of Elmer the Safety Elephant. On the road into town, it's true, there was a security booth and a long, mechanized arm that, when down, blocked all traffic but, by the time we moved there, people were stopped and questioned far less routinely than they had once been.

In Ottawa, my parents had lived in a tiny apartment not far from the Rideau Canal. When they met, in Fredericton, New Brunswick, my father had just completed graduate school and gone to work for Nuclear Energy of Canada, producing pilot studies on sites for possible nuclear power stations. My mother, Anne, was waiting tables in a fish and chip café, saving up money in order to travel across the country she'd just landed in. She'd been born on the island of Malta, of parents who mingled French and English and Jewish and Spanish blood between them, although her parents moved, when she was two, to the South Island of New Zealand. Travelling genes, she said, hybrid genes, although as an adult, I think she longed as much to settle down. My father had grown up partly in Toronto and partly in Boston, where his father had worked as a mechanical draughtsman. His mother was born in Italy, his father a Canadian raised in England. Another hybrid.

My father believed that naming children was not something that you undertook lightly — that names should mean something, herald something, have a certain resonance. My mother has told me how he would come bursting through the door of their tiny apartment, snow in his dark hair and nestled in the tweed of his winter coat — a man in motion — and shout out possible names. Bliss. Adam, if it was a boy. Atom. Or Molecule. My mother had argued against my name, on the grounds that I was bound to be teased in the school yard, but my father had argued back that children will be teased no matter what their names are, no matter how common or peculiar, the ingenuity of childhood will always think up something, and I tend to agree with him.

His passion convinced her — the light in his face, the fervour stretched tight beneath his skin; his brightness, his idealism, his enthusiasm. He would lean beside her at the kitchen counter, she said, or kneel down by her rocking chair, pressing his cheek to the sleeve of her butter-yellow cardigan, dreaming a landscape for her. He'd rub her fingers and ankles, swollen in the late stages of pregnancy, and pull loose the barrette holding back the nearly black, growing-out bob of her hair. A blue fluorescent strip light burned above their heads. A north wind hissed in the pine tree outside the window. I don't believe he imagined idyllic fields and rolling green hills dotted with sheep, no quaint pastoral landscape — but giant trees and brilliant light and bare knees of granite poking up through the earth.

What did she believe in? Love. A progressive world. The future.

I switched off the portable telephone and set it down on the desk. So Lux was coming. Rising to my feet, I swivelled the Venetian blinds closed, hiding the outside stairs that led down to my door. I flicked on the standing lamp beside the old gas fire place, and sank down on the tiny sofa, loveseat really, backed against the far wall. Loveseat, ha.

Unlacing my black boots, I tugged off first one, then the other. I unrolled my black nylon socks, and, with my thumbs, massaged the arches and soles of my bare feet. Then, barefoot, I padded down the narrow hall to my tiny bedroom, where there is room for no more than a double bed and a closet and an electric fan. Nor is there a window — but the walls, like all the walls in the flat, are painted glossy white, and the fine cotton bed linens are white, and mostly I light the room by candlelight, which makes it pleasant enough.

Opening the closet, I unzipped my silky skirt and stepped out of it, unbuttoned my thin linen blouse and pulled on instead the sleeveless white cotton dress that I often wear about the flat, now that the weather has turned warm, in these days of new English drought and heat. I don't know why it should seem so extraordinary, to some people, that a woman who writes about war should love the sensual feel of silk or linen or old cotton next to her skin, or that I should rinse my face with rose water or salve my arms and legs with botanical creams. But it does — to some people.

I have a friend named Lola Race, a military historian specializing in World War Two aerial bombing techniques, who likes to wear bright stockings — fuchsia, lemon, lime — and short-skirted black suits, and complains how often men seem surprised that she shaves her legs and underarms.

Now if we were war correspondents, there wouldn't be this problem, Lola says. And it's true. For female war correspondents are naturally deemed to have a touch of glamour about them. It isn't seen as incongruous. They may be fascinated by war but they are also women who thrive in dangerous situations — who race through sniper fire gathering stories about human suffering, who win the confidence of hot-blooded, sex-starved young men brandishing AK-47s, who dash lipstick over their lips by candlelight in a room in the partly bombed-out Sarajevo Holiday Inn.

I'm not sure I'm a woman who thrives in dangerous situations.

In the kitchen, at the back of the flat, I opened the fridge and poured myself a drink: a glass of water with a splash of vodka in it. I pulled stray strands of hair out of my mouth.

Waning sunlight still fell through the glass panel of the back door and the window above the kitchen table. Long rays trembled across the garden, too — for this is indeed a garden flat, though the garden is a very small one. When I opened the window and unlocked the back door, the sweet scent of early honeysuckle drifted in; a hint of rose; the piney tang of the ancient rosemary bush. Blossoms from the gnarled and tiny apple tree at the bottom of the garden lay strewn across the patch of grass. Orange nasturtiums glowed.

I dragged a chair into the open doorway and sat down. Someone, several houses away, was practising the saxophone. I closed my eyes. When you live by yourself, there is no one to tell you when bits of food are stuck between your teeth. There's no one to notice if you stuff newspapers in the freezer instead of food, or get up at two a.m. to water the garden, no one to stop you from eating a pear and letting pear juice dribble pleasurably along your arm or down your chin.

Whenever Lux came, she unsettled things. She roused the possibility of rupture, a threat of invasion, and could not help herself. She came trailing shreds of Toronto, shreds of the past, stirring the air around her like the flutter of a butterfly's wing.

Whenever I knew that Lux was coming, I began to dream, and always the same sorts of dreams. I dream of Evan and Neil. My radar angels — this is how I think of them. Like the ghost images that appear on an airplane radar screen and befuddle a pilot. There but not there. Although in some sense they are always there, carried with me, encoded in neuropeptides and combinations of proteins, mapped in muscle, in sinew, in tissue. I'm not sure there's ever any complete escape.

I dream of Evan, sometimes Evan as he was when I left — tawny-haired and small and muscular — and sometimes Evan as he might now be. I run across a field towards him, grab him by the shoulders, shake him until his jaw begins to rattle. We'll be in a room together. I'll graze my hand across his cheek. Or I'll be walking down a Toronto subway platform — Rosedale, or Davisville, one of the outdoor ones where you can feel the wind — towards Neil slouched on a bench, hands bunched in the pockets of a wool overcoat, pulling it tight around him. I can't see the blood but I know it's there.

Making my way in a dream along a dark alley, I'll hear — it's like having all the breath squeezed out of me — the sudden throb of a motorbike engine igniting. The clatter of a streetcar in its tracks. The click of a gun.

* * *

I came to London seeking refuge, believing it was possible to escape the past, frightened that at any moment my new life could be taken away from me.

I worked odd jobs, the sort where you can get paid in cash, under the table. I made sandwiches in a tea shop owned by a Polish couple, sliding the sandwiches into little white paper bags and twisting the corners into ears for customers to take away. I served quiche with leeks and Bosnian pie. I worked in a pub near the law courts, one which barristers frequented, their hair flattened or sticking up in twigs after being squashed by a wig all day. I avoided the sharp gazes of policemen. I had never heard of War Studies, although I had abandoned a four-year history degree, discarding history back in Toronto. I wanted to cross an ocean, a border, and transform myself. I let my voice slip a little, vowels rounding, as if I were holding different-shaped fruits in my mouth. I copied the voices I heard around me. Right, I said and felt the thrill of metamorphosis, the seductiveness of reinvention. Brilliant. Ring me. I dowsed my new London A to Z in the bathtub to make it look more weatherworn, once I'd discovered that everyone, not only tourists, carried about maps of the city. At least my name seemed to attract less attention, its weirdness accepted as an English sort of eccentricity.

Nine months after I arrived in London, I met Martin Cale in a vegetarian café just off the Tottenham Court Road. As he sat down across from me, on the far side of a refectory table, the sleeve of his raincoat tipped over the sugar — raw sugar, naturally. Together we scooped sticky palmfuls back into the bowl. Out of embarrassment or residual boldness, or perhaps as an act of contrition, he started talking to me. "Are you all right?" he asked with a note of such solicitude that something opened wide inside me. This was, at that moment, exactly what I wanted — to be regarded with deep attentiveness and asked, "Are you all right?"

And again, when he opened the door to me, the first night that he invited me to his flat. "Are you all right?" He stood there, dark-haired, long-limbed, in an unironed shirt, arms crossed tightly over his chest. He had a bony, narrow face. For an instant, I felt a frizzle of caution — as if something might be exposed that I didn't want to be, some glimpse of flagrancy or recklessness or disarray, some hint of what I'd abandoned by fleeing Toronto, which made me want to hide this all the more, to start anew and prove that, yes, indeed, I was all right.

* * *

Three weeks after we met, I moved in with Martin Cale, which was made easier by the fact that I had been living in a squalid shared flat miles west of central London and where Martin lived, in Brixton, I rather liked. Three months after that, I married him.

He worked as an electrician — that was how he put it. He did not say he was an electrician but made it clear that although this was how he made a living, there were other things he also did. He'd once played bass in a band called the Poisoned Lollies. They had put out two albums and had one single reach the charts before the band collapsed amidst the usual acrimony. Now he played session gigs occasionally, wrote music reviews for magazines, and composed for small strange performance companies. As an electrician, he worked in television sometimes, though more often he worked on reno jobs, warehouse or flat conversions. And because this was the mid-eighties, there was a great demand for the work he did.

He liked to cook, if almost always fish fried in great slathes of butter and dollops of wine. When he stood at the cooker, his shoulder blades sloped a little, at the top of the long curve of his back. At night, the freckled expanse of his shoulders glowed smooth in the blue cast of moonlight. He was filled with wishful enthusiasms, and an eagerness to please. He could be moody, and stubborn sometimes. At others he slumped around or lolled indolently, flashing a winsome smile, or sat, nervously twisting a strand of hair at his temple, as if waiting to see what I would do. Left alone, he'd sleep until noon. At night, without his round, metal-framed glasses, his narrow eyes and the thin slip of his eyelids gave him an almost feline cast. He chewed his fingernails, only the tips, and never in front of me.

Together, we basked in our own romantic allure — and the deliciousness of other people's awareness of it. We married young, as almost no one we knew had — and not simply for immigration reasons. We knew other people who had immigration marriages — a Danish friend of Martin's, for one — but no one else who had married three months after meeting purely by chance in a crowded café.

I married Martin because I wanted to start anew. (And for immigration reasons.) To escape the sense that everything could so easily be taken away from me. Because I wanted to prove I still believed in romance. In love. Love did not necessarily have to lead to destruction.

I told him I'd had a falling out with my family and this was why I'd run away to London. That my father worked in the nuclear industry, though nothing military. This was, after all, in the months after Chernobyl. People stared dubiously into their milk when they drank it. Radioactive sheep roamed the Welsh hills.

We all still lived in terrible fear for our safety. Martin and I had both come of age believing our future could at any instant burn up in a flash of light. You did not have to grow up upstream from a nuclear research station to succumb to this. It's so easy these days to forget exactly what that felt like.

Now and again I sent postcards home. I wrote that I was fine and not to worry. I wrote announcing that I had gotten married. I never gave a return address and mailed each from the same central post office and since there was no telephone registered in my name, I assumed it would be difficult for anyone to track me down. Everything, I told myself, was going to be all right.

Yet at night I still woke out of dreams that I couldn't shake away. I dreamed Neil walking unscathed towards me. I dreamed myself on a rooftop, leaping between slanted gables, closing my eyes as I hurled myself across the chasm between them. I clutched the latticed wood trim that ran along the steep peaks of brick houses and when I glanced down, Evan was there, staring up at me.

I saw them on the street. My heart raced at the sight of a young man in a brown leather jacket, whose dark hair made a thick dip at the back of his neck and who lurched along with a sharp limp. Palpitations shook me as a smaller figure, with a flare of straw hair and a swift stride, blazed around a corner ahead of me. I'd be stalled by a figure glimpsed entering a bookstore or a blur of lips framed by a black cab's window.

Out walking by myself, I was convinced that someone with a gun was following me. I waited to be shot anywhere, anytime. A man would come bursting into the pub, scattering barristers, as I drew off a pint of real ale, or into the tea shop as I passed a jacket potato across the counter. He would leap out of a phone box or follow me through the retractable flaps of the ticket turnstiles and into the stations of the underground, onto platforms where smoky winds blew. Walking home by myself at night through the streets of Brixton, I carried fear and a certain fearlessness with me — past the boarded-up market, reduced now to a jumble of cardboard boxes and shifty incense sellers where during the day an automated loud-speaker blared Beware of Pickpockets; past Beauty Tandoori and the Oh So Keen Chinese Takeaway; past the cheap cosmetics shop on the corner where you gathered what you wanted in a plastic basket and the owner gave you a boiled sweet when you paid. Disaster could happen anywhere, anytime. I waited for explosions, to walk around the corner and see our building going up in smoke. Nothing would surprise me.

In the dark, as I opened my arms to Martin, I heard a little voice — a voice I tried to squelch — go, Look at me. Even as I tried to vanquish the past through touch. An arm. A leg. A nipple. Touch me.

As Martin's long-limbed body slept beside me, I felt the grip of my father's hands on my shoulders, felt him shake me and shake me. I thought of the first time Martin and I had gone to visit his parents in Suffolk, driving north and east out of London past fields smelling of fog and peat. Martin's father, a solicitor who worked for the county council, had stepped out of their red brick house to greet us and kissed Martin on the cheek. "Are you all right?" he'd asked. Then Martin's mother, who taught in a comprehensive, stepped forward, holding out both hands. "Are you all right?" The next day, outside the local chemist's, we ran into an old high school girlfriend of Martin's, a girl with a voice as bright and sweet as jam, and I listened as the two of them greeted each other — Are you all right? — the way, where I came from, we asked How are you? and expected only the most cursory answer.

In the dark, eyes wide open, I swallowed and touched my fingers to the hollow at the base of my throat. I felt like a girl in a fairy tale who has something stuck in her throat and does not know, when she opens her mouth, what will come tumbling out — frogs or stones or pearls. I slipped from the bed and poured myself a glass of water. In front of the bathroom mirror, I pressed my mouth open wide.

Back in the bedroom, I set the glass of water on the orange crate beside the bed. I pulled on the silk robe that I'd brought from Toronto, one that Evan had once given me. From the bed, Martin was watching. I knelt on the sheets beside him, tucking long strands of hair behind my ears, digging my freezing fingertips into my palms. "Martin," I said. "I want to tell you something."

He looked frightened, as if I were about to announce any one of the usual things: a loss of love or a new lover; that I was a bigamist. My own heart skittered, as if a wind blew through it. He rolled cautiously onto one side, keeping his eyes on me, shoving one hand beneath his head.

"I know I should have said something before this — it's just so hard, it sounds so outrageous." My tongue tasted like photo emulsion, as if in the midst of chemical transformation. "I left Toronto because I had a duel fought over me."

"A what?" I don't know what I expected. Afterwards I discovered how often this would happen when I told people. At first they didn't hear me; or they disbelieved me.

"A duel," I said. "It's true. I swear. With pistols."

He sat up then. "Was anyone killed?"

"Shot. Not killed. I don't think. He was in hospital when I left. But wounded quite badly, in the groin, near an artery — he was incredibly lucky."

Martin lowered himself onto his back, staring up at the cracked plaster ceiling. He seemed remarkably, unnervingly calm. "Who were they?"

"Evan." I'd told him about Evan — that I'd had a boyfriend for three years during university with whom I'd broken up at last, and it had been horrible and messy. "I met someone else right near the end. We started to get involved and Evan freaked out. He issued this challenge."

"How did you find out?"

"Someone else told me. They didn't tell me. But I never believed — "

"Where did they fight it?

"In a ravine. At dawn."

He kept staring at the ceiling. "What was the name of the other one?"

"Neil Laurier."

"He must have loved you, too."

"Martin, it doesn't change anything — "

He rolled onto his side again. "How did it make you feel?"

"Make me feel? Horrified. Shocked. Martin, it doesn't change anything. I left. I came here. I don't want anything more to do with either of them." He'd shifted once more onto his back and began twisting strands of hair at his forehead between his fingers. "It's over," I said and touched my hand to his bare shoulder. "It's history."

"Kiss me," he said. His lips looked particularly full and sulky, and when I leaned over, I caught a flicker in his eye — pleasure in the form of vindication — for this was proof, after all, that I had chosen him over the two of them.

There were signs Martin might have noticed, if he'd looked. On the bottom bookshelves, which I'd claimed as my own, I kept my collection of Russian literature — Lermontov, Pushkin, Turgenev, Chekov. Russia wasn't the only thing these works had in common. Also Pirandello's *Collected Plays* and Thomas Mann's *The Magic Mountain*. A collection of Joseph Conrad stories. Behind these, carefully shoved out of sight, I stored two other books: *A Short History of Dueling*, and *The Duel in England*, which included a brief chapter on the transplantation of dueling practices to the colonies.

I had no official accreditation that would have allowed me to present myself as a researcher at the Reading Room of the British Library. Instead, I traipsed among the second-hand bookshops on Charing Cross Road and made friends with a bookseller named Tom Frane, a beetle-eyed man with skin of vampiric paleness to whom I finally confided exactly what I was looking for. "Books about duels," I blurted. "Anything to do with duels." Ah, was all he said, as if this request were, after all, not so unusual.

I ranged across the tussled hump of Primrose Hill, where an army colonel and a navy captain had once fought a pistol duel over the merits of their Newfoundland dogs. Duels, so I discovered, had been fought over all sorts of things — points of honour, lies, women, an angora cat. I read about French duels, Russian duels, Italian duels, the barrier duel, the back-to-back duel. In turn-of-the-century Germany, three levels of insult could lead to a duel; the insult of seduction was graded at the highest level, along with landing someone a physical blow. I walked through Islington where two seventeenth century court favourites had slaughtered each other in a duel; Covent Garden and Lincoln's Inn Fields had once both been popular dueling sites. I became a dueling expert. I wondered how much of all this Evan had known.

If I'd wanted, I could have drawn up a duelist's map of the city of London. I read about a duel fought from balloons, and about the last duel fought in Toronto, in which an eighteen-year-old had died, although the words on his tombstone, still visible in the entry of St. James' Cathedral, read "killed by a blight."

Hands bunched in the pockets of my overcoat, I squinted up at the sooty English sky. What does it mean to dream more of the city left behind than the one inhabited? To run towards the thing you think you've fled?

* * *

I met Evan when I was eighteen, the autumn of my first year at university. I chose him for myself. I picked him out — picked him out by sight even before I'd met him.

One afternoon, walking along Hoskins Avenue, I saw a young man locking up a bicycle outside a college. As he knelt over the frame, sunlight caught in his hair, turning it wheaten, then even brighter, nearly white. A yellow canvas knapsack rode up his shoulders. He wore grey flannel trousers, not a private school pair but old pleated ones, from the forties perhaps. On someone else they might have looked mannered or merely idiosyncratic, but on him they had a quaint, intentional flare. His hands, shunting the lock around the wrought-iron fence and clasping the bike frame to it, were small and birdlike. What moved me was this suggestion of vulnerability, something not quite balletic, grace mixed with abruptness. Yet he moved with compressed energy, a honed purpose—as if each gesture bore weight, were the exterior sign of some interior thrust.

Two days later I saw him again, on the steps of his college, in the rain. He'd just finished a run. Slowing to a stop at the top of the steps, he heaved over breathlessly, hands on his knees—not calling attention to himself, oblivious, it seemed, to everything but his own rigorous propulsion. His hair was matted to his scalp, the skin beneath his flimsy gym shorts—the sinuous muscles of his exposed thighs—shockingly wind-chilled and red.

A week later, I went with some friends to a party at his college and left early, sick of the yeasty beer smell on the slick floors and all that desperation hiding in the semi-darkness. I'd searched with private urgency for the wheat-haired boy but hadn't seen him.

Outside there was dew on the grass. Falling leaves smelled like smoke. I walked down a small set of stairs, quelling disappointment, under a stone archway and into the college courtyard. Left behind the wa-wa of amplified music, the frenzy of people away from home for the first time, let loose on their own in Toronto. Voices rose faintly from the wooden benches at the edges of the courtyard lawn—the murmur of couples perhaps. More music wailed from a room upstairs. Longing swelled everywhere, the whole complicated dizzying surge of college life. Lit windows shone like tender, mysterious beacons.

On the far side of the courtyard, the wooden door that led into the main entrance hall stood open, propped ajar. Inside, the smooth floors were flagstone. Corridors led away in either direction beneath glazed lanterns hanging from the ceiling. The bulletin board beside me was scattered with posters for French Lessons Private Group Affordable! Toronto-Montreal Bus Tickets CHEAP!! Sweet Bird of Youth Auditions The Godfather One Screening Only!!! Friday 7 p.m. Medical Sciences Auditorium. Across the vestibule a light shone in the porter's lodge.

The main door rattled, swinging open. From his shoulders hung the same yellow army-surplus knapsack. His hair lay scattered across his head like straw. Over one thin wrist he'd shoved a pair of bicycle clips, which clinked like bracelets. No doubt I looked startled. I scrambled for purpose, a way to funnel the ricochet of yearning—any reason to be in the hallway other than what I'd intended, which was to slip out the door through which he'd just entered, down the front steps, and into the night.

Before I could say anything, he'd come to a stop, not unfriendly. "Do you know what a blue moon is?" His voice had a faintly nasal twang. His manner was blunt, but there was also a note of genuine appeal—and something unabashed, as if he were daring me to find his question strange.

"What a blue moon is?"

"Not what the expression means, not like 'once in a—' but what it actually refers to, the scientific phenomenon."

"A blue moon." As if spinning out the words a few seconds longer would offer me something—a missing piece of information. "I've probably read it somewhere but I don't—Sorry." Desolation swept me. Given this charmed, this perfect moment, I'd failed. I'd disappointed him irrevocably. I listened to the slap of his shoes over stone as he bounded upstairs to the second floor.

I found him ten days later in the library. Now and again I'd seen what I convinced myself was his bicycle locked in one of the jammed racks outside—although it was practically impossible to distinguish one scuffed red ten-speed from another. In any case, I would have trawled the reading rooms in search of him, the banks of plastic chairs in the ground-floor cafeteria, the four floors of stacks, the wooden benches by the xerox machines where people gathered to chat. Which wasn't to say I didn't study. The plague in medieval Europe. Plato's *Symposium*. Heaving my books around in my own canvas knapsack.

I found him one afternoon at a table in the periodical room, between current periodicals and encyclopedias. A chemistry textbook was propped open in front of him. He looked up as I seated myself in the empty seat across the table. "I found out what a blue moon is."

One of his cheeks was flushed—from the rampant heat of the building; from having a palm pressed against it. His lips had a delicate, roseate plushness. "Just a sec." He stood briskly, slipping the metal cap of his fountain pen back over the nib.

Outside the doors of the reading room, we found an empty corner in that odd-cornered, cement-walled building. He leaned back against the concrete pillar behind him, arms crossed.

"If there's a second full moon in a single month it's called a blue moon."

He looked down at his scuffed running shoes before he spoke. "It's funny. That's not even an old, old wives' tale, it's actually very new. Interesting, in its own way. That is, why is it circulating now, and where did it come from? But if you look in a good astronomical dictionary, that's not what a blue moon is. For a start, you need something much rarer. There's a second full moon in a month every couple of years. That isn't rare enough. But every so often, say once in a lifetime in a particular place on earth, dust particles, maybe from a forest fire or volcanic eruption, dust particles barely longer than the wavelength of light, filter the light of the moon. Filter out the red light and leave the blue. And you have a blue moon."

Dust particles barely longer than the wavelength of light. Another tide of despair washed through me. A tendril of bafflement poked up, too. "Why did you ask me if you already knew?"

"To see if you knew." Tenderness and enthusiasm gripped his face. "And you looked—" He wasn't mocking me. He seemed uniquely moved.

Already there was no going back. Already it seemed clear to me that there could be no one else like him. "I'm Arcadia," I said.

If my name surprised him, he didn't show it. "Evan Biederman," he said.

We went for walks together, heading north, away from the campus, across Bloor Street, past the old red-brick mansions of Bedford Road. Neither of us had come to the city to go to university and we felt that bond: the disjunction between those of us who already slipped knowingly through the streets and those who'd just arrived. We shared the maps of the city that we'd already made for ourselves, dotted with personal history.

"Tell me things," Evan would say fervently. "Tell me things about yourself." I told him I'd been born in Ottawa, and shortly afterwards we'd moved to the little town of Deep Creek. He nodded, as if it were somewhere he had actually heard of. I told him, as I did not tell many people, that my father worked in the nuclear industry. Usually I simply said he was an engineer, as if he built roads or bridges, spanning the fissures of geography not of atomic particles. But I was curious to observe Evan's response: this was, in its own way, a kind of test. I told him my father worked for Ontario Power but was also a member of an international team working on the development of an experimental fusion reactor. "Using tritium," he said, and nodded again—moved or unmoved? As if the differences between fusion and fission were not unfamiliar to him.

I told him that I was planning to major in history (far from the domain of nuclear science), and thinking of becoming a medievalist. That I lived at home because I hadn't been able to get into residence and I didn't have the money to move out. How, the autumn we'd moved to Toronto, the year I'd turned ten, I would take my little sister and ride the subway for hours, from Islington to Warden, St. George to Finch, leaping off at every station to run upstairs, punch the transfer machine, grabbing the paper transfers that it spat out before racing down to the platform again.

"Your mother let you?"

She'd travelled halfway round the world, I said. Geographic exploration didn't frighten her. "Yours wouldn't have?"

"Oh, sure," he said.

I told him, when we moved out of the forest and into the city, my father had promised my mother a house on a ravine and we did live in a house on a ravine, north of Eglinton, even if it was a small tributary with a drainage culvert running through the middle of it.

"Tell me about yourself," I said.

He told me he had been born in Toronto, and grown up here, although in the last two years his whole family had split apart and fled the city. He was the only one left. He had two sisters, twins named Karin and Maya, who were two years older than he was and had moved away to go to university — Maya to Boston, Karin to Vancouver. He told me about the day in March that Peter, his father, had appeared on television. It was the middle of the month, during March break. Maya was home from the Boston, the two of them sprawled on that particular evening on the lumpy old sofa in the sitting room just off the kitchen, Maya idly flicking channels on the cable box. So it was just chance that she happened to hit that particular local news broadcast at that particular moment — just as Delia, Evan's mother, appeared in the doorway, cat draped like a stole around her shoulders, a gin and tonic in one hand. A car had burst into flames on the 401 near Islington. And there was Peter, in his beige overcoat, arm around a young, dark-haired woman they would come later to know as Isobel Melo, the Portuguese investment analyst, the pearl-grey Scirocco a pyre of flames behind them, the two of them too flagrant in the ecstacy of their twin survival to be aware of anything else.

The next morning, when Evan came downstairs, pieces of furniture, books, records were marked with little red dots that Delia had placed on them — like auction items. It was Peter who moved out. He lived in Philadelphia, teaching in the economics department at the University of Pennsylvania. Delia had held onto the house, although in July she had rented it out and run off with a Buddhist art dealer named Giorgio Ferrari to Montréal.

Evan took me to see the house one afternoon and we stood outside, on Summerhill Avenue, while leaves skirled at our feet and a brisk wind buffeted us. It was bigger than our house, dark brick, the thick skeleton of a vine climbing up the front. "Gondwanaland," Evan said and it took me a moment to recall, right, the enormous protocontinent from which all the current, drifting continents had broken off. He said the cat's name was Eddypuss. He'd named the cat. His mother had taken him. "Get it? Eddypuss?" He gave a sharp, bleak, nasal laugh.

It amazed us that we hadn't met before this. We knew people who knew people even if we'd gone to different schools. As if we'd been held back by what — fate? luck? — until the right moment. Our own blue moon.

We wandered among the secondhand clothing stores that we both loved — Tresor, Tango — searching for opalescent cufflinks, antique collar pins, chiffon scarves, elbow-length kid gloves, Evan in the grip of a collector's passion. We sat in Queen's Park talking, among the falling oak leaves, while a thick mist turned to heavy rain around us.

We walked in the ravines, which Evan loved — the wild places, the unobserved places. We carried buttery croissants and brioches in paper bags stuffed into our pockets. From the forest floor, we picked up shiny conkers that had tumbled from chestnut trees, smoothing our fingertips across their silky skins. Duff, I taught him, cradling a handful of pine needles and rotting compost. I pointed out birds: pileated woodpecker, nuthatch. North of St. Clair, beyond the skinny men with sassy hips who lurked at the entrances to overgrown paths, we unlatched the wire-mesh gate that led to the Mt. Pleasant Cemetery and let ourselves in. Some days we roamed even farther north through the ravines nearer my house, tree-filled crevasses that wound behind back gardens. We dreamed of houses we'd like to own, old brick houses, with fireplaces.

We kissed goodbye outside subway stations. On the Glen Road bridge, under a fading indigo sky, we kissed while traffic raced through the Rosedale ravine beneath us. From this bridge, Evan said, years before, he and his friend Fergus had once tossed long fluorescent tubes stolen from the garbage dumpsters of the apartment towers to the south. Did you hit anyone? No, he said tersely, of course not. The press of his lips was velvety soft. Just the touch of his fingers at the nape of my neck, fingers wound through my hair, made me ache in the gut. Love, I thought.

Back in his residence room, which was unlike any other residence room I'd been in, I called home and said I'd be eating dinner at one of the colleges while behind me Evan poured boiling water into a white china teapot. On the shelf behind him stood two brandy snifters, balloons of fantastically frail glass. He'd saved them from the house, he said, when his mother had packed up her belongings. That is, his mother had allowed him to take them, along with the goatskin rug on the floor, which had lain at the foot of his bed all his life.

He lit two candles, in antique brass candlesticks, on his dresser. Above them hung a framed reproduction of a William Blake engraving: the daughters of Albion combing their hair. Evan studied English as well as chemistry, Romantic poets as well as polymerization, and while in anyone else this might have seemed an odd combination, in him it seemed anything but. And the work of William Blake, that idiosyncratic visionary, he loved with a fervent and eloquent attachment. For his poetry but more than that, more than that, Cay, for his cosmology. Here he is in the eighteenth century, this absolute radical who says he believes in the marriage of opposites, the body isn't separate from the soul, it isn't contaminated, sex isn't sinful, eroticism's divine.

We were lying on the floor. As I watched, Evan pulled a long, loose hair from the shoulder of my sweater, opened his mouth, laid it on his tongue, and swallowed it.

Then he took my wrists in his hands, rolling me onto my back — opening my arms so that he could press his head against my chest and I breathed in the humid, yeasty tang of his breath. After a moment he looked up, wide-eyed, strangely ecstatic. "Don't mess with me, Arcadia," he whispered. "I'm not interested in frivolity. You have to be prepared to be serious."

Everything ticked. The walls shone. "I'm serious," I said.

Untitled (libertad)

Phil Jackson

Lisbon Revisited

Fernando Pessoa, Álvaro de Campos,

Alberto Caeiro, Ricardo Reis,

Bernardo Soares

Translated by Paulo Lemos Horta

Álvaro de Campos (1890–1935)

Born in the city of Taviras on the coast of the
Algarve, Álvaro de Campos studied naval engineering in Glasgow and travelled widely through the
East before settling in Lisbon and founding —
alongside Mario de Sá Carneiro and Fernando
Pessoa — the avant-garde literary magazines *Orpheu*
and *Portugal Futurista*. His 1915 Futurist *Ultimatum*
to Europe proclaims the advent of a perfect and
mathematical humanity, contingent on the purging
of Europe's aesthetic and political ills — among
them George Bernard Shaw, "vegetarian of paradox,
charlatan of sincerity, cold tumour of Ibsenism."
Impressed by the force and ambition of Campos'
"Triumphal Ode," Mario de Sá Carneiro ventured
that Campos' poetry would outlast his own and
Fernando Pessoa's.

Álvaro de Campos
Lisbon Revisited (1926)

Nada me prende a nada.
Quero cincoenta coisas ao mesmo tempo.
Anceio com uma angustia de fome de carne
O que não sei que seja —
Definidamente pelo indefinido ...
Durmo irrequieto, e vivo num sonhar irrequieto
De quem dorme, irrequieto, metade a sonhar.

Fecharam-me todas as portas abstractas e necessarias.
Correram cortinas por dentro de todas as hypotheses
    que eu poderia ver da rua.
Não ha na travessa achada o numero de porta que me
    deram.

Acordei para mesma vida para que tinha adormecido.
Até os meus exercitos sonhados soffreram derrota.
Até os meus sonhos se sentiram falsos ao serem
    sonhados.
Até a vida só desejada me farta — até essa vida ...
Comprehendo a intervallos desconnexos;
Escrevo por lapsos de cansaço;
E um tedio que é até do tedio arroja-me á praia.

Não sei que destino ou futuro compete á minha
    angustia sem leme;
Não sei que ilhas do Sul impossivel aguardam-me
    naufrago;
Ou que palmares de litteratura me darão ao menos
    um verso.

Não, não sei isto, nem outra cousa, nem cousa
    nenhuma ...
E, no fundo do meu espirito, onde sonho o que
    sonhei,
Nos campos ultimos da alma, onde memóro sem
    causa
(E o passado é uma nevoa natural de lagrimas falsas),
Nas estradas e atalhos das florestas longinquas
Onde suppuz o meu ser,
Fogem desmantelados, ultimos restos
Da illusão final,
Os meus exercitos sonhados, derrotados sem ter sido,
As minhas cohortes por existir, esfaceladas em Deus.

Álvaro de Campos
Lisbon Revisited, 1926

Nothing holds me to anything.
I want fifty things at once.
With a hungry, carnal anguish I crave
I know not what —
Definably for the undefined ...
I sleep a disquiet sleep, and live the dreamt disquiet
Of him who sleeps, disquietly, half to dream.

All abstract and necessary doors have closed on me.
And curtains drawn inside all hypotheses I might see
    from the street.
On the given sidestreet my number is not to be found.

I wake to the same life which put me to sleep.
Even my dreamt armies suffered defeats.
Even my dreams felt false as I dreamt them.
Even a life alone desired exhausts me — even this
    life ...

I apprehend at disconnected intervals;
I write through lapses of fatigue;
And a tedium even of tedium itself casts me ashore.

I know not the destiny or future in store for my
    anguish without helm;
I know not what islands of the impossible South
    await my shipwreck;
Nor what literary palm trees will yield me at least a
    verse.

No, I know not this, nor something else, nor any
    other thing ...
And, in the depth of my spirit, where I dream what I
    dreamt,
In the last fields of the soul, where I reminisce
    without cause
(The past a natural fog of false tears),
In the roads and shortcuts of far-away forests
Where I supposed my being,
Flee, dismantled,
The last remains of
Final illusion,
My dreamt armies, defeated without having been,
My unborn courts, sphacelated in God.

Outra vez te revejo,
Cidade de minha infancia pavorosamente perdida …
Cidade triste e alegre, outra vez sonho aqui …
Eu? Mas sou eu o mesmo que aqui vivi, e aqui voltei,
E aqui tornei a voltar, e a voltar,
E aqui de novo tornei a voltar?
Ou somos, todos os Eu que estive aqui ou estiveram,
Uma série de contas-entes ligadas por um fio-memoria,
Uma série de sonhos de mim de alguem de fóra de
    mim,
Outra vez te revejo,
Com o coração mais longinquo, a alma menos minha.

Outra vez te revejo — Lisboa e Tejo e tudo —,
Transuente inutil de ti e de mim,
Extrangeiro aqui como em toda a parte,
Casual na vida como na alma,
Phantasma a errar em salas de recordações,
Ao ruido dos ratos e das tabuas que rangem
No castello maldicto de ter que viver …

Outra vez te revejo,
Sombra que passa atravez de sombra, e brilha
Um momento a uma luz funebre desconhecida,
E entra na noite como um rastro de barco se perde
Na agua que deixa de se ouvir …

Outra vez te revejo,
Mas, ai, a mim nao me revejo!
Partiu-se o espelho magico em que me revia identico,
E em cada fragmento fatidico vejo só um bocado de
    mim —
Um bocado de ti e de mim! …

Once more I view you,
City of my childhood vertiginously lost …
Sad and joyful city, once more I dream here …
I? But am I the same as he who lived here and here
    returned,
And here took to returning and returning,
And come here again to return?
Or are we, all the I that was or were here,
A series of bead-beings threaded by memory,
A series of dreams of me dreamt by someone outside
    me?

Once more I view you,
With heart more distant, soul less my own.

Once more I view you — Lisbon, Tejo and all —,
A useless passenger of you and myself,
Foreign here as in all parts,
Casual in life as of soul,
Phantom to err through halls of remembrances,
To the sound of rats and creaking planks
In the damned castle of the obligation to live …

Once more I view you,
Shadow which passes through shadows, and shines
For a moment in an unknown sepulchral light,
And enters night
As the trace of a ship loses itself
In the water which ceases to be heard …

Once more I view you,
But alas I cannot see myself!
The magical mirror where I perceived myself
    identical has shattered,
And in each fateful fragment I see only a morsel of
    myself —
A morsel of you and of me! …

Alberto Caeiro (1889–1915)

Like his master Césario Verde (1855–1886) Alberto
Caeiro was a native of Lisbon who preferred the
life and sensibility of the village, which he sung in
his works *The Keeper of Sheep* and *The Amorous
Shepard*. Caeiro's uneventful life in Ribatejo led
Ricardo Reis to remark: "One cannot narrate
Caeiro's life because there is nothing there to narrate. His poems are the only things which happened
in his life." The most influential Sensationist poet
of his generation, Caeiro believed sensation was
"everything," and held that thought was "a disease."
In his estimation Sensationism entailed stripping
perception bare of convention, sentiment, and
reason. Once asked by Álvaro de Campos if he was
content with *himself*, Caeiro replied: "No, I am
content." Comments Campos: "It was like the voice
of the Earth, which is everything and no one."
Soon after his return to Lisbon in 1915 Caeiro died
of tuberculosis.

Alberto Caeiro
Do *Guardador de Rebanhos*, 1914

Ao entardecer, debruçado pela janela,
E sabendo de soslaio que há campos em frente,
Leio até me arderem os olhos
O livro de Cesário Verde.

Que pena que tenho dêle! Êle era um camponês
Que andava prêso em liberdade pela cidade.
Mas o modo como olhava para as casas,
E o modo como reparava nas ruas,
E a maneira como dava pelas cousas,
É o de quem olha para árvores,
E de quem desce os olhos pela estrada por onde vai
    andando,
E anda a reparar nas flôres que há pelos campos ...

Por isso êle tinha aquela grande tristeza
Que êle nunca disse bem que tinha,
Mas andava na cidade como quem anda no campo,
E triste como esmagar flôres em livros
E pôr plantas em jarros ...

Alberto Caeiro
From *The Keeper of Sheep*

In the evening, leaning over the window sill,
And obliquely acknowledging the fields before me,
I read Cesario Verde's book
Until my eyes burn.

How I pity him: he was a peasant
Who walked through the city imprisoned by liberty.
But the way he looked at houses,
And the way he observed streets,
And the manner he came by things,
Was that of one who looks at trees,
Who lowers his sight along the street he walks on,
And walks prone to observing flowers in fields ...

Thus he felt that great sadness
Which he never admitted outright,
But walked in the city as if through the country,
Sad as the pressing of flowers in books
And the placing of plants in pots ...

Ricardo Reis (1887–1936?)

Poet of a sad Epicureanism, master of highly
wrought, metaphysical and neoclassical odes,
Ricardo Reis was born in Porto and educated by
Jesuits. A doctor by profession and monarchist
by conviction, Reis sought exile in Brazil after the
proclamation of the first Portuguese Republic in
1919. The cause and date of his death are uncertain.
Antonio Tabucchi, one of Reis' foremost critics
and translators, believes Reis to have died peace-
fully in exile toward the end of 1935. Novelist
José Saramago, however, speculates that Reis mys-
teriously passed away in Lisbon a year later,
unwittingly entangled in the revolts which spilled
over from the Spanish Civil War into Lisbon.

Ricardo Reis
Os Jogadores de Xadrez (1916)

Ouvi contar que outrora, quando a Persia
    Tinha não sei que guerra,
Quando a invasão ardia na Cidade
    E as mulheres gritavam,
Dois jogadores de xadrez jogavam
    O seu jogo contínuo.

Á sombra de ampla arvore fitavam
    O taboleiro antigo,
E, ao lado de cada um, esperando os seus
    Momentos mais folgados,
Quando havia movido a pedra, e agora
    Esperava o adversario,
Um pucaro com vinho refrescava
    A sua sobria sêde.

Ardiam casas, saqueadas eram
    As arcas e as parêdes,
Violadas, as mulheres eram postas
    Contra os muros cahidos,
Trespassadas de lanças, as creanças
    Eram sangues nas ruas ...
Mas onde estavam, perto da cidade,
    E longe de seu ruido,
Os jogadores de xadrez jogavam
    O jogo de xadrez.

Inda que nas mensagens do ermo vento
    Lhes viessem os gritos,
E, ao reflectir, soubessem com acerto
    Que por certo as mulheres
E as tenras filhas violadas eram
    Na vitoria proxima,
Inda que, no momento que o pensavam,
    Uma sombra ligeira
Lhes passasse na fronte alheada e vaga,
    Breve seus olhos calmos
Volviam sua attenta confiança
    Ao taboleiro velho.

Ricardo Reis
The Chess Players

I heard that long ago, when Persia
    Waged I know not which war,
When invasion flamed in the city
    And women screamed,
Two chess players played
    Their continuous game.

In the shadow of an ample tree they gazed
    Fixedly upon the ancient board.
And at their side, awaiting an
    Idler moment—
When one, having moved a stone,
    Now waited for the opponent—
A jug of wine refreshed
    Their sober thirst.

Smouldering houses, sacked
    Walls and arks ...
Raped, women were left
    Against fallen walls,
Run through with spears, children
    Were blood in the streets ...
But there, close to the city,
    And far from its noise,
The chess players played
    Their game of chess.

Though the messages of the desolate wind
    Brought them cries,
And, upon reflection, they ascertained
    That for certain wives
And tender daughters were raped
    In the near victory,
Though in the moment they thought this
    A light shadow
Passed by their vague and distracted brow,
    Soon their calm eyes
Turned with confident attention
    To the ancient board.

Quando o rei de marfim está em perigo,
    Que importa a carne e osso
Das irmãs e das mães e das creanças?
    Quando a torre não cobre
A retirada da rainha alta,
    O saque pouco importa.
E quando a mão confiada leva o cheque
    Ao rei do adversario,
Pouco pesa na alma que lá longe
    Estejam morrendo filhos.

Mesmo que, de repente, sobre o muro
    Surja a sanhuda face
D'um guerreiro invasor, e breve deva
    Em sangue alli cahir
O jogador solemne de xadrez,
    O momento antes d`esse
É ainda entregue ao jogo predilecto
    Dos grandes indiff'rentes.

Caiam cidades, soffram povos, cesse
    A liberdade e a vida,
Os haveres tranquillos e avitos
    Ardem e que se arranquem,
Mas quando a guerra os jogos interrompa,
    Esteje o rei sem cheque,
E o de marfim peão mais avançado
    Prompto a comprar a torre.

Meus irmãos em amarmos Epicuro
    E o entendermos mais
De accordo com nós-proprios que com elle,
    Aprendamos na historia
Dos calmos jogadores de xadrez
    Como passar a vida.

Tudo o que é serio pouco nos importe,
    O grave pouco pese,
O natural impulso dos instinctos
    Que ceda ao inutil goso
(Sob a sombra tranquilla do arvoredo)
    De jogar um bom jogo.

When the ivory king is in danger,
    What matter the flesh and bone
Of sisters, of mothers and of children?
    When the rook does not cover
The retreat of the tall Queen,
    The raid matters little
And when the trusted hand places under check
    The opponent's King,
The soul weighs the distant death of sons
    Lightly.

Should suddenly above the fort
    Appear the fierce face
Of an invading warrior, and soon
    In blood fall
The solemn chess player,
    The moment before
Is still devoted to the favourite game
    Of the indifferent great.

Cities may fall, peoples suffer,
    Liberty and life cease,
Tranquil and inherited possessions
    Tear and smoulder,
But when war interrupts the game,
    May the king not be in check,
And may the ivory pawn most advanced
    Be about to take the rook.

My brothers, in loving Epicurus,
    In understanding him
On our own terms rather than his,
    We learn from the story
Of the calm chess players
    How to live.

Everything serious concerns us little,
    We weigh the grave lightly,
In us the natural impulses of instinct
    Yield to the useless pleasure
(Under a grove's tranquil shadow)
    Of playing a good game.

O que levamos d`esta vida inutil
    Tanto vale se é
A gloria, a fama, o amor, a sciencia, a vida,
    Como se fosse apenas
A memoria de um jogo bem jogado
    E uma partida ganha
    A um jogador melhor.
A gloria pesa como um fardo rico,

    A fama como a febre,
O amor cança, porque é serio e busca,
    A sciencia nunca encontra,
E a vida passa e dóe porque o conhece…
    O jogo de xadrez
Prende a alma toda, mas, perdido, pouco
    Pesa, pois não é nada.

Ah, sob as sombras que sem qu'rer nos amam,
    Com um pucaro de vinho
Ao lado, e attentos só á inutil faina
    Do jogo de xadrez,
Mesmo que o jogo seja apenas sonho
    E não haja parceiro,
Imitemos os persas d`esta historia,
    E, enquanto lá por fora,
Ou perto ou longe, a guerra e a patria e a vida,
    Chamam por nós, deixemos
Que em vão nos chamem, cada um de nós
    Sob as sombras amigas
Sonhando, elle os parceiros, e o xadrez
    A sua indifferença.

What we take from this useless life
    Is worth as much if
Glory, fame, love, science, life ensue
    Or just
The memory of a game well played,
    And a game won
    Against a better player.

Glory weighs like a rich garb,
    Fame like a fever,
Love tires since it is serious and seeks,
    Science never finds,
And life passes and aches because it knows…
    The game of chess
Engages the entire soul, but, lost, weighs
    little, since it is nothing.

Under the shadows that unwittingly love us,
    With a jug of wine
At hand, and attentive only to the useless task
    Of a game of chess,
Even if the game is but a dream
    And there is no partner,
Let us imitate the Persians of this story,
    And, while outside
Near or far, war and nation and life
    Clamour for us, let them
Call us in vain, each of us
    Under the friendly shadow
Dreaming, each his partner, and chess
    Its indifference.

Bernardo Soares (1888–1935)

Lisbon is the protagonist of Bernardo Soares' diary
O Livro do Desassossego (*The Book of Restlessness*).
For Soares Douradores Street, where he worked as
an assistant book-keeper, constituted "an entire
life." His fragmented and incomplete journal details
his wanderings through the streets of his favourite
commercial district in Lisbon, the Baixa. Soares
made no attempt to publish *O Livro do Desassossego*
and it was only discovered and published in Portugal
in 1982.

Bernardo Soares
do *Livro do Desassossego*

Nas vagas sombras de luz por findar antes que a tarde seja noite cedo, gozo de errar sem pensar entre o que a cidade se torna, e ando como se nada tivesse remédio. Agrada-me, mais à imaginação que aos sentidos, a tristeza dispersa que está comigo. Vago, e folheio em mim, sem o ler, um livro de texto intersperso de imagens rápidas, de que vou formando indolentemente uma idéia que nunca se completa.

Há quem leia com a rapidez com que olha, e conclua sem ter visto tudo. Assim tiro do livro que se me folheia na alma uma história vaga para contar, memórias de um outro vagabundo, bocados de descrições de crepúsculos ou luares, com aléias de parques no meio, e figuras de seda várias, a passar, a passar.

Indiscrimino a tédio e outro. Sigo, simultaneamente, pela rua, pela tarde e pela leitura sonhada, e os caminhos são verdadeiramente percorridos. Emigro e repouso, como se estivesse a bordo com o navio já no mar alto.

Súbito, os candeeiros mortos coincidem luzes pelos prolongamentos duplos da rua longa e curva. Como um baque a minha tristeza aumenta. É que o livro acabou. Há só, na viscosidade aérea da rua abstrata, um fio externo de sentimento, como a baba do Destino idiota, a pingar-me sobre a consciência da alma.

Outra vida, da cidade que anoitece. Outra alma, a de quem olha a noite. Sigo incerto e alegórico, irrealmente sentiente. Sou como uma história que alguém houvesse contado, e, de tão bem contada, andasse carnal mas não muito neste mundo romance, no princípio de um capítulo: "A essa hora um homem podia ser visto seguir lentamente pela rua de ..."

Que tenho eu com a vida?

Bernardo Soares
from *The Book of Restlessness*

In the vague shadows of light to end before evening turns night, I err without thinking amid what the city becomes, and walk as if nothing had remedy. A diffuse sadness accompanies me, more pleasing to the imagination than to the senses. I roam, and leaf, without reading, a book whose text is interspersed with rapid images, idly forming about it an idea which will never be complete.

Some read with the speed of sight, and conclude without having seen everything. And so I take from the book leafed through in the soul a vague story to tell, memories of another vagrant, morsels of descriptions of sunsets and moonlight, with avenues of parks among them, and figures of various silks, passing, passing.

I do not discriminate between boredom and other states. I follow, simultaneously, the street, the afternoon, and the dreamt reading, and the paths are actually traversed. I migrate and repose, as if on a ship on the high seas.

All of a sudden, along the double lanes of the long and arched streets, the dead street lamps coincide alight. My sadness increases with a thud. The book, you see, has ended. There is only, in the aerial viscosity of the abstract street, an external thread of sentiment, like the slavering of an idiotic Destiny, dripping over the conscience of soul.

Another life for the city which darkens. Another soul for him that looks on. Uncertain, allegorical, unreally sentient, I follow. I am like the story that someone might have told, and told so well that I would walk carnal but not quite in this romance world, at the beginning of a chapter: "At this hour a man could be seen walking slowly along such and such a street ..."

What have I with life?

Fernando Pessoa

One of the most original poets of European mod-
ernism, Pessoa maintained that literary texts should
be appreciated apart from the names and reputations
of their authors. Toward that end he sublimated
his own genius through the creation of heteronyms:
imaginary poets possessing distinct influences and
phases, grammar and style, biographies and even
horoscopes. Among his most celebrated heteronyms
are the philosopher Antônio Mora, the poet Coelho
Pacheco, and short-story writer Pero Botelho. After
a ten year sojourn in Durban, South Africa, he
returned to Portugal at age 17 and thereafter never
ventured far from his native Lisbon. Pessoa considered Mario de Sá Carneiro's insistence on living in
Paris an exemplary case of Portuguese provincial-
ism: "Had you been educated abroad as I was, under
the influence of a great European culture, you
would realize that the great cities are within you."

Fernando Pessoa
do drama estático, "O Marinheiro." (1913)

Sonhava de um marinheiro que se houvesse perdido numa ilha longínqua. Nessa ilha hava palmeiras hirtas, poucas, e aves vagas passavam por elas. Nao vi se alguma vez pousavam. Desde que, naufragado, se salvara, o marinheiro vivia ali. Como êle não tinha meio de voltar à pátria, e cada vez que se lembrava dela sofria, pôs-se a sonhar uma pátria que nunca tivesse tido; pôs-se a fazer ter sido sua uma outra pátria, uma outra espécie de país com outras espécies de paisagem, e outra gente, e outro feitio de passarem pelas ruas e de se debruçarem das janelas. Cada hora êle construía em sonho esta falsa pátria, e êle nunca deixava de sonhar… Durante anos e anos, dia a dia, o marinheiro erguia num sonho contínuo a sua nova terra natal. Todos os dias punha uma pedra de sonho nesse edifício impossível. Breve êle ia tendo um país que já tantas vêzes havia percorrido… Ao princípio êle criou as paisagens; depois criou as cidades; criou depois as ruas e as travessas, uma a uma, cinzelando-as na matéria de sua alma — uma a uma as ruas, bairro a bairro, até as muralhas do cais de onde êle criou depois os portos. Uma por uma as ruas, e a gente que as percorria e que olhava sôbre elas das janelas. Passou a conhecer certa gente, como quem a reconhece apenas. Ia-lhes conhecendo as vidas passadas e as conversas… E assim foi construindo o seu passado. Breve tinha uma outra vida anterior. Tinha já, nessa nova pátria, um lugar onde nascera, os lugares onde passara a juventude, os portos onde embarcara.

Um dia, que chovera muito, e o horizonte estava mais incerto, o marinheiro cansou-se de sonhar. Quis então recordar a sua pátria verdadeira. Mais viu que não se lembrava de nada, que ela não existia para êle. Meninice de que se lembrasse, era a na sua pátria de sonho; adolescência que recordasse, era aquela que se criara. Tôda a sua vida tinha sido a sua vida que sonhara. E êle viu que não podia ser que outra vida tivesse existido. Se êle nem de uma rua, nem de uma figura, nem de um gesto materno se lembrava. E da vida que lhe parecia ter sonhado, tudo era real e tinha sido. Nem sequer podia sonhar outro passado, conceber que tivesse tido outro, como todos, num momento, podem crer.

Fernando Pessoa
from the static drama *O Marinheiro*.

I dreamt of a sailor lost on a distant island of scarce and rigid palm trees. Vague birds passed among the trees. I could not discern if any of them alighted. From the time of his shipwreck the sailor lived on the island. As he had no means of returning home, and suffered each time he thought of it, he set out to dream a homeland he had never had; to make for himself another homeland, another kind of country with other kinds of landscapes, and another people, who possessed another form of walking along streets and leaning over window sills. Each hour he built in dream this false homeland, and he never ceased to dream… Day after day, year after year, the sailor erected in a continuous dream his new homeland. Every day he lay a dreamt stone on this impossible edifice. Soon he possessed a country he had traversed so many times… At first he created the landscapes; then he created the cities; then he created the streets and side-streets, one after another, chiseling them from the matter in his soul — one by one, the streets, until the quay's fortress walls from which he created ports. One by one the streets, and the people who crossed them and observed them from the windows. He came to know certain people, as if merely recognizing them from before. He came to know their lives and conversations… And so he constructed his past. Soon he had another original life. In this new homeland he had a birthplace, realms where he had spent his youth, ports from which he had departed.

Then one day of heavy rain and uncertain horizon the sailor tired of dreaming. He wished to remember his true homeland. But he saw that he remembered nothing, that it did not exist to him. The childhood he recalled was one spent in his dreamt homeland; he remembered only his created adolescence. All his life had been his dreamt life. And he saw there could not have been another life for him. For he could not remember a street, a figure, a maternal gesture. Everything was real and had happened in the life he seemed to have dreamt. He could not even dream another past, nor conceive he had possessed another, as we all, at times, are want to believe.

Exam Questions

Andrew Ross

If you were a "new democrat," which authority would you be likely to recognize?
- ☐ The Tennessee valley authority
- ☐ The port authority of New York
- ☐ The Chicago housing authority

If you were a pugilist, would you be living
- ☐ In a riverfront condominium
- ☐ Near a townless highway
- ☐ In a stucco bungalow

If you were an anarchist, would you be admiring
- ☐ Corbusier
- ☐ Geddes
- ☐ Rouse

If you were an antidisestablishmentarian, would you be living within sight of
- ☐ A city on a hill
- ☐ A dome on the rock
- ☐ The Coliseum

If you were a liberation theologian, would you be living near
- ☐ A *favela*
- ☐ A *colonia proletaria*
- ☐ A *hacienda*
- ☐ A *barriada*

If you were a millenarian, would you be figuring out what the future holds for
☐ Evanston, Illinois
☐ Toxteth, Liverpool
☐ Hong Kong

If you were a teuchter, would you be living in
☐ A zone in transition
☐ A *ciudad lineal*
☐ A *gartenstadbewegung*

If you suffered from condominia, would you be living in
☐ A high-rise apartment block
☐ A ranch house
☐ A satellite town

If you were a homesteader, would you be living in
☐ A garden city
☐ A gated development
☐ A pre-electric farm

If you had to choose between the following, what would it be?
☐ Gridlock
☐ Dry rot
☐ Athlete's foot

Para-site

Yelda Nasifoglu

Yelda Nasifoglu has used the covered bazaar in Istanbul, the city of her birth, for her primary investigations on architectural typologies. Her examination of this site resulted in a text which she contends is a dictionary of architecture, a dictionary which neither privileges text or image; "it is an appendix to any book on architecture." Her text troubles the space between two representational systems, that of architecture and its false, formal completion, and, an architecture of exchange whose units of measurement (gold) resists any spatial geometry.

 Para-Site anxiously supplements the bazaar's own self-replication and sprawl. The walls of the covered bazaar are hidden beneath a *veil* of consumer goods, which are then taken away (dis-placed) by a mobile social body who come to *stand-in-for* the very architecture of the bazaar itself. Nasifoglu's *text* is a work in progress, perhaps never to be finished; it seeks an origin forever deferred. —C. H.

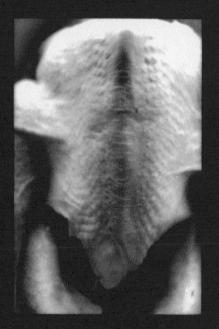

I escape the subject

Before consumption, the body is gutted, the remaining hairs are plucked out or burnt. Then it is filled with stuffing, sewn up, and cooked at 350°F . . It will be ready for consumption in 3 hours.

What has been lost in the market?

The loss is the bazaar's consumption of itself where its crumbling stones are swallowed by a ground plane, that is merely a skin over the underground chest.

Yet nothing is taken away from the bazaar. A labyrinth is constructed to keep the loss within itself, to continue consuming its own excess.

That piece from the 1461 construction which fell
off the column during the 1894 earthquake is
placed 5 kilograms away — but that is a secret, so
they hide it.

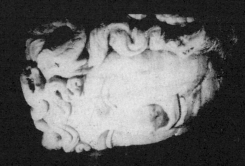

It could not take the column any more and it broke off. It could not take the sewer running
beneath the city, so it sank down. It could not lay still, so it rolled off into the Bosphorus.

For Loos, I turn serious
now. In its place is left
a crypt, an architecture
created by *dépense*.

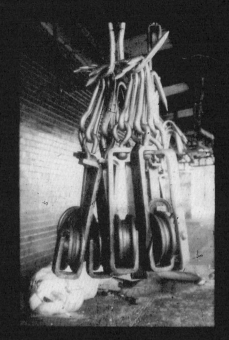

The walls are hastily dressed with leather; with fabric, with gold and silver and copper; with veils.

And soon enough, these layers themselves become the doubles of architecture.

There is only one column hidden; that is the address of the tomb. A woman has dressed it with evil eyes to interrupt the flow of the current that runs through the matter. As the eyes turn inward they mirror the blank faces, the blank spaces, the blank lights. The column forgets about itself and is lost in the bazaar.

And as the veils double for the walls,

the woman doubles for architecture in her dark veil.

The column becomes the embodiment of a loss of order that it disrupts.

Matter, as such, is only visible through the reflection of light as reflection.
Yet when enough light is gathered,

it eats through architecture. Then it becomes

space as light —
the way shadows eat through the plane.

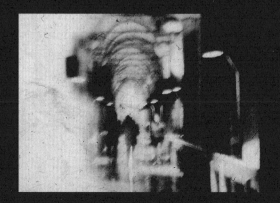

Yet something happens when there is no
base, when there is no head. Or when it is
subverted and turned sideways.

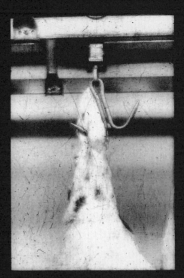

The column itself gets lost in depth; no more fixations. Through reflection, it flows endlessly into
the same sewer underneath the city. And it suddenly ends up within the wells carved through the
pilasters of Hagia Sophia.

Everything turns dark. Then.

A Thousand Shapes of Death

Eric Miller

Photographs by Guntar Kravis

> Directional signals have been added in a pitiful and revealing, rather desperate, attempt
> to restore the coordinates of an older space.
> —Jameson

> Did you ever chance to hear the midnight flight of birds passing through the air
> and darkness overhead, in countless armies, changing their early or their late summer
> habitat? It is something not to be forgotten.
> —Whitman

1.

That brightness is no star. The towers of high finance, whose lights never dim, twist the wind at hard angles. Though deflected so many times, this wind cannot spin free from a stagnating smell that keeps up with every subterfuge, every ricochet. Cornered air accelerates. In the gulf between glass walls, it drives night, damaged by lamps, hunched like a rail through cattails. Wind turns loose from their white and red cardboard boxes the bones of fried chicken lunches, and rolls those memorials to rest on manhole gratings, or in the locked bays of revolving doors, or against the leaves, as tough as the straps that dangle in subway cars, of corporate flowerbeds. Yesterday's fast food bags migrate rustling up and down cul-de-sacs. Only the wind's own image escapes enlistment into the currency of the mirror-sided buildings.

3:45 a.m. Your eyes become keener but less accurate, concentrated by the hour's too-lucid coffee. Your eyes invent from the crumpled carbon paper of a credit-card receipt the shape of a dazed thrush. Beauty dilates helplessly. Rats go by on feet lit like dusky sparklers in their speed. Why would anyone hallucinate a thrush, the mottles of a thrush, the idea of the forest that costumes a thrush? Keep walking to keep awake. The wide flagstones occasionally wobble under you with a grinding sound like millstones. Slammed on obduracy, the discs of your sneakered heelbones dart pain upward at your high resolve. You twitch quarters in your pockets.

When they fly south and north birds of many kinds navigate, as mariners used to, by the stars. But birds confuse lamps with stars, and resistant glass with the steep, permeable air; so that the windowed promontories of our transparent, interposed cities deceive them, disfigure them, and kill them. A window's thin membrane of melted silica won't yield breath or sustain a bird's flight. Truths too stupid to enunciate—but these are incommunicable or intransitive truths. With mildly appealing novelties, we shatter skulls of organic astrography, bone maps.

The skyline of Toronto has stretched into the night since the sixties a labyrinthical net. Welders' torches melt the vitreous mesh-work together; later, the offices buzz with continuous light; and the great idée fixe harvests the most comprehensive flocks of birds for no one. Or rather: for rats, for gulls, and for crazies, whom I attempted to outrun in my patrol for casualties. I kept records, a random opening of which recalls one ruby-throated hummingbird the Royal Bank Plaza's golden windows intercepted twenty years ago. "Golden" is no trope: the glass derives its mica glamour from an actual infusion of the metal.

Yet who couldn't love downtown? I did. I admired its skeleton crew, among which I was a kind of stowaway; I adored the profound plazas and insights from the dregs of styrofoam cups, warm as the cheeks of fevered children. Those city blocks correspond to a recurrent vacancy in the mind. Thought sometimes amounts to a residue on the bottom of the skull, like lichen or the coagulate of a kid's spilled drink on the sidewalk. At the foot of so much glass, you diminish to the abstract cuffs of your pants tugged by that musty, vigorous wind which feels as though it were never outside, but bred in arcades by the desire of kids to go into the forest they can't imagine beyond the flogged trash of a highway margin. Lassitude amid too many potentials, as after imagined love.

I was sixteen and had slept, as usual, till 3:15 on an itchy couch in a lobby, a knapsack full of paper bags by my side. The properties of a paper bag make it ideal for transporting injured birds. Fluttering in such a prison, some of them small enough to hover and become the sun of that close space, they never encounter a resistant angle. Paper breathes, and supplies its captives with sufficient air.

Paper bags are extraordinary. They age quickly. If you acquire a new one, its face is as clear as a child's. Use it several times, and it resembles the withered countenance of a mummy. I filched and salvaged dozens of paper bags. How many slogans, names of fast food outlets, pharmacies, shoe stores I collected and carefully folded! This axiomatic diversity offered a pleasure like the one you get from reading on the plywood hoardings around the eruption of new towers the bright handbills advertising bands, protests, and film festivals.

With my bags and a stapler to close them firmly, I left the insomniac dormitory of the lobby. I walked down a lane between a warehouse and a hotel, passing only a couple of maritimers, their heads tucked into packing crates, the toes of their flaking boots pointing skyward where the voices of warblers and thrushes swirled as thinly and as poignantly as the gases of a galaxy.

I mentioned a hummingbird. At 5:30 on the morning of the twenty-sixth of August, 1977, I wrote in failing ballpoint that the "collector forced a rat to drop this specimen," which was "partially eviscerated." I measured the wings of the corpse: forty-six millimetres. Carrion hummingbirds, given their magnitude, rot rapidly. The bird's belly was torn. Her flake-like feathers came loose and stuck under my thumbnail. Her mandibles were askew like a cosmetician's tweezers found deranged in the rubble after the bombs of an air-raid. I buried the metallic-backed bird in a patch of marigolds and Japanese yew, ornamentals whose tints complemented her own. Her smell remained across only part of my palm. My stomach simmered with anxiety's old coffee. Day was approaching — wide, untended hours like parched municipal lawns. School with its clocks and lockers would resume soon.

2.

My mother died in a hospital room, from which I could look down and see the yard of the high school I had attended for a year and a half, before dropping out. On the day she died the robin in this yard sang into her open window. Sounds such as that one only just cling to the outer side of filmy hospital curtains, and sift through the mesh, breath from a yellow beak distant as Jericho. Traffic continued. Strong fury passed in a breath.

There was no fateful warning that she would die just then. Her belly was enormously swollen by accumulation of fluids, but her legs were eerily girlish. She had been somewhat overweight (she had had that plumpness which seems eternally cool, as if her flesh were always in the shade, always by the side of a well); illness trimmed her thighs down until they appeared like an eighteen year-old girl's. She had danced when young and was so powerful that she could pace Marilyn Bell, the first woman to swim across Lake Ontario. Lake Ontario was visible, fuzzy with a blend of heat off flat roofs and pollution.

My brother happened to be in the hospital room with me. I was working as an usher at a movie theatre. I had a night shift, so that I was frequently in the hospital during the days. I had my dress shoes on, whose soles were coming detached, and which seemed more comfortable for their disrepair, disintegrating and reassembling with every step I took, breathing a trace odour of persistent cinematic popcorn. Apart from the disdain of the well-heeled young, ushering was pleasant; I could duck into one of eight films showing simultaneously, and flood my eyes with an enormous story. The cinema resembled an eight-sailed ship whose redemptive wind was the certainty of tight plotting.

One afternoon, already wearing the white shirt mandatory for an usher, I visited my sister Freja's. A gust of crying overtook me so violently that my nose began to bleed with extraordinary profuseness. My shirt was dyed almost entirely red, as if my chest, theatrically rosy, had been struck open. Freja conjured up a white shirt to replace the red one, and I went off to work with the light-headedness of a person who has lost a lot of blood.

After a nosebleed, you become conscious of the narrow apertures that ensure existence; you follow after the knowledge of their recent occlusion, and feel yourself hollowly, continuously, reliant on air. People drift by you on the sidewalk like varieties of wind, Portuguese men-of-war, bags, balloons. Trucks and streetcars seem as slim as whippets. How could the thin air bear such heavy shadows along! We are told that tears cleanse the system of certain intrinsic venoms. This nosebleed was more on the order of a sacrifice, a prelibation, as you might cut off a little finger in order to forestall the loss of a hand. The pain may truly be of the same intensity in either circumstance; more remains serviceable, however, in the former case.

Just before she died, my mother raised a hand level with her eyes. She held it horizontal, and observed it with a smile on her face. Her eyes gleamed their swimming grey, the area of their exposed white augmented by the action of a drug. Then her forehead began to work lightly, no more and no less fretful than the surface of calm water on which a single waterstrider executes its buoyant dashes. I have never seen a waterstrider fall through the lucid borderline on which it dwells.

I remember how irritated she had been earlier in her illness when my brother and I read books or newspapers: the sound of pages turning irked her no end. Some time later a woman I know told me that she had read a manual for housewives in pioneer America, a book with a taut crumbling texture like a poplar leaf in the fall. The pages were as frail as the pressed flowers with which they were here and there interleaved. One of the tasks a housewife had to be readied for was the trick of flipping pages in a sickroom without chagrining the invalid. I wish I had been acquainted with this manual, I needed its counsel, everything turned to powder in my hands — as if the substance of time were crucially dusty, like moth's wings, and I continually rubbed off with thumbs as wide as highways and as dirty as bicycle chains every available mediating film of grace.

My brother was so earnest that he carefully displayed to me the reading material he intended to bring into our mother's room. "Would she approve of this?" he asked, and showed me a book on the frugal society of the Inuit. This pale green book debunked the formerly common assumption that these arctic people don't experience sexual jealousy. The author told, in undistinguished prose, perhaps translated, of a man driven to murder by this passion — a passion ludicrously exaggerated among dwarf willows and birds that can nest only on the ground. The author wrote more feelingly on the kindness of the Inuit to their children.

My mother's face still expressed life after I believe she had actually died. There was a stirring of the lips, nostrils, forehead for what seemed seconds after she had given a conclusive sigh. For

some time prior to her death she had been troubled by a terrible rasping respiration, but her final breaths were like those of someone leaning against a flower and trying its perfume.

I remember being struck by how delicate, how almost like a play of light or of leaves, the tremor of her lips was. The lips operate with a musculature that exceeds the facts of their own anatomy. The image of her quivering lips, flesh even more ethereal than hair, belongs to me now, an altogether strange inheritance. It is a memory of severance and of transitivity, of something gliding swiftly from the eyes and from the impulsive, too-slow hands, as when you let a bird go or hand a gift over as a child.

My brother stood — he had realized before I did that she was dying — and while her forehead still worked he laid his hands on it. I rose after him and stood on her other side. I laid a hand on her slim forearm. My brother, of a more religious bent than I, said to what was now a fresh body, "Bless you." My reaction was mingled incredulity and admiration. Someone later told me in tones of peculiar mild reproach that a lay person can indeed administer such benediction on the dying. My brother has a certain grace most efficacious just when other people's charity fails from inhibition, disgust or embarrassment. As a boy he walked fearlessly in the senile ward where so many of our farmer relations ended their lives, and spoke — I could not do this — to the stinking and demented as if they were playmates in whose companionship no violence could occur. My mother had died, it remained in the months ahead to kill her.

3.

Rose-breasted grosbeaks smell not of roses, but of maple syrup. This is a truth imparted only to those who hold them, to those who sniff them as you might a flower. To handle live birds, to raise them to your face, as if to tip them directly into the ports of your senses — I set this among the supreme pleasures. Louis Agassiz Fuertes, the artist, is said to have held "in his lap" the dead birds that were to be his models and to have preened with his painter's fingers the disordered plumage, "an act of empathy," we are told, "that put him in a trance beyond reach of his field companions."

Fuertes was not so strange. A cadaver can become an object of beauty; while our own life, like an ineffectual corona, a superfluous plumage of tangential solicitude, busies its fluttering hands around the dimming and stiffening vacancy. Our voices are always calling for those whom we know have died; our hands have briefer opportunities. How quickly the eyes of a bird pucker and sink! That starry look evaporates, almost exhales into the air, the most acute vision becomes a sigh and a sinking.

I had to kill many birds too badly injured by collision with towers to convalesce. I flip through my notes — they are extensive — and observe randomly that I "euthanized" a Canada warbler and an American redstart. They succumbed to heart attacks induced by the educated pressure of fingers. My records omit the rose-breasted grosbeak whose torment is so robust in my memory. It was September, when gnats dangle in cyclones and starlings turn flycatchers and execute among the poplars of Toronto parks airy evolutions far more extempore than their terrestrial marching. These signs used to fill me with dread of school. Nighthawks on the verge of migration stooped twisting low to the ground as if the sky itself pressed them down, a viaduct shaken by passing planes, filthy shelf fit only for the abortive nesting of rock doves.

The rose-breasted grosbeak had hit Commerce Court's silver-blue glass, and now he pulsed and gasped, half-paralytic in a shoebox on top of soft dishtowels. Despite his winter colours' incipient muffling and obscuration, he illustrated his name better than most birds do, for his breast was blood-rosy and his beak large, like a pair of ivory pliers. Who can repress a smile at what looks so magnanimously oversized? The bird was stout in every particular but his fine toes. He could not move his legs at all.

It is a common misconception that birds, when they strike windows, break their necks. The suppleness of birds' necks encourages this error: the troubled person who picks up one of these bright, soft corpses observes how its head dangles freely, all too freely; but what kills such birds is in fact intracranial haemorrhaging. Birds' skulls are as translucent as thumbnails, especially those of birds of the year, before the milky ossifications of maturity. A fatal bruise to the brain is visible even through bone to anyone examining the remains of a window-kill closely.

My grosbeak had suffered permanent brain damage. He would not take water or food, but neither would he die. Instead he convulsed with quiet vigour through a long day. I couldn't stand his repetitive pain, and yet I kept hoping that the bird would recover. Often dazed birds Lazarus-like rallied. A thrush collided with the Royal Trust Tower at 6:20 on the twenty-fourth of August. Assuming it dead, I scooped up this "limp and unresponsive" thrush; but by one o'clock that afternoon, it fled from me into pines with "sustained flight," a valedictory dropping, a poignant rather than an angry note, and a trace of the musky smell with which millennia on millennia have infused thrushes. Nothing on earth lacks a perfume.

So I watched the grosbeak. He thrillingly unfolded and refolded one wing and his tail. The opening of a bird's wing is the disclosure of a secret, even when you have memorized the disposition of the flight feathers and the pigment. You gasp at this beauty as at the lightning that threatens you; but there is no threat, apart from the identity of vulnerabilities you may experience, all aloft in the flight of time, the weak eye and the wing it sees.

The day was hot, the grosbeak didn't drink, and I didn't have fingers strong enough, I thought, to induce a heart attack in this broad- and rose-breasted bird. I took him outside with vague mind. It was dusk. Park Drive Reservation Ravine, cooled by a stream smelling slightly of solvent and sewage, sank down submissively from our street, shaded by crack willows, Manitoba maples and white oaks. Joggers and dog-walkers must not witness my murder.

I went up a far incline where no path led, among forsythia, wild grape and hawthorns. Over ivy and poison ivy a cardinal irritably snapped. As in many city valleys, fragments of demolished buildings had lodged themselves on the slopes and formed terraces of architectural talus, where ferns still unscrolled themselves and moss thickened beside tinted bottles. I paused on such a terrace. I began to cry and laid the grosbeak, which still unfurled and closed rhythmically like a winged heart, on a chunk of concrete from which rusted steel rods stuck out.

I lifted a half brick and brought it down on the bird's head. The head gave at once with a rupture of eyes. As usual with birds, little blood showed or leaked. The continuing motions of the wings and tail appalled me. I struck again and again, and finally all motion subsided, but for a tentative stirring of the toes, relieved in this extremity of the paralysis which had gripped them. It was as if they reached even for this paralysis, as a token of retained life. The grit of the brick against my hand felt like a bite; my palm was minutely mottled red and white.

I cried, my vision itself bursting painfully forward like fruit trodden underfoot. I had seen security guards step on broken birds while patrolling the wind-beaten courtyards between towers, and janitors sweep the living bodies up; at least the grosbeak was good and dead. Already a red ant fluttered its antennae along the enigma of the bird's smooth beak. I got to my feet, bent various branches, snapped several knotweed stems flat, walked with abrupt, ungainly ease across a mani-cured lawn, and — after washing the odour of grosbeak from my palms — inspected a dozen more fortunate birds still in my custody but likely to live.

Waiting for the Barbarians

C. P. Cavafy (1904)

Translated by Elias Polizoes

—What are we waiting for, assembled in the forum?

    The barbarians are to arrive today.

—Why is there such inactivity in the Senate?
Why do the Senators just sit and do not legislate?

    Because the barbarians will arrive today.
    What kind of laws can the Senators make now?
    The barbarians, once they come, will do the legislating.

—Why has our emperor risen so early in the morning,
and why is he sitting at the city's largest gate,
on the throne, in state, wearing the crown?

    Because the barbarians will arrive today.
    And the emperor is waiting to receive
    their leader. In fact, he prepared
    a parchment for him. On it
    he has spelled out for him a host of titles and names.

—Why have our two consuls and the praetors come out
today with the scarlet, the embroidered togas?
Why did they put on bracelets with so many amethysts,
and rings with bright, glittering emeralds?
Why should they today take-up precious walking-sticks
exquisitely inlaid with silver and gold?

ΠΕΡΙΜΕΝΟΝΤΑΣ ΤΟΥΣ ΒΑΡΒΑΡΟΥΣ

— Τί περιμένουμε στὴν ἀγορὰ συναθροισμένοι;

    Εἶναι οἱ βάρβαροι νὰ φθάσουν σήμερα.

— Γιατί μέσα στὴν Σύγκλητο μιὰ τέτοια ἀπραξία;
Τί κάθοντ' οἱ Συγκλητικοὶ καὶ δὲν νομοθετοῦνε;

    Τιατὶ οἱ βάρβαροι θὰ φθάσουν σήμερα.
    Τί νόμους πιὰ θὰ κάμουν οἱ Συγκλητικοί;
    Οἱ βάρβαροι σὰν ἔλθουν θὰ νομοθετήσουν.

— Γιατί ὁ αὐτοκράτωρ μας τόσο πρωΐ σηκώθη,
καὶ κάθεται στῆς πόλεως τὴν πιὸ μεγάλη πύλη
στὸν θρόνο ἐπάνω, ἐπίσημος, φορῶντας τὴν κορώνα;

    Γιατὶ οἱ βάρβαροι θὰ φθάσουν σήμερα.
    Κι ὁ αὐτοκράτωρ περιμένει νὰ δεχθεῖ
    τὸν ἀρχηγό τους. Μάλιστα ἑτοίμασε
    γιὰ νὰ τὸν δώσει μιὰ περγαμηνή. Ἐκεῖ
    τὸν ἔγραψε τίτλους πολλοὺς κι ὀνόματα.

— Γιατί οἱ δυό μας ὕπατοι κ' οἱ πραίτορες ἐβγῆκαν
σήμερα μὲ τὲς κόκκινες, τὲς κεντημένες τόγες·
γιατί βραχιόλια φόρεσαν μὲ τόσους ἀμεθύστους,
καὶ δαχτυλίδια μὲ λαμπρά, γυαλιστερὰ σμαράγδια·
γιατί νὰ πιάσουν σήμερα πολύτιμα μπαστούνια
μ' ἀσήμια καὶ μαλάματα ἔκτακα σκαλιγμένα;

Because the barbarians will arrive today,
and such things dazzle barbarians.

— Why too, have the worthy orators not come as always
to have their say, to speak their minds?

Because the barbarians will arrive today,
and they tire of eloquence and speeches.

— Why should this restlessness and confusion
begin all at once? (How serious the faces have become).
Why do the streets and squares empty so quickly,
and everyone makes for their homes so deep in thought?

Because night has fallen and the barbarians have not come.
And some have returned from the border
and said that barbarians no longer exist.

And now what will become of us without barbarians?
These people were some sort of solution.

Γιατὶ οἱ βάρβαροι θὰ φθάσουν σήμερα·
καὶ τέτοια πράγματα θαμπώνουν τοὺς βαρβάρους.

— Γιατί κ' οἱ ἄξιοι ῥήτορες δὲν ἔρχονται σὰν πάντα
νὰ βγάλουνε τοὺς λόγους τους, νὰ ποῦνε τὰ δικά τους;

Γιατὶ οἱ βάρβαροι θὰ φθάσουν σήμερα·
κι αὐτοὶ βαρυοῦντ' εὐφράδειες καὶ δημηγορίες.

— Γιατί ν' ἀρχίσει μονομιᾶς αὐτὴ ἡ ἀνησυχία
κ' ἡ σύγχυσις. (Τὰ πρόσωπα τί σοβαρὰ ποὺ ἐγίναν).
Γιατί ἀδειάζουν γρήγορα οἱ δρόμοι κ ἡ πλατέες,
κι ὅλοι γυρνοῦν στὰ σπίτια τους πολὺ συλλογισμένοι;

Γιατὶ ἐνύχτωσε κ' οἱ βάρβαροι δὲν ἦλθαν.
Καὶ μερικοὶ ἔφθασαν ἀπ' τὰ σύνορα,
καὶ εἴπανε πὼς βάρβαροι πιὰ δὲν ὑπάρχουν.

Καὶ τώρα τί θὰ γένουμε χωρὶς βαρβάρους.
Οἱ ἄνθρωποι αὐτοὶ ἦσαν μιὰ κάποια λύσις.

[14, 1904]

Not Spain

Richard Sanger

Sie ahnten nicht, dass es nicht die Hoffnung war, die die Bürger Sarajevos höflich sein liess (denn in Sarajevo über die Hoffnung laut zu reden ist ebenso unanständig, wie im Hause eines Verstorbenen vom Tod zu sprechen). Wir verhielten uns so, um den Besuchern nicht die Illusion zu nehmen. Und um ihnen zu helfen. Das gehört zu den alten Gebräuchen dieser Welt: Barmherzigkeit gegenüber Bettlern, Reisenden, in Not Geratenen zu üben.

Ivan Lovrenović, *DIE ZEIT*, 10 September 1993.

They would never imagine that it was not hope that led the citizens of Sarajevo to be polite (since to speak out loud of hope in Sarajevo is bad manners, just like speaking of death in the houses of the deceased). We behaved in such a way so as not to destroy the dreams of these visitors. And to help them. It's one of the old customs of this world: to practise charity towards beggars, travellers and those in need.

Not Spain was first performed at the Tarragon Theatre in Toronto as part of the 1994 Summerworks Festival; this version was produced in 1996 at Theatre Passe Muraille, Toronto and at the Grand Theatre in London, Ontario, with music by Peter Kiesewalter, set by Steve Lucas and lighting by Martin Conboy.

Deborah Lambie and Naomi Campbell directed both productions jointly; for both, the cast was as follows:

Sophie: Cynthia Ashperger

Andrei: Arturo Fresolone

I am grateful to all involved, especially to Deborah and Naomi, for their help and advice.

—R. S.

All rights to *Not Spain* are retained by the author. Applications to produce, perform, or give public readings from the play should be made to him, c/o The Playwrights Union of Canada, 54 Wolseley Street, Toronto, Ontario M5T 1A5, Canada.

Not Spain will be published in book form by Playwrights Canada Press in 1998.

Not Spain
Order of Scenes

Ballad of the Bridge

Flies on a Wound

The Pie

Carousel

Hello

Stories 1

Everything/Nothing

Candlesticks 1

Stories 2

Hello, Hello

Candlesticks 2

Sky

Stories 3

A Song from the Bazaar

Stories 4

Jigsaw

Stories 5

The Guide-Book

Candlesticks 3

The Mexican Correspondent

Tell the Truth

Stories 6

Propositions

Not Spain

The End of the Song

Not Blood

Goodbye Presents

A city in a war zone.

Sophie is in her hotel room. She visits Andrei in the building where he takes shelter. There, everything is provisional: bucket, blanket, boxes for furniture, a brass candlestick. Wartime debris.

Ballad of the Bridge

(Sung as the lights come up.)

Three brothers are building a bridge
    King John, Count Mark and George
They are building a bridge at Talar
    There where the Duna roars.

Don't waste your time, don't waste your money
    Cried the voice of the witch.
You will never outsmart the river
    Never finish the bridge.

Flies on a Wound

Sophie: Like flies …

Andrei: Like flies on a wound.

Sophie: An open wound on the face of the earth.

Andrei: They come from all the corners of the earth.

Sophie: A little gash that by chance opened up in one particular point, and spread — the place, who knows? — someone chose for everything to spill out so we could see what we are like inside.

Andrei: You know they're from the same tribe by their eyes, their eyes that seem so friendly, so interested, so compassionate, yes, but can't keep still —

Sophie: We look at them, we try to see them but we can't, we can't look long. How can people live like this?

Andrei: They scan the background behind you just in case there's something there that's more alive, that's more to their taste, more succulent …

Sophie: Look, how quickly they discard everything that has no purpose, apartments, friendships, tractors, how they move from village to village, turning each one upside down to search for something of use, then —

Andrei: They feed, their eyes shift —

Sophie: And they're off again.

Andrei: Like flies.

Sophie: Flies on a wound.

Andrei: And they keep coming from all over the world, the Americans, the British, the French, the Germans, the Mexican correspondent —

Sophie: It happens like this: one appears, he looks just like you or me, same jeans, same running shoes, except that there's something about him that tells you he hasn't used those shoes to play tennis, or perhaps they weren't his to begin with, he's restless, he bends over to pick something up, some barely edible scrap —

Andrei: They come in planes, in helicopters, in jeeps, in armored personnel carriers; they come, swarms of them, and some of them are women *(Glances at Sophie.)* and all of them bring with them bags and cases full of up-to-the-minute equipment, everything black and chrome and plastic —

Sophie: Just then another appears, to demand his share, and soon there's a whole swarm of them, each wanting a piece of that scrap, each believing it must be good because there are more and more of them wanting it.

Andrei: Cameras with zooms and enormous convex lenses, cellular phones, radios with antennae and tripods with spindly, thin, black legs, and cables, miles and miles of cables.

Sophie: And the more of them there are the less human they become, scrambling, scavenging, trampling each other under their feet, willing to fight a neighbour, a brother, over anything.

Andrei: All that technology just to look at us. It's almost flattering. And then their adjectives.

Sophie: Unfathomable, unprecedented, inconceivable, atavistic, on a scale hitherto unimagined, unspeakable.

Andrei: But they'll speak, and speak as long as they have something on which to —

Sophie: So desperate they'll do anything —

Andrei: To feed.

Sophie: To feed.

Andrei: Or else they fly away.

Sophie: Or else they die.

The Pie

Sophie: The day I arrived, I was starving, I don't know why. I went straight to the hotel to sleep, which I hadn't done on the plane, nor the night before, because there was a party in London. You see, I met someone at it, I almost missed the plane. At the restaurant downstairs, they were between meals but I couldn't go out, I'd just arrived. So the waitress brought me something that looked like pastry, that they hadn't eaten at lunch, and I ate it right there in front of her. It was cherry pie: very sweet and very red inside. Then I went upstairs to sleep, and I slept. I dream of the party or the man I've met or home. I dream of myself, of my body and this thing inside me, that put itself back together out of all the bites I've taken, that looks like a map of somewhere that shows all the counties in patchwork and stitches, except that it bleeds at the seams.

Carousel

Andrei: I see the road, very close up for a long time. It's chalky, pale yellow limestone, with bits of broken cinder blocks and rock and a shiny belt-buckle right near my nose and some broken black plastic. Then there's noise — my neck hurts but I look from the corner of my eye and then hide my face in the road. It's four soldiers coming up the hill behind me, with big boots that crunch, they are coming closer, they are singing "Deux milles à pied, ça use, ça use — " and, just when the chorus ends, one kicks me in the ribs. "ça use les SOULIERS!" UGH. And they march on. Behind them comes an older man, with a crutch, and he cries "Wait for me! Wait for me! I'm the dead Goran's father! Wait!" But one of the boys just throws a stone at him and says "Get lost, Grandad." And behind him I hear a woman crying "You promised, you promised" but he doesn't answer, and she goes by dragging two big suitcases. And there are lots of people, they are speaking and screaming and sobbing and some are dragging metal on the stones but I don't see them, I keep very still. And then it's quiet, and far-off I hear a woman's voice singing an old song from the mountains:

Three brothers are building a city:
King John, Count Mark and George.
They are building the city of Talar,
There where the river roars.

I look and there's an old woman in a shawl pushing a wheelbarrow slowly up the hill like she's in no rush, like this, going from side to side. She is singing and at the same time talking in a low voice to something in the wheelbarrow, a baby or maybe an animal. But about ten yards beyond me, she stops. Something has fallen from the wheelbarrow. She picks it up — I see it's an arm with lots of hair and blood and bone — she looks it over closely and drops it back onto the road, and then she continues on up the hill, humming that song.

They build the tower, they build the square,
The streets, the gates, the wall.
They build the city stone by stone
And soon they've built it all.

Hello

Sophie: I had to get away, so I took a day off to visit a village in the safe zone. Tufa.

Andrei: A little village two hours from here where I first saw the world — I hide my treasure there.

Sophie: I wanted to see the monastery, all the treasures the Crusaders had deposited there on their return.

Andrei: When I go back it's always changed. Little things disappear like that.

Sophie: I went but I couldn't find it. I spent the day in the orchards with the cherries.

Andrei: The store is empty, the cafe is boarded up. Now there is writing on the door. I enter.

Sophie: I was waiting in the square. The bus, I should have known, was late.

Andrei: In the safe zone, I tell her, it is safest.

Sophie: There is no one in the square; no one but a dog and his shadow.

Andrei: I bring her vegetables and cans and apricots for the children. We drink tea — there's no time, no place to make love. We laugh and laugh.

Sophie: I have a book and a bag of cherries I picked.

Andrei: Suddenly I'm late. I rush for the bus.

Sophie: I'm reading and eating in the empty square. I look up.

Andrei: There's no one — the bus I think has gone — no one but —

Sophie: There's a man running into the square.

Andrei: There's a woman in strange clothes.

Sophie: A man I think I know.

Andrei: She's reading a book.

Sophie: Or perhaps I don't. *(Faces him.)* Hello.

Andrei: Hello.

Stories 1

Sophie: I don't need much. I can get everything I need most places. A bed, a sink or shower to wash myself, a stove to make tea, and a desk to write at. And a book or two — whatever I'm reading at the time. I used to keep every book I read, I used to think I couldn't live without them, and I needed them to keep track of who I was. Then I came back from a trip and realized that I didn't miss them at all. I enjoyed being away from them. I could be myself, I could be someone else. So I had a big big sale, I cleared out everything, donated the proceeds, and swore to use the library. If it doesn't stay with me, why should I keep it? Travel lightly — write in pencil — pay your fines.

Andrei: The apartment was on the ground floor at the back. It wasn't very big or bright but we liked it because there was a courtyard where Katya and Boris could play. We left their toys out there, left the pram, hung our laundry. Then one day they hit the building and Mrs Santic's new TV landed in the courtyard. Azra left that evening with the children. That night I went walking in the city; there is more shooting and more shooting, but I don't care, and when I get to my aunt's apartment, I see flames on the horizon, something big and orange and glowing like a new planet I've never seen. It was the National Library. I've never been inside.

Everything/Nothing

Sophie: I have everything.

Andrei: I have nothing.

Sophie: I have a lover, I have an apartment, I have friends, I have a name!

Andrei: I had a wife and two children, I had an apartment, I had a job and a perfect happy life with family portraits on the mantelpiece.

Sophie: The human side of the story. That's what I do. They call me when they want it, and I don't say yes to everyone.

Andrei: But there was always a little skull in the corner of the picture. And the skull said: "Everything is vanity."

Sophie: Now I wake up sometimes and ask myself: Is this the name I wanted? Is this everything?

Andrei: I didn't know that my attachments to my family were also vain, that my love for my children was vain.

Candlesticks 1

Andrei: Nothing. No candle, no light, no match. Nothing but this candlestick. Once there were two. Azra noticed them the first time I took her to my mother's house. Up till then I hadn't really seen them — they'd always just been there, in the house, forever. When my mother gave them to us after we got married, Azra was so happy she cried. She said this made our house a real house now, that we were the rightful heirs and the candlesticks would carry on their journey through us. My mother told me not to tell her where they came from and then muttered to herself, "In the house of the unbelieving, let there be a true flame."

Stories 2

Sophie: But I have to have a window. I always have to have a window to look out on the outside world. Just so I know it hasn't gone away, and that the seasons continue in their lovely, mindless repetition. At home I'm spoilt — I have two bay windows that overlook a quiet square where an old man in a jacket with gold braids sells the newspapers, and a woman comes to feed stale bread to the pigeons at eleven every morning.

Andrei: I went back with Petrus the next day, he's my neighbour, there had been more shooting and bombs and shells, and the building was completely empty — just Petrus and I and a couple of other men trying to load the biggest of our possessions onto carts. The televisions, the VCRs, a chest-of-drawers, and Petrus's deep freezer, which was very heavy and kept slipping off, which he wanted to take to his sister's villa because he had a feeling this was going to last a while... I told him, "no," he didn't need it, now that Michaela and his children had gone, I'd left mine behind and was going to go back to eating dried sausages and cabbages from the root cellar the way my mother and I had before I married Azra. But the freezer was very heavy, it was hot outside, and Petrus insisted and I began to understand that the freezer wasn't empty.

Hello, Hello

(Andrei is looking at himself in a mirror, or doing something likewise mildly embarrassing; Sophie enters.)

Sophie: Hello. Hello.

Andrei: Hello.

Sophie: I came.

Andrei: Who?

Sophie: You invited me to your house. I've come.

Andrei: Oh yes. Of course.

Sophie: We were on the same bus back from Tufa. I had gone to see the monastery.

Andrei: There is no monastery in Tufa.

Sophie: That's what you said. I thought perhaps you.... At the roadblock, you remember, when everyone got off the bus, that was when my camera disappeared, and I thought perhaps you ...

Andrei: You are mistaken. I was not on this bus.

Sophie: You said I should visit you. You're Andrei.

Andrei: Correct.

Sophie: I'm Sophie.

Andrei: You're a journalist.

Sophie: Now you remember. You do.

Andrei: I must give you some information.

Sophie: You see, when you invited me to visit you, I thought you were going to give me my camera back.

Andrei: You want your camera. What do I know about your camera?

Sophie: But you did take it, didn't you?

Andrei: You know what they would have done? They would have shot you.

Sophie: Yes, yes. I know. That's why I really came. I wanted to, to thank you. You saved my life.

Andrei: Hospitality is a custom in this country.

Sophie: Yes, it's one of your nicer customs, isn't it?

Andrei: In every house, the biggest, the best room will be reserved for receiving visitors.

Sophie: For me, you don't have to bother.

Andrei: No, no, the room must be nice for me. I am your host.

Sophie: But I'm happy anywhere.

Andrei: It's the custom. And sometimes when we invite people it's just the custom too. The tradition is that we are always available. It is a shame, a disgrace on our house, if we let someone think that we are so poor or so busy trying not to be poor that we can offer our guests nothing.

Sophie: You are a very warm and hospitable people.

Andrei: I say these things to help you in your visit. Because if we all accepted every invitation we received and every guest we invited accepted our invitation, well, you see —

Sophie: It would be awkward.

Andrei: Very difficult.

Sophie: You'd spend your whole lives inviting and being invited.

Andrei: And sometimes it would be even worse. I would have to be a guest at my brother's, say, at the same time you were being a guest with me.

Sophie: And I would have to be a guest in three places at once. But we could all be guests and hosts together all the time. Wouldn't that be fun?

Andrei: So, to avoid this problem, sometimes we say, "yes, yes, of course," but we don't go.

Sophie: You didn't mean it. I'm so sorry. I didn't realize.

Andrei: I say these things to help you on your visit in our country.

Sophie: It's hard to know everything.

Andrei: But no one invited you to this country either and you came. That must be your custom.

Sophie: It's my job. I go where there's a story, something happening.

Andrei: And you get paid. We make the news and they pay you!

Sophie: I'm sorry. I'll go.

(A siren sounds.)

Andrei: Wait.

Sophie: No, I'm going.

Andrei: You're crazy. You can't go now. It's the siren.

Sophie: I'm going anyway. It's not far. You don't want me here.

Andrei: You must stay. Stay.

Sophie: But you don't want me here.

Andrei: I have no choice.

Sophie: I understand you not feeling like having guests. I live alone and there are times when I just can't see people.

Andrei: Did you like Tufa? There are many things to see.

Sophie: I wanted to see the monastery.

Andrei: The cherries from Tufa are famous.

Sophie: I know. I went for a walk in the orchards.

Andrei: They have the best flavour and there are so many, so many that the branches must sink with their weight and sometimes they break.

Sophie: No one had picked them. They were going rotten.

Andrei: For this reason, when we want to say that there is a lot of something —

Sophie: I wanted to see the treasures —

Andrei: When there are so many things you can't count them —

Sophie: All that gold and silver.

Andrei: We say —

Sophie: What?

Andrei: "Like cherries under a tree in Tufa."

Candlesticks 2

Andrei: The candlesticks came to my mother from my uncle who was — what do you call it? — the Bishop. When I was young, he was the only man I knew from outside the village. At first, he frightened me. He was old, he had a long beard, which he dyed, and his black robes stank in the heat. He came to stay in the summer and he brought presents. The whole village wanted to see him, but he, it seemed, only wanted to see me. I began to like him. The village was where he got away from all the important people in the city, but the people who thought they were important in the village didn't understand. We would be sitting outside in the garden, and he would be telling me stories about the Knights of the Crusades and the Battles against the Infidels, and sometimes my mother would come in and say there was someone at the door for him. My uncle would wink at me and say, "Tell them I'm busy spreading the word." And then through the slats of the gate, I would catch sight of the mayor or whoever, who never came near our house at any other time, walking off slowly, explaining to his friends that the Bishop couldn't see them: even though it was the evening, it was August, and it was the holidays, the Bishop was busy spreading the word.

The Sky

Andrei: You are enjoying your visit here?

Sophie: It's work.

Andrei: Oh, I'm sorry. You are enjoying your work here?

Sophie: Yes, yes I am. Though it's difficult to know who to trust. Who to believe.

Andrei: It is.

Sophie: The other journalists say you can't trust anyone. Ever. Who do you trust?

Andrei: Not the journalists.

Sophie: What about your family?

Andrei: No.

Sophie: Your wife and children?

Andrei: Two children. Boris. Katya.

Sophie: What about them?

Andrei: My family are dead.

Sophie: Oh. *(Pause.)* I'm sorry. I didn't know.

Andrei: You didn't know them. Why are you sorry? You didn't kill them.

Sophie: I should go.

Andrei: No. *(Pause.)*

Sophie: I said, "I'm sorry," because you must be devastated because they're ... I didn't know them. But I know you a bit.... They died. I can't say anything — can I? — and there's no use in you saying anything about them because they're dead. That's it.

Andrei: They're dead. That's all. It's simple.

Sophie: I should go.

Andrei: Have some.... *(Reaches in pocket.)* What do you call this? Nuts?

Sophie: Sunflower seeds. Thanks.

(They eat a few each, him spitting the shells on the floor.)

Andrei: Like this. It's a custom.

Sophie: *(Spits some that land on her dress or chin.)* Shells — that's what they're called. We're spitting out shells.

Andrei: It's a custom.

Sophie: I went to the monastery. With some Englishmen. It's a very beautiful place. Peaceful. Why did you tell me it wasn't there? *(Pause.)* I wanted to visit it and you told me it wasn't there. Why?

Andrei: *(Sarcastic.)* You wanted to visit the monastery? Just like you wanted to visit this country?

Sophie: It's a beautiful place. In other countries, you don't have —

Andrei: And you don't have this war. That's not just a monastery.

Sophie: It's a wonderful piece of Romanesque architecture.

Andrei: Do you know what they do in there? Do you know what they tell the children that go on their retreats there?

Sophie: That's not the building —

Andrei: Those people are the building. They keep it standing. They hold up the walls, the roof. They keep the stones in place. I know. I did it too. I went there on Sunday afternoons. My mother spent the happiest hours of her life in their chapel or claimed she did just to get my father angry. And her brother was the Bishop. My uncle was the Bishop! Yes, the monastery is very beautiful, the churches are very beautiful. But you know what would be more beautiful to me? You know? It would be to burn them all to the ground, starting with that monastery there. That's correct. It would make me very happy to see the fire rise and melt the lead in the stained-glass windows, to watch those little coloured panes fall out one by one and smash on the flagstones. Ping — there goes St. Sebastian's halo. Ping — Oh, St. Stephen's arm. Yes, yes, smashed on those famous flagstones that the Crusaders trod and that visitors from all over the world came to stand on in their expensive American running shoes. And while all this was going on, and the flames rose higher and higher, you know what I would do? I would round up all the people in the village, all the nice faithful parishioners, and make them stand around the burning ruin and sing, "Hallelujah. Hallelujah!" That would be beautiful.

Sophie: *(Pointedly.)* Yes, and then what?

Andrei: Then we would start from zero.

Sophie: But how? How?

Andrei: *(Slowly.)* We would look at the blue sky above us instead of the dark church roof and the tortured stained-glass saints. And I would remind the people of the village that, in our language, the word for sky is the same as the word for heaven, and that we only have one sky, one heaven, and that's what we would all believe in.

Stories 3

Sophie: And sometimes, sometimes, Lewis is there. Lewis. Louis. My lover. My paramour. My louis d'or. Not my partner, no. We don't live together. I don't live together well. Louis, my by-love, my for-love, my paramour. Now he wants a bigger part, he's got all ambitious. It's perfect the way it is, I tell him. I can be by myself, I can be myself, I can be unhappy when I want to. And I don't have to explain. And then sometimes, sometimes when I come home, he's there, he's let himself in and cooked supper for us, a surprise, say, asparagus, and I can forget everything and be happy being with him. Then in the morning, he goes down and gets bread from the bakery in the square and the paper from the old man — who speaks to him but never to me — and by the time we've finished breakfast and the paper the woman is there feeding the pigeons.

Andrei: The freezer was full but I knew I couldn't ask Petrus what was in it. He pretended it was empty and I couldn't see inside because it was locked. But I began to get very very hungry just thinking about all the things in there. I remembered what dishes I had eaten recently in Petrus's house, I ate very well there, and, at the same time, I had to think how I could get him to open it up. Petrus said since it was the heaviest thing on the cart, we should deliver the freezer first. I knew he was scared it would defrost before we got to his sister's villa. I knew, too, that if the freezer opened with Petrus and me there, Petrus would be obliged to give me a share of the contents. So I devised a plan.

A Song from the Bazaar

Andrei: What about the Horse Bazaar? This would be a very good place for you to visit. It's in a suburb a bit hard to get to.

Sophie: On the other side of the river?

Andrei: Yes.

Sophie: I thought it was called the Turkish Market.

Andrei: Some people call it that.

Sophie: I've already been there.

Andrei: It's wonderful, don't you think? You know this suburb used to be a village of its own. It was where they bought and sold horses and where the ironsmiths and leather-workers lived. Then when the Austrians were here, they taxed all the street-traders in the city, so most of them went to this village and the market got bigger and more variety. Now you can buy everything there: horses, leather, silver, carpets, birds.

Sophie: That's what everyone told me but there wasn't much to see when I was there.

Andrei: No?

Sophie: It must be the war.

Andrei: I don't think so.

Sophie: What?

Andrei: The market is doing very well now. Lots of people selling things, all kinds of things, their possessions, their family valuables. And lots of soldiers, journalists, buying with dollars and Deutschmarks.

Sophie: I didn't see anything like that.

Andrei: You have to go early in the morning.

Sophie: When I went all they had were rows and rows of sports clothes, and cassette tapes.

Andrei: That's Saturday; it's the Young People's Market.

Sophie: There weren't many of them.

Andrei: Then you went too late, I think.

Sophie: Eleven in the morning.

Andrei: Much too late. Everyone has gone home for lunch.

Sophie: I wanted to find a carpet.

Andrei: Of course. A carpet.

Sophie: But there weren't any, so I looked at the jeans and the cassettes and I went into a café.

Andrei: The café with the stained-glass windows?

Sophie: Yes.

Andrei: This is very typical.

Sophie: They were very nice to me. They gave me some hot sausage to eat and some brandy to drink. I tried to explain I wanted coffee.

Andrei: This is very late for them, you see.

Sophie: Then the barman understood and gave me coffee. And after he gave me another brandy and then another one.

Andrei: It's the end of the week for them. They celebrate.

Sophie: And he pointed to a blind man in the corner. I took the second glass to him while the barman yelled at him, and he started to play on his accordion.

Andrei: Of course, of course.

Sophie: *(Sings.)* Three brothers live in a city —

Andrei: No, no.

Three brothers are building a city
   King John, Count Mark and George
They are building the city of Talar
   There where the Duna roars.

Sophie: It's a very beautiful song.

Andrei: And very sad. It's about a bridge.

Sophie: A bridge?

Andrei: Yes, it tells the story of how the bridge at Talar was built:

They build the tower, they build the square,
   The streets, the gates, the wall.
They build the city stone by stone
   And soon they've built it all.

All they have left is one little thing,
   All they have left's the bridge.
They need a bridge over the river,
   The river that laughs and sings.

They start to build one morning
   Before the sun gets hot.
"A bridge is beautiful thing"
   Says John; his brothers nod.

They know what beautiful things are,
   They have three faithful wives:
Queen Margaret, Countess Anne and Lena,
   Lena from the other side.

Stone by stone they start to build
   Two arches and a pillar;
By night it stands two horses high
   Above the silent river.

Sophie: It's silent now.

Andrei: Yes, the river is sulking because the bridge is standing. Bridges are very important here.

Sophie: Yes, yes, I see. A connection, a link, a bridge between places. Between people.

Andrei: *(Standing up.)* Yes, but the river keeps washing it away.

But the next day when they come down,
   Oh-oh! The pillar's gone.
The river runs right past them and laughs,
   The river runs along.

Stories 4

Sophie: Lewis had the magazine and was reading to me this long article about art forgery — how, in these old European families, when they ran out of money, the father would secretly sell off the original work and commission a fake from a tradesman to fill its place on the mantelpiece.... He did this imitation of the excitable offspring swearing up and down and by all the most obscure Sicilian saints that this was the authentic Etruscan statuette they'd inherited as a dour art expert shook his head in the corner. And while I was listening to him do all this, my eyes ran over the front section and there was this picture of these people lining up at some camp staring me in the face — the war had just broken out and they had a chart explaining which people were on what side and why they were fighting those other people.... And I thought: Why can't we live together?

Andrei: On the way to Petrus's sister's villa there was a little bar where we would go to drink beer after we played soccer, when we played soccer. I told Petrus I had to see the owner, Milos, about some business, and, since we were going right by, we could just stop there for a second. I went in and told Milos what I needed. We came out, carrying this big piece of calf and Milos said, "Petrus, I have no room in my freezer for this calf. Would you like it?"
"Yes, Yes."
"Good, let's put it in your freezer so it doesn't go bad."

"No, just put it on the cart. I want to eat it today."

"You're crazy. You can't eat all this in one day. Put it in your freezer."

"No, on the cart."

Like this, back and forth, and finally Petrus opens up the freezer. It's full, absolutely full, with food, with meat, with soup, with fish, with fruit, and even with ice cream.

Jigsaw

Andrei: Canada, Canada, Canada, Canada.

Sophie: I heard shells last night.

Andrei: No, no. We have that every night now. Last night was normal.

Sophie: I thought I heard them over here.

Andrei: No, it was the lower quarter last night. Tell me about Canada. Canada.

Sophie: What it's like?

Andrei: Yes, what it's like.

Sophie: It's very beautiful. There are forests, there are lakes and rivers, there are mountains.

Andrei: And what's it like in … in autumn?

Sophie: Oh then it's especially beautiful. The leaves change colour, and they go yellow and orange and red, and they fall.

Andrei: They all fall?

Sophie: No, not the pines and the cedars. They don't have leaves; they have needles instead. But the maple, the oak, the birch, and all the other leaves fall to the ground and they're bright, bright, bright —

Andrei: Like cherries.

Sophie: Like cherries?

Andrei: Under a tree —

Sophie: Under a tree in Tufa!

Andrei: Really?

Sophie: No, no. It must be different. You should see it.

Andrei: But I've seen the cherries in Tufa.

Sophie: But it can't be the same. You have to see it, to see the leaves, the hillsides. I hope you'll come someday.

Andrei: No.

Sophie: You don't want to come to Canada?

Andrei: No.

Sophie: Even if you could get a visa?

Andrei: No. It's not for me. I can't.

Sophie: I could try. I know some people.

Andrei: This was — is — my country. I can't leave.

Sophie: Why?

Andrei: I can't. I don't want to go to Canada. I just want to know.

Sophie: Oh. Well, it's a very, very beautiful country.

Andrei: But you don't live in the forest. Not with all those beautiful leaves falling on you.

Sophie: No, I don't live in the country.

Andrei: You don't?

Sophie: I live in a city in Canada. In Montréal.

Andrei: Montréal?

Sophie: It's a city in the country of Canada.

Andrei: Yes, yes, there's a company there; they make very good puzzles, jigsaws.

Sophie: Really?

Andrei: I have three of them. I had. No piece is the same. Each one is different, not just different parts of the picture but different shapes for each piece.… Very difficult.

Sophie: You like jigsaws? You do lots of them?

Andrei: Before. Then I would give Azra a new one every winter. We would work on it together. She loved it, but she would get so angry when she couldn't find the piece she wanted, she wouldn't come to bed. So sometimes I would make it myself with wood and paper and hide it on the table and not tell Azra and wait for her to see it.

Sophie: She didn't know?

Andrei: I made very good pieces. Once there were too many pieces, one too many, there on the table, all by itself when we finished the puzzle. I pretended this was the company's mistake.

Sophie: You cheated!

Andrei: No, no. We know this problem here. A little mistake far away; someone forgets to put one little thing in a box. He's watching the girl in the window or telling a joke, and then the box comes here and we spend days trying to fix the damage.

Sophie: But they didn't forget the piece.

Andrei: No, not this time. And this is what I know Montreal for. Very good, very difficult jigsaw puzzles. It must be very nice, Montreal.

Sophie: It's peaceful.

Andrei: You like, ah —

Sophie: Peace. Same word.

Andrei: You like peace?

Sophie: Yes. Well, not always.

Andrei: You're a writer. You need peace, to write.

Sophie: Sometimes.

Andrei: You have a good life. You're like some kind of people we know here.

Sophie: What do you mean?

Andrei: You get everything you want. You get peace. And you get war when you want it.

Sophie: I don't want war. Nobody wants it. I came here because I want it to end. I want to help stop it.

Andrei: And how will you do that?

Sophie: I will talk to people like you. I will find out what's going on here. I will write about it — write about what it's like to live here — about how people here need warmth, need water, need food, need hope.

Andrei: Yes, yes, we know this song here. It's …

Sophie: And maybe if enough people read what I write, maybe they will understand that they must, and their governments must, do something, too.

Andrei: It's — it's Beatles. You liked The Beatles?

Sophie: Why?

Andrei: I did too. Such stupid, happy music.

Stories 5

Sophie: Lewis looked up and said, "Let's." It was a lovely spring morning: I had put daffodils in a vase, and there was bread and jam and coffee and fruit on the table. Let's what? Let's live together, he said, and reached out for my hand. I'll move in, I'll pay rent. I looked down at the newspaper, and at the pictures of those people and their bombed-out towns. It seemed so obvious, lying there on the table between us like some carcass we were about to be obliged to come to terms with. So obvious I don't know why I needed to say it: We'll fight.

Andrei: So Milos went back inside with his calf. Petrus said, "When we get to my sister's villa, I must give you some of this food, I insist, but we'll leave it here for now and it won't go bad." We locked up the freezer and pushed it back into the road, which was now uphill with more potholes and stones. A shell exploded. I dove for cover. I saw the freezer on the cart like a big white coffin; Petrus was gone and then, KA-BOOM.

The Guide-Book

(Andrei is rolling a cigarette out of butts he's collected.)

Andrei: That moment you are on the bus, surrounded by people you don't know, the bus arrives somewhere you have never been, perhaps it's the station —

Sophie: Everyone gets off except —

Andrei: Except you, and you sit there not knowing what to do, not wanting to ask anyone because they're all so busy, because you don't want them to know that you don't know where you are.

Sophie: And you don't know. It's frightening.

Andrei: When I first came here the bus pulled in to a shed. Later I learnt it was attached to the station. The bus driver yelled something in slang I didn't understand. I sat on the bus alone. He yelled again at me and I got off. And that day I walked out. I was fifteen. I had just come from Tufa. All I had was my bag, and I was frightened — frightened that the whole city was waiting, just waiting to take this bag from me. When I asked people the way to the boarding house, they would say the names of streets and churches I didn't know. But I didn't dare say.

Sophie: You have to. I know — I feel that all the time.

Andrei: And then this became my city. There are streets I walked up that first evening that I would later live on, and buildings I saw then like fortresses or banks, which later became familiar places I entered to visit friends or conduct business. I made it my city, with my routes, my paths to work, windows I looked in and faces I saw and nodded to.

Sophie: And now buildings are burnt and the windows are smashed.

Andrei: I take a new route every day, I never know what I'll meet. It's the same for me as it is for you.

Sophie: We've both arrived somewhere we don't know where, and we're alone. Why did you come?

Andrei: What? I live here.

Sophie: Do you need a match?

Andrei: What?

Sophie: A match, a light. *(Gives him a box.)*

Andrei: Oh, that match. Thanks.

Sophie: What other matches are there?

Andrei: I played soccer. We would have a match every Saturday.

Sophie: Ah yes, a game.

Andrei: Yes, a match.

Sophie: Why did you come here from your village?

Andrei: I had a job. A real job. In a printing house.

Sophie: It must have been interesting.

Andrei: It was busy.

Sophie: What kind of books?

Andrei: I don't know. I didn't read them. That wasn't my job. I set letters up when I started. And later when we got new machines I worked on the pages.

Sophie: You didn't read them?

Andrei: That wasn't my job. My boss said, "It's like a cake: here we make the cake, we don't eat it. Make the book, don't read it."

Sophie: But didn't you want to know?

Andrei: It was lots of writing. Words and words. Sometimes at night when I was trying to sleep I would see them in my head. Some of the books were for the church. My uncle, the Bishop, got me the job, you see. Menus for the restaurant, too, and, oh yes, we did the city tourist guidebook with maps and all kinds of things. We printed it in English, too. For the tourists and the relatives in America who come and have forgotten how to talk.

Sophie: *(Pulling out a book.)* Is this it?

Andrei: That's it.

Sophie: It's a bit out of date.

Andrei: Look at the maps. Look at the colours. Do you know how we —

Sophie: Lots of these places aren't there anymore. They're gone.

Andrei: Yes. But they're in the book. And the book's in my head. There's the train station the Austrians built — see how grand and elegant it is? — and here's the National Library.

Sophie: Which you never went inside.

Andrei: Everything I need I keep in my head. See, on page sixty-two, there is the river, the river where I used to go walking in the spring, and the girls would wear their new dresses for the first time.

Sophie: They've chopped down the plane trees for firewood.

Andrei: Of course, they would.

Sophie: And the bridge —

Andrei: Yes, I know that. It is really very beautiful that walk by the river.

Sophie: It's gone. I can't see it.

Andrei: It's beautiful. The plane trees are reflected on the waves of the river, and the leaves float on the river's surface drifting slowly under the —

Sophie: I should have come before the war.

Andrei: You will never know how it was. There were cafés and long evenings and nights outside eating in the square. But you only come now, to see the rubble, to see the bombs —

Sophie: It's my job.

Andrei: The barricades, the barbed wire — it's not my city any more.

Candlesticks 3

Andrei: I was right. I should have been frightened of him. He was spreading the word. He wanted me to be a Bishop, too. He gave the candlesticks to my mother when I was born. They came, he told her, from a church that was burnt a long time ago, in another village. Each time they are lit, he said, remember that fire, those flames.

The Mexican Correspondent

(*Andrei is evidently upset over something; Sophie enters.*)

Sophie: You heard the news?

Andrei: Tufa?

Sophie: I don't understand. It's a safe area. These people are protected there by peacekeepers. For six months, they've been there and they haven't been killed. They've survived. And today a report came that they're leaving the village en masse.

Andrei: Perhaps they think the safe area is not so safe.

Sophie: And it was a Mexican reporter who discovered this. None of us believed him. We thought it was propaganda.

Andrei: People will say anything here.

Sophie: Then someone checked and discovered that it was true.

Andrei: Yes.

Sophie: All those people streaming out of Tufa, leaving their homes and possessions, their whole lives behind. It's crazy.

Andrei: Stupid people.

Sophie: But what if they know something we don't, if they sense it? Think of animals. Salmon finding their way home to their spawning grounds, geese sensing the onset of winter and setting off south.

Andrei: No, no. They're like sheep. One person gets frightened, runs away, and the rest all follow.

Sophie: But you're from there. You should know.

Andrei: They're just frightened.

Sophie: Of what?

Andrei: I don't know. I haven't been back there for a long time.

Sophie: That's not true. I met you there.

Andrei: Oh yes, I went back once.

Sophie: And this reporter seems to know what they know as well.

Andrei: It's a lot of stupid people from my village who don't understand. They don't trust the radio but they believe these medieval rumours.

Sophie: And you know what? He's one of the worst. He laughs, he makes jokes, he doesn't care. And he won't share his — you're shaking again.

Andrei: It's nothing.

Sophie: What is it? Tell me?

Andrei: I can't ask you.

Sophie: Ask me.

Andrei: I have a sister. You have friends.

Sophie: Go on.

Andrei: My sister wants to know —

Sophie: She wants a visa?

Andrei: She needs it very badly. I will be very, very grateful.

Sophie: Is it just for her?

Andrei: For her family.

Sophie: Her whole family?

Andrei: A very nice family. Two beautiful children. Perfect for Montréal.

Sophie: She's married?

Andrei: Yes, she has a husband.

Sophie: Then she can't marry someone.

Andrei: You must try. She's frightened of the war. The children are young.

Sophie: I'm not sure I can help.

Andrei: Please.

Sophie: I'll ask. I will.

Andrei: Thank you. Thank you.

Sophie: *(Picking up a radio.)* Where'd this come from?

Andrei: A friend.

Sophie: But what about the blockade? It's a Japanese make.

Andrei: He's a friend from the outside.

Sophie: Oh?

Andrei: Like you, a journalist.

Sophie: What's his name? I probably know him.

Andrei: Yes, you do.

Sophie: Tell me his name. Oh no. It's not him.

Andrei: He visited me.

Sophie: He's the worst. I told you, the very worst.

Andrei: He gave me a radio.

Sophie: You know what his stories are like?

Andrei: I'm not interested.

Sophie: He comes from a country where the government slaughters people. He wants to pretend to his readers that this is normal behaviour, to tell them that here things are much worse. So they read his reports in the official news service, and pat themselves on the back and say how barbaric. And he visited you.

Andrei: Yes.

Sophie: And you took the radio he gave you?

Andrei: It's very useful. Short-wave.

Sophie: Are you sure you didn't just take it without him giving it to you?

Andrei: What do you mean?

Sophie: I didn't give you my camera. You —

Andrei: Your camera! What do I know about your camera?

Sophie: I just want to know.

Andrei: You need a camera? Go buy a new one. And then get yourself killed.

Sophie: Is that what you live from?

Andrei: He gave me the radio. He gave it to me.

Sophie: What did you give him?

Andrei: We talked.

Sophie: He wanted something from you. What did you give him?

Andrei: I gave him information.

Sophie: You told him about? —

Andrei: Yes.

Sophie: How do you know?

Andrei: I'm from there.

Sophie: Yes, and you go back there every now and then, don't you? You're my friend. Why didn't you tell me?

Andrei: Because I told him.

Sophie: You don't think I'm a real journalist, do you?

Andrei: No, no. I just didn't want to tell you.

Sophie: Why?

Andrei: I didn't want to tell you more bad things about my country.

Sophie: But I'm a journalist. I need to know. Tell me everything. Tell me the truth.

Andrei: You're my friend.

Sophie: Tell me.

Tell the Truth

Andrei: There is writing on the door of the house in Tufa. I don't erase it, as I wish: signs of life, that might be dangerous. But what bothers me, is I notice a mistake, I think, in the spelling.

Sophie: Lewis wants to live with me. He knows me, he thinks, and it seems he wants to get to know me better. Ha!

Andrei: Mr. Andric said there were mistakes in every book if you looked closely enough. If you want to find mistakes, you will find them. If you want to find something else, you will find that also.

Sophie: It'll be some wondrous, self-forgetting, nectar-sipping idyll, he thinks. All our best moments strung together and multiplied by two.

Andrei: "In most other ways," he said, "books are perfect. They sit on the shelf happy beside each other, they don't want food or water, and they only speak to us when we pick them up."

Sophie: Logical flaw. Because we have been happy together, it does not follow that whenever we are together we will be happy, or that if we are together the whole time, we will always be happy.

Andrei: I preferred people, and being together with them. But then everyone wanted to be apart, to be themselves, their true, their perfect selves. How hard it has been for them all these years sharing their houses, their streets, their villages. How cramped and unnatural they have become.

Sophie: Couldn't we just leave it at that? But it's never enough. There always has to be more. These two parallel lines, meeting each other so enjoyably at times, have to run on and on through the night, vainly trying to merge, to become one, till they run themselves out, till they crash.

Andrei: We never said, they never said, anything was wrong. We knew each other, we thought, and what we didn't know was not important. It was just some quirk of table manners or decorative mark above the door.

Sophie: And there has to be more. More to have, more to know. What father did, what mother didn't do. The shadow falling across the delighted crib.

Andrei: Now all these quirks, these little faults they found add up.

Sophie: Ah, yes, the truth.

Andrei: The mystery solved.

Sophie: The dark little secret that explains it all.

Andrei: The truth about them.

Sophie: The truth about us.

Stories 6

Sophie: And so we fought. "Look at them," I said. "That's nothing to do with us," Lewis replied. "That's…" and he used a word, I can't remember what, some phrase from the paper or such, that made you think he knew all about it. How did he know? He was like everyone else reading that newspaper that morning. They were all judging, making pronouncements, using words to label the world. How could he be so sure he knew how things would be, so sure that he knew me? I took the next assignment I could abroad to mull things over and that, as it turned out, was here. Right in the thick of it.

Andrei: I lie in the road a long time and people stop coming. It's dark and cold. I'm not frightened of people anymore. I don't care if someone comes and kills me. I just want someone to come. To help me, to kill me. It's the same. And I lie here a long time. And then there's a new sound, something like an insect buzzing, one I haven't heard in a long time. It's a motorcycle, a motorcycle! It's Red Cross, Red Crescent, come to take me to hospital. To the American hospital! I know no one else has gasoline in the city. The motorcycle pulls up, a man in a big smile and sunglasses and safari clothes gets off. He is very nice, very polite. He has a big black box strapped over his shoulder, and he pulls out this thing, which, at first, I think is a new anaesthetic. It's bright and shiny and he puts it in my face. It's a microphone. He smiles some more and asks, "Are you dead yet?"

Propositions

Andrei: You asked?

Sophie: I couldn't.

Andrei: I told them you would ask.

Sophie: I'm trying to get hold of my friend.

Andrei: Please.

Sophie: I can't promise anything. Where were you yesterday? I came to take you out for dinner.

Andrei: What restaurant?

Sophie: To the Petit Europe.

Andrei: I don't eat in restaurants.

Sophie: You weren't here.

Andrei: I'm sorry.

Sophie: Where were you?

Andrei: I couldn't answer the door. I'm sorry.

Sophie: You weren't here. The door was padlocked from the outside.

Andrei: We must be very prudent in this city. Very, very prudent.

Sophie: You were in Tufa, weren't you? What were you doing there?

Andrei: I didn't go anywhere.

Sophie: You weren't here. Don't lie —

Andrei: I didn't go anywhere. I tried to go somewhere. But the road is cut off now.

Sophie: What do you do there?

Andrei: I visit.

Sophie: Visit who? Everyone left.

Andrei: I visit graves.

(Pause.)

Sophie: I want you to tell me about your wife.

Andrei: No.

Sophie: Please. I don't want to know how she died.

Andrei: Yes, she's dead.

Sophie: I want you to tell me what she was like, what kind of person she was, what she liked, what she didn't like.

Andrei: Why?

Sophie: I want to know about her, for myself. I want to know what kind of person you married.

Andrei: She's dead. I married a dead person.

Sophie: She wasn't dead then. Pretend she's alive. I want to know what kind of person you would fall in love with.

Andrei: I see.

Sophie: So she's not forgotten. What did she look like?

Andrei: I've forgotten.

Sophie: Don't forget. You can't forget.

Andrei: I'm trying.

Sophie: Was she as tall as me? *(He looks away.)* Was she this tall?

Andrei: I don't know.

Sophie: Look at me. Please. Was she? —

Andrei: I don't want —

Sophie: I need to know.

Andrei: *(Looking at her.)* She was shorter.

Sophie: How short? *(Hand at nose level.)* This short?

Andrei: *(His hand at her eye level.)* This short.

Sophie: And her hair? Was it black?

Andrei: Yes, and longer than yours. And her skin was dark, too. But her eyes were green.

Sophie: And was she...? *(Hands signalling larger hips than her own.)*

Andrei: She was heavier, rounder than you. I made her like that. I gave her children. I gave her food. You are more beautiful, I think.

Sophie: But you loved her — her roundness.

Andrei: But she was more beautiful when I met her. More beautiful than you. Yes.

Sophie: You were very young then, weren't you?

Andrei: I was seventeen. I was working but I went back to Tufa on weekends. Her father took over the hardware store there. Before it was a crazy mess, with boxes and boxes piled up on top of each other, with nails in one place and screws in another, with bolts in one place and the —

Sophie: Nuts.

Andrei: The nuts for them somewhere else. Most likely spilled on the floor.

Sophie: It's a custom, isn't it?

Andrei: She was there at the counter one day. I asked her where something was, she went to find it, and I followed her down the aisle. I noticed that the farther she got from the counter where her father was the slower and more interesting her walk became, so I came back and I began to ask for the things that were the farthest away, like rope, and wire, and fence materials. And one day it was cold but very sunny outside....

Sophie: You didn't need any more rope.

Andrei: I had lots, all tied up in knots to make one long rope.

Sophie: And your tongue was tied in knots.

Andrei: How do you know?

Sophie: You think women don't fall in love?

Andrei: No, it was my, ah, intestines in knots. Because I went to the store just before closing and I asked if she would like to go for a walk? She was with her sister and they laughed. "A walk?" "Yes," I said. "Inside the store, or outside?" And so we went for a very long walk, except we didn't know how long it was.

Sophie: You should have taken a rope. Like what's his name in the labyrinth. You know …

Andrei: I don't know this story.

Sophie: Theseus.

Andrei: But didn't get lost.

Sophie: You know a match can be something else as well. If you have one thing, and then you have another one that's exactly like it, the second one is a match for the first. It's its match.

Andrei: Oh, a pair of things.

Sophie: Yes, a pair of matching gloves, say. And people, too. If two people are very like each other, or if they get on well, we say they're a good match.

Andrei: So they make fire together.

Sophie: Yes. Yes. Andrei and Azra, it's a very nice story.

Andrei: It's a normal one for here.

Sophie: I wish I could tell a story like that.

Andrei: You don't sound happy.

Sophie: I have everything I want.

Andrei: Are you happy?

Sophie: I have everything I want.

Andrei: That's why you came here. You have something unhappy inside, you wanted to go somewhere where you can see the same unhappiness outside.

Sophie: I came here to do something, to help.

Andrei: Do you want to sleep with me?

Sophie: What?

Andrei: Do you want to sleep with me? Would that make you happy?

Sophie: I didn't come here for that.

Andrei: Do you want to?

Sophie: No.

Andrei: You don't want to? You don't find me desirable?

Sophie: No. I don't know. I'm thinking about Azra and how you met. You miss her, don't you? I know your heart stops but your body keeps on wanting food, wanting…. I'm silly to think you should stop—

Andrei: I don't want to sleep with you.

Sophie: What?

Andrei: I don't.

Sophie: Oh. *(Pause.)* What do you want from me?

Andrei: You came here. You found me. What do you want from me?

Sophie: I don't want to sleep with you. *(As if it had just suddenly occurred to her.)* I, I want to interview you. On tape.

Andrei: So you want a story.

Sophie: I want an interview.

Andrei: Not today.

Sophie: No.

Andrei: I have a headache.

Sophie: I'm sorry.

Andrei: It's a joke. *(Pause.)* It is getting dark. You should get to your hotel.

Sophie: *(Noticing candlestick.)* That's very beautiful.

Andrei: It's from the family. My mother gave it to me when we married.

Sophie: It's lovely. Where did she?—

Andrei: You won't find it anywhere. There's only one in the world.

Sophie: Such a beautiful candlestick.

Andrei: But no candles. It's getting dark.

Sophie: Can we do it on Friday?

Andrei: What?

Sophie: The interview.

Andrei: Monday is better.

Sophie: Monday.

Andrei: And my sister?

Sophie: I'll call again tonight.

Not Spain

Sophie: Do something. What? I try to sleep. I can't. I go to the hotel bar. There are a lot of them drinking there and laughing, all men, and the young woman who gives them drinks looks frightened. One sees me and comes up to me waving his arms and stamping his feet in a kind of grotesque flamenco imitation while the others cheer him on. "It's not Spain," he says and leers at me. "It's no holiday," he says, baring his awful British teeth.

> "Auden, Spender, Orwell, Hemingway
> Fighting Franco
> Writing poetry in the barranco
> Throwing paper darts across the sand
> Oh, this isn't no war for them —
> This is a war for men."

Then he cackles and goes back to the bar, and the others all buy him drinks.

The End of the Song

(Sophie and Andrei with a tape recorder.)

Sophie: I called my friend in London — he's sending the papers.

Andrei: He's sending them!

Sophie: The papers, the forms your sister has to fill out.

Andrei: And then they get the visa?

Sophie: No. Then they decide.

Andrei: How long?

Sophie: I don't know. It takes time. And they might say no after that. In fact, they'll probably —

Andrei: They won't say no.

Sophie: They might.

Andrei: No.

Sophie: Let's start. Once I've turned it on, I'm not going to stop it. OK?

Andrei: Very good.

Sophie: *(Pressing both 'start' and 'record' buttons.)* Andrei is a Christian, originally from the village of Tufa, who nonetheless believes the church is to blame for much of the bloodshed.

Andrei: When I was a boy I wanted to go on a crusade. This is what the church taught me — to be a crusader.

Sophie: And now?

Andrei: Is it bad to be a crusader? Is this what you think?

Sophie: But hasn't the church contributed to the violence by encouraging this intolerance, this animosity? You yourself told me —

Andrei: The church teaches what it must. If you are a Christian, you cannot question it. You can only pray for the people who are dead. Perhaps that is necessary.

Sophie: Your wife and children were killed. Do you feel that was necessary?

Andrei: In war many things we don't understand become necessary.

Sophie: Do you really believe that?

Andrei: You want me to say that everything we do here is wrong?

Sophie: Killing people isn't very good, is it?

Andrei: You want me to tell you that the way you live is right, the way we live is wrong, and that if we are more like you, everything will be right.

Sophie: I just want this to stop.

Andrei: *(Turning off tape recorder.)* So do I.

(Pause.)

Sophie: I thought because of your wife you thought differently, you thought —

Andrei: I changed my mind.

Sophie: So you did. *(Getting ready to leave.)* I suppose that's all.

Andrei: Yes. You're going soon.

Sophie: Next week. I'll come by before with the papers to fill out.

Andrei: Have you found your carpet yet? You should go to the market again. Before you leave.

Sophie: But I don't want anything.

Andrei: There are all kinds of treasures there. Have a look. Go early. Before they pull out the brandy.

Sophie: I have so many things. I don't need anything.

Andrei: There are lots of very old and very beautiful things. Family heirlooms, silver, china vases, the antique carpets that mothers gave their daughters when they got married...

Sophie: Really?

Andrei: They call it the Vultures' Market now.

Sophie: I thought it was the Horses'.

Andrei: Now it's the Vultures'. Everything they sell comes from the dead, from people who have been killed, that's why it's so good.

Sophie: I'm not a vulture. I can't buy something that belonged to someone.

Andrei: Why not? Anything really old belonged to someone else before. Why do you feel so guilty about your money? Spend it, enjoy it. You can find something very old and very beautiful to take home, and you don't have to know where it came from and what it meant.

Sophie: I don't want anything.

Andrei: You wanted a carpet.

Sophie: I wanted — I want — something that has meaning.

Andrei: You could have a wonderful antique Persian carpet the colour of the cherries in Tufa for nothing. For a song.

Sophie: For what?

Andrei: For a song. I like that expression. I sing a song and you give me something.

Sophie: But you never —

Andrei: I did sing you a song.

Sophie: You never finished it. There is a bridge at Talar, you know.

Andrei: Of course, there is.

Sophie: You said the bridge keeps getting washed away by the river. But, in the end, the bridge got built. It must have, because there is a bridge there now, a very old one.

Andrei: I'll tell you the end.

Sophie: I want you to sing it to me.

Andrei: It's very sad. I can't.

Sophie: But it's about building a bridge, a connection, that still stands today.

Andrei: The three brothers go to the old woman of the hill, who is like a witch, and ask for her help to finish the bridge:

Don't waste your time, don't waste your money
 Cried the voice of the witch
You will never outsmart the river,
 Never finish the bridge.

—Never? — Not in a thousand years,
 Unless your wives are true
And you wall one up in a pillar,
 That way the bridge won't move.

They must bury her in the pillar. That way the bridge will be faithful, too. So the three brothers all promise not to tell their wives, they swear to leave it to chance which one will come. But that night each of them goes to his wife and watches her with sad eyes. They go to bed: I can't tell you the things they did there or what they might have said. But the next morning, it happens that the wives of the two older brothers are sick and ask Lena to go.

Sophie: Their husbands told them!

Andrei:
I'd be happy to go, said Lena,
 And do as you request
But I have all this linen to wash
 And a baby at my breast.

Oh, I'll take care of him, said Margaret,
 I'll wash your sheets, said Anne.
Lena put on her best white dress
 To take lunch to the men.

His brothers smiled to see her come
 But George, her husband, cried.
She looked more beautiful than ever,
 Lena from the other side.

Why is your face so wet? she asked
 Why do you look so sad?
I've brought you rabbit for lunch, my love,
 Rabbit and wine and bread.

Sophie: She thinks she's safe.

Andrei:
Stone by stone the masons wall her up
    Beginning at the toes.
At first she thinks it's just a joke,
    A joke that grows and grows.

At her knees, it's stopped being funny.
    At her hips, she calls for George.
At her waist, she begs for mercy,
    But her voice is growing hoarse.

At her breast the masons take pity
    And leave her two small holes
Two holes to suckle her son through
    They leave, and lay the next row.

Up and up the pillar rises
    Past her neck, past her crown.
The next morning a new bridge stands
    But Lena's voice is gone.

Not Blood

Sophie: I gave away the books and things that were me. Those that are me I left behind. I'm going back to them soon, but even they seem far away, like the apartment I'll return to, renewed and less forgiving, like a student returning home. There will be a knock at the door and Lewis will want in, to move in, merely to discover that I am not what he thought I was. If only we could live together. We can't. But let's imagine we could. There will be a knock. "No," I'll say, "don't come in. Let's go out." The world flows through me and I don't know it, don't know what secrets, what flaws run through me. Not blood. You see, I don't even know what one month does to my body, to me, what other sorrows I'll miss. I know this: before I leave I will go to Tufa, not to the monastery, but to the cherry orchards, to walk among the trees and imagine how they must look in season, and how the cherries must fall, how like the thick red carpets in the bazaar. They fall and no one cares or knows how or when exactly or what particular branch they fell from. They fall and all we say is they were many, they were red, they were sweet.

Goodbye Presents

(Andrei is rearranging his boxes so that Sophie, who has just arrived, will have somewhere to sit.)

Andrei: Excuse me. It was close last night.

Sophie: What was?

Andrei: You didn't hear?

Sophie: Oh, the shells.

Andrei: One landed right at the corner. I put this here so the glass wouldn't hit me when the window exploded.

Sophie: I'm sorry. I've got used to them.

Andrei: And now you're leaving.

Sophie: What will happen?

Andrei: I didn't think it could be worse. It can. I'm very worried for my, my sister's family.

Sophie: Look, I brought you the papers. I've signed them, so if there are any questions, they can contact me.

Andrei: *(Accepting them.)* I'm very grateful.

Sophie: Thank you for the interview. I did use it, even though I didn't expect you to be so —

Andrei: Things are very complex. You can't tell everyone what happens.

(Pause.)

Sophie: Is Azra still alive? Is your family alive? The visa is for her, isn't it?

Andrei: I can't tell everyone. I have to protect —

Sophie: Are they?

Andrei: I can't tell you.

Sophie: They are. I know. You lied to me, didn't you?

Andrei: I lied? No, no. I tried to survive.

Sophie: I trusted you and you lied to me. You realize if the other journalists find out, my name will be ruined.

Andrei: And my family.

Sophie: What?

Andrei: If they find out about them —

Sophie: What?

Andrei: They'll be killed.

Sophie: I'm sorry, I'm sorry. Where are they?

Andrei: I can't tell you.

Sophie: I know. They're in Tufa. They can't go out and you can't visit, and all they can do is wait.

Andrei: It's a safe zone.

Sophie: But all those people were leaving.

Andrei: Not them. I told them not to. I told them it's safe.

Sophie: And now you've got the papers for them.

Andrei: Thank you.

Sophie: I wish you'd told me. Then I could have—

Andrei: That's not what you wanted.

Sophie: I wanted you to lie to me?

Andrei: A story, the front page, a headline, news!

Sophie: I wanted the truth.

Andrei: Otherwise you talk to someone else.

Sophie: I wanted to talk to you.

Andrei: You wanted news.

Sophie: About the war.

Andrei: About the death of my wife, my children.

Sophie: Your family aren't dead.

Andrei: But I talked about their death. *(Smiles.)* For you.

Sophie: Yes, you did. Thank you.

Andrei: You did your job, and I helped you. And now you're going.

(Pause.)

Sophie: Yes. Thank you for being my friend here.

Andrei: It's nothing. Hospitality is our custom.

Sophie: Yes, it is.

Andrei: Did you go back to the bazaar?

Sophie: Actually, I've just been there.

Andrei: Did you get a carpet?

Sophie: Not a carpet.

Andrei: No. A painting?

Sophie: No.

Andrei: Some china for your friend, Lewis?

Sophie: No, it's for me, for my dining room table.

Andrei: Let me think.

Sophie: It's beautiful and old.

Andrei: Show me.

Sophie: It's just like yours. *(Revealing a candlestick.)* Look!

Andrei: *(Seizing it.)* Oh no. No. No. No.

Sophie: What?

Andrei: It's Azra's! I gave it to her when I left.

Sophie: I found it in the bazaar.

Andrei: They've got her! And Katya and Boris, too! *(He hands both candlesticks to Sophie, who accepts them silently, and then he walks away from her, muttering as if in prayer.)* Dear father, what I most loved, you have taken from me. It was dark, I did not see you, so I asked you to speak. You spoke and said, "Everything is vanity." Azra, Katya, Boris—vain, vain, vain. Take this one, too, I say, take them both. And in the house of the unbelieving—

Sophie: And in the square, there is an old man who sells newspapers and at eleven a woman comes to feed stale bread to the pigeons. How can I know what the paper doesn't say? How or when exactly or what particular people died waiting for that bread? And where they would be safe? Tonight Lewis is coming for dinner and I'm cooking. Wine, bread, pasta, salad, candles, candlesticks. I have everything!

(Blackout.)

Berlin

Maurice Blanchot

Translated by Aris Fioretos

For everyone, Berlin is the problem of division. From one point of view, this is strictly a political problem, for which — we must not forget — strictly political solutions exist. From another point of view, it is a social as well as an economic problem (and therefore political, but in a larger sense): in Berlin, two systems, two socio-economic structures, confront each other. From still another point of view, it is a metaphysical problem: Berlin is not only Berlin, but also the symbol of the division of the world, and even more: a "point in the universe," the place where reflection on the both necessary and impossible unity imposes itself on each and every one who lives there, and who, while living there, has not only the experience of a domicile, but also that of the absence of a domicile. This is not all. Berlin is not only a symbol, but a real city in which human dramas unknown to other big cities are performed: here, division is a name for tearing apart. This is not all. Berlin presents, in unusual terms, the problem of opposition between two cultures within the same cultural context, of two languages without inner relation inside the same language, and thus challenges the assumption of intellectual security and the possibility of communication normally granted to those who live together by virtue of sharing the same language and historical past. This is not all.

To treat or question the problem of Berlin as a problem of division, it is not enough to enumerate, however completely, the different forms in which they are given to us to comprehend. Concerning the problem of division, we must say that Berlin is an indivisible problem. At the point at which we isolate provisionally — if only for clarity of exposition — this or that particular given of the situation "Berlin," we run the risk of falsifying not only the question in its entirety, but also this particular given, which it is nonetheless impossible to grasp without considering it by itself.

The problem of division — of fracture — which Berlin poses not only to the Berliners, not even to Germans only, but, I believe, to all thinking human beings — and in a compelling, I would say painful, way — is a problem that we cannot formulate adequately in its complete reality if we do not decide to formulate it fragmentarily (which, however, does not imply partially). In other words, each time we happen to be confronted with a problem of this nature (after all, there are other such problems), we must remember that to speak of it in a just way entails speaking of it in such a way that the profound gap existing in our words and in our thought also be permitted to speak, in order to articulate the impossibility in which we find ourselves when we speak in terms that strive to be definitive. This implies: 1. that omniscience, if it were possible, is of no use in this case: the essence of this situation would elude even a God alleged to know all; 2. that in general it is not possible to dominate, survey, or encompass in one sweep the problem of division, and that — in this as in other cases — the panoramic vision is not the correct one; 3. that the deliberate choice of the fragment is not a sceptical retreat, the lazy renouncement of a complete synthesis (though it could be the case), but a patient-impatient, mobile-immobile method of searching, and the affirmation, furthermore, that meaning, the entirety of meaning, is not to be found immediately, either in ourselves or in what we write, but that meaning is still to come, and that, by examining the sense, we consider it a pure becoming and a pure future of questioning; 4. this implies, to conclude, that we must repeat ourselves. Each fragmentary speaking, each fragmentary reflection, requires repetition and infinite plurality.

I would like to add two (fragmentary) observations. The enforced political abstraction which Berlin represents found its most acute expression the day the wall was erected, which is nonetheless something dramatically concrete. Until

August 13, 1961, the absence of a visible sign of separation — well before this day a series of regular and irregular controls that had already prompted premonitions of the enigmatic advance of a line of demarcation — gave the partitioning an ambiguous character and signification: what was it? A border? Certainly? But it was also something else: something less than a border, since large numbers of people cross it every day, avoiding the controls; but also, something else in addition, because the fact of crossing did not signify the passage from one country to another, from one language to another, but the passage within the same country and the same language, from "truth" to "error," from "evil" to "good," from "life" to "death," and it implied being subjected, almost without knowing, to a radical metamorphosis (but in order to determine where this "evil" and "good" were properly located — as brutally opposed as they are — one could only rely on a partial reflection). The almost instantaneous construction of the wall substituted for the still indecisive ambiguity the violence of a decisive separation. Outside of Germany people became aware of, in a manner more or less intense, more or less superficial, the dramatic changes this event announced, not only in relations between fellow human beings, but also in the economic and political domains. Yet one problem, I believe, passed unnoticed (perhaps even in the eyes of many Germans): the fact that the reality of this wall was destined to throw into abstraction the unity of a big city full of life, a city that was not and is not, in reality — its profound reality consists precisely in this — a single city, not two cities, not the capital of a country, not any important city, not the centre, nothing but this absent centre. In this way, the wall succeeded in abstractly concretizing the division, to render it visible and tangible, and thus to force us to think henceforth of Berlin, in the very unity of its name, no longer under the sign of a lost unity, but as this sociological reality constituted by two absolutely different cities.* The wall's "scandal" and importance consists of being, in the concrete oppression it represents, essentially abstract, and it thus recalls what we continually forget: that abstraction is neither simply an inexact manner of thinking nor a manifestly impoverished form of language, but that abstraction is our world, the world in which we live and think day after day.

Meanwhile, we have at our disposal a considerable quantity of writings on the situation of Berlin. I am struck by the fact that among all these texts, two novels offer, at least to non-Germans, the best approach to the situation, two novels which are neither political nor realist. I do not attribute their merit only to the talent of Uwe Johnson, but also to the truth of literature. The difficulty itself and, to put it more succinctly, the impossibility of the author to write such books in which the division is put into play (and thus the necessity, for him, to reassess this impossibility of writing as well as in what is written) — this is what brings the literary operation into accord with the singularity of "Berlin," precisely by this hiatus it had to leave open with an obscure and never relaxed rigour between reality and the literary grasping of its sense. Perhaps the impatient reader or critic will say that, in works of this genre, the relationship toward the world and toward the responsibility of a political decision concerning it remains distant and indirect. Indirect, yes. But one must ask precisely if, in order to accede to the "world" by way of speech and, above all else, by writing, an indirect route would not be the correct one, and moreover the shortest.

[Translated from the Italian translation and its French translation.]

* The wall pretended to substitute the sociological truth of one situation, its factual state, with a deeper truth, one which could be called — but only by simplifying considerably — the dialectics of this situation.

Beirut / Tokyo

Rodolphe el-Khoury

"The city I am talking about offers this precious paradox: it does possess a centre, but this centre is empty" [Barthes, 30–32]. The city is Tokyo and the statement is Roland Barthes', taken from his quasi-utopian account of Japan in *The Empire of the Signs*. I say "utopian" because Barthes does not approach the Orient as a reality that can be contrasted historically and politically to the West, but rather as a reserve of features whose inventive manipulation allows him to entertain the idea of an unprecedented symbolic system. For Barthes, the centre of the European city is always full; it is the site of truth, where the values of civilizations are condensed. In Tokyo, where the urban traffic is forced into a perpetual detour around the imperial residence, Barthes can entertain the notion of the voided centre, a city where "the system of the imaginary is spread by circularity, by detours and returns the length of an empty subject."

Barthes' utopia may well have been realized in Beirut, quite fittingly a city which has historically negotiated and frustrated the extremes of Orientalist fantasy. In Beirut's centre-city, where the busiest and densest structures once stood, now lies an empty field. For the last few years it has attracted crowds of curious Beirutis and held the attention of international media. Visitors to the centre-city have yet to exhaust their fascination with this dusty field. Some are supposedly interested in the ancient artifacts that archeologists and bulldozers have recently unearthed. Others are invested in the development of the Central Business District: they come to survey what PR slogans have promoted as the largest construction site in the world. In fact, Beirut's CBD project is dwarfed by dozens of other developments across the globe. Do not be fooled by the subterfuge: their curiosity for the excavated past and the speculative future is an alibi for a morbid fixation on the present scene of the absent centre.

The combined effects of thoroughly destructive warfare and the equally uprooting reformulations of property law and zoning ordinances — namely, the forces of capital — have created a *tabula rasa* at the very heart of the city. This cleared ground has no discernible physical differentiation: all traces of streets and building masses are now erased. Also obliterated are the property lines, zoning envelopes and other invisible but no less "real" demarcations which customarily determine or reflect urban morphologies. The homogeneity and superficial neutrality of this clear slate may have been compromised, when the archeological strata were exposed in the recent surveys, but the excavations finally participated, perhaps most effectively, in the systematic erasure of modern Beirut by challenging the primacy of the surface, by eventually replacing one ground with several others. By the time the survey is complete, the valuable artifacts collected and the trenches filled up, the new ground will be artificial, and therefore arbitrary: abstract and more vacant still.

If the war period saw more construction than actual destruction, and if reconstruction entails the systematic deployment of efforts and resources in the transformation of Beirut, we may then argue that the most radical if not substantial result of this project has already been realized in the "deconstruction" of the centre. By "deconstruction" I mean literally a systematic dismantling of preexisting physical, political and legal structures; "deconstruction" also refers to the symbolic assault on the plenitude of the centre. To go downtown or to the centre-city, Barthes reminds us, is "to encounter the social 'truth,' to participate in the proud plenitude of 'reality'" [Barthes, 30]. This ritual persists in Beirut's centre-city in its inverted form: in today's Beirut we go downtown to encounter another truth in the spectacle of a sublime emptiness.

The ritual engagement with the centre, be it the positive participation in logos or the negative but still gratifying encounter with the sublime, may be altogether lost once this site is reclaimed for development. In fact, despite the efforts of planners, legislators and investors, Beirut has survived for twenty-two years without its downtown and its centrifugal energy is not about to waste its momentum. No matter what we build on the site, be it the developer's fantasy of a miniature Manhattan where enclaves of wired office buildings will rival the inscrutability of Tokyo's walled precinct, or the nostalgic reconstruction of a vanished historical district where simulation can only hasten cultural degradation, loss will linger on and indifference will grow.

And yet as long as this terrain vague persists in its vagueness, its vacancy and vagrancy [de Sola Morales, 1996], our Beirut could be Roland Barthes' Tokyo: we may see in the emptiness of the evacuated centre "the possibility of difference, of mutation, of a revolution in the propriety of symbolic systems" [Barthes, 30]. At the site of Beirut's sacrificial immolation, we may recognize an opportunity for the remorseless détournement of a negative yet potentially liberating violence. Beirut is dead: long live Beirut.

Works cited

Roland Barthes (1982), *Empire of the Signs*, Richard Howard, trans., New York: Hill and Wang

Ignasi de Sola Morales (1996), *Terrain Vague*, *Quaderns* 212

Call for Submissions

Social Insecurity / 1999

The vertigo, fright and solitude of Pascal's world, Borges tells us, was not an infinite sphere, but rather originally, effroyable: a fearful sphere, whose center is everywhere and whose circumference is nowhere.

When the Federal Building in Oklahoma City was bombed in April 1995, the heartland of America met the enemy and it was them. In the wake of the bombing, a new escalation of the rhetorics of insecurity took hold, the manifestations and logic of which are not locatable—lacking a proper name and familiarity.

To speak of social insecurity is to recognize the ephemerality and slippage of social relations, the nuanced communicative elisions within which such relations occur. Such insecurity may be found in the tension between urbanism's organizational strategies and the forced intimacy of virtual social relations. This insecurity can also be read as the result of the increasing globalization of local communities, states and nations, and inscribed into a thereby troubled political economy of space—the lost dimension within which such relations mutate and shift.

The 1999 issue of *Alphabet City* will address the implicit insecurities built into and generated by social formations. *Social Insecurity* may suggest an examination of the following among other ideas; the re-imagining of "differences" within racial and ethnic identities as reflected in nostalgic, utopic and dystopic notions of the constructed spatialities of film, literature, architecture and other media—the cacophony of boundaries made-liminal.

Alphabet City welcomes submissions on any appropriate topic, from health to economics, homelessness, migration, ecology, terrorism, security, the police, vigilantism, militias, state-supported housing, virtual cities, prostitution, sex, surveillance, insurance, or unemployment.

A savage, upon meeting others, will at first have been frightened. His fright will have made him see these men as larger and stronger than himself; he will have called them Giants. After much experience he will have recognized that, since these supposed Giants are neither bigger nor stronger than he, their stature did not fit the idea he had initially attached to the word Giant. He will therefore invent another name common both to them and to himself, for example the name man, and he will restrict the name Giant to the false object that had struck him during his illusion.
—Jean-Jacques Rousseau, *Essay on the Origin of Languages*

Issue editors
Cornelius Heesters *mrykos@interlog.com*
Kyla Wazana *ktompkin@chass.utoronto.ca*

Lost in the Archives / 2000

For more clarity they chose as a mnemotechnic base their own house, their home, and attached to each of its elements a distinct fact; — so the courtyard, the garden, the surroundings, the entire countryside no longer had any other point than to aid their memory. Boundary markers out in the fields delimited certain epochs, apple-trees were genealogical diagrams, bushes were battles, the world became a symbol. They looked on walls for all sorts of absent things, wound up seeing them, but no longer knew the dates they represented.
—Flaubert, *Bouvard et Pecuchet*

In the middle of Bebelplatz in central Berlin, between the National Opera and the former Royal Library, Micha Ullman has installed a memorial to the Nazi bookburning on that site in 1933: a negative monument, a submerged chamber lined with empty shelves and provided with a transparent ceiling flush with the level of the square. Meanwhile the political careers of former East Germans aspiring to office in the unified Bundestag have been held hostage to kilometres of freshly exhumed Stasi files, detailing in meticulous minutiae the banality of surveillance; and in the Kulturforum near Potsdamer Platz, a major exhibit of archival practices in modern art proposes a celebration of those same technologies. Can we read in these three uses of the archive — empty tomb, unquiet mass grave, and raw aesthetic stuff — a reminder of the dangers to which memory is susceptible, an index of the memorialist's dilemma at the end of this viciously forgetful and obsessively documenting century? And just what is an archive? What is it today, when the capacities for storage, classification and circulation of information have increased astronomically? While the spread of data retrieval networks may be rendering obsolete both the monumental institutions of the nineteenth century and the romance of the collector, what continues to be at stake is nothing less than control over the means of production of the past.

Issue editors
Rebecca Comay *comay@chass.utoronto.ca*
Rafaël Newman *110026.1160@compuserve.com*

Editorial policy
Alphabet City encourages submissions to the editorial board in all disciplines and genres. They should be received both on hard copy and on disk. While the editorial board will comment on proposals, final decisions will be made only on the basis of completed works.